The Distorted Economy

The Distorted Economy

Hans C. Blomqvist
Professor of Economics
Swedish School of Economics and Business Administration
Finland

and

Mats Lundahl
Professor of Development Economics
Stockholm School of Economics
Sweden

palgrave
macmillan

First published 2002 by
PALGRAVE MACMILLAN
Houndmills, Basingstoke, Hampshire RG21 6XS and
175 Fifth Avenue, New York, N.Y. 10010
Companies and representatives throughout the world

PALGRAVE MACMILLAN is the global academic imprint of the Palgrave
Macmillan division of St. Martin's Press, LLC and of Palgrave
Macmillan Ltd. Macmillan® is a registered trademark in the
United States, United Kingdom and other countries. Palgrave
is a registered trademark in the European Union and other countries.

ISBN 0–333–80208–X

This book is printed on paper suitable for recycling and made
from fully managed and sustained forest sources.

A catalogue record for this book is available from the British Library.

Library of Congress Cataloging-in-Publication Data
Blomqvist, H. C. (Hans-Christer)
    The distorted economy / Hans C. Blomqvist, Mats Lundahl.
        p. cm.
    Includes bibliographical references and index.
    ISBN 0–333–80208–X (cloth)
        1. Economic development. 2. Welfare economics. 3. Developing countries—
Economic conditions. I. Lundahl, Mats, 1946- II. Title.
HD75.B5795 2002
330.12'6—dc21   2002022416

10   9   8   7   6   5   4   3   2   1
11   10   09   08   07   06   05   04   03   02

Printed and bound in Great Britain by Antony Rowe Ltd
Chippenham and Eastbourne

Contents

List of Figures   x

Preface   xii

1 Welfare, Government Intervention and Political Economy   1

   Equity   2

   Efficiency   2

   Distortions and government interventions   3

   Market failures   5

   Distortions as policy: an overview   8

2 Some Analytical Tools   13

   Linearly homogeneous production functions   13

   The factor diagram   16

   The box diagram   19

   The production possibility curve   20

   The shape of the production possibility curve   24

   Social indifference curves   27

   The commodity price line   31

   Equilibrium in the commodity market   33

   Commodity prices and factor prices   34

   Conclusions   37

3 The Gains from Foreign Trade: The Fundamental Theorem   39

   The formal model   39

   The fundamental theorem of foreign trade   41

   Tariffs and free trade   45

   Dynamic effects of free trade   46

Possible objections   48

Conclusions   51

4 Trade, Distortions and Welfare   **53**

A classification of distortions   53

The country can affect its terms-of-trade   55

The optimum tariff   56

External effects in production   58

Mark-ups by the intermediaries   63

The economy does not produce on the efficient
production possibility curve   63

Factor-generated externalities   68

Conclusions   71

**5 Instrumental Distortions: Swedish
Agricultural Policy**   **74**

Emergency policy   76

An import restriction   78

A 'relative' contingency target   79

An 'absolute' contingency target   82

Capital use as a restriction   83

Limited flexibility of techniques: 'market failures'   86

Conclusions   89

6 Import Substitution in Developing Countries   **91**

The background   91

The dynamic argument: 'infant industries'   93

The theoretical alternative   95

The actual policy   95

The consequences of import substitution   98

The export-based development model: an alternative   103

7 Urban Bias	**108**
What is 'urban bias'?	109
Efficiency	110
Equity	110
The components of urban bias	111
Public investment	111
Taxation	112
Optimal taxation	114
Taxation and equality	115
Price policy	115
Effects on agricultural incomes	120
Migration and urbanization	121
Does an urban bias exist?	123
The analytical scheme	123
The empirical material	125
Conclusions	128
8 The Apartheid System in South Africa	**131**
Segregation of the land market	132
'Civilized labour market policy'	135
Influx control and crowding-out	138
The breakdown of apartheid	144
9 The Socialist Planned Economy: The Price System Eliminated	**147**
Principles of a planned economy	147
Reforms of the price system	150
The planning routine	151
The incentive problem	152
The input problem	154

General scarcity of goods   155

Overemphasizing the production of goods   156

Foreign trade   157

A model analysis   159

Conclusions   161

10 Interest Groups and Collective Action   164

The behaviour of lobbies   165

The demand for tariff protection   166

The supply of tariff protection   167

Endogenous tariffs   168

When can lobbies be formed?   170

Small groups and collective goods   172

Applications of the theory   174

An example: urban bias   180

Conclusions   181

11 Directly Unproductive Profit-Seeking Activities   184

Directly unproductive profit-seeking activities and their costs 184

A classification   187

Case 1 (DD)   188

Case 2 (DF)   194

Case 3 (FD)   195

Case 4 (FF)   197

Conclusions   197

**12 The State as an Interest Group: The Economic
      Logic of Wielding Power   199**

The view of the role of the state in the economy   200

Different types of state   204

The state as a predator   206

Techniques of predation 211

Factors that limit predation 214

The productive predatory state 215

The developmental state 220

Conclusions 221

13 **The Predatory State: Haiti and the Dominican
Republic** **224**

The emergence of a predatory state 225

Haiti in the nineteenth century 226

The predatory state as a club 228

The pattern of Haiti 232

The Dominican Republic in the nineteenth century 233

Trujillo and Duvalier 234

Concealing the truth 238

Some Haitian tricks 239

Conclusions 241

14 **From the Perfect Economy to the Predatory State:
The Internal Logic of Distortions** **243**

Index 248

List of Figures

1.1	A tax on luxuries	4
1.2	Welfare loss from an externality	6
2.1	Production isoquants	16
2.2	The box diagram	19
2.3	Derivation of the production possibility curve	21
2.4	The production possibility curve	22
2.5	The convexity of the production possibility curve, I	25
2.6	The convexity of the production possibility curve, II	25
2.7	Indifference curves	27
2.8	Intransitivity of preferences	28
2.9	Social indifference curves	29
2.10	Relative commodity prices	32
2.11	Equilibrium in the commodity market	33
2.12	Cost minimization per unit of output	36
3.1	Welfare maximization in a small, open economy operating under perfect competition	42
3.2	The gains from foreign trade	42
3.3	Tariffs and free trade	46
3.4	Dynamic effects of free trade	47
3.5	Factor immobility	48
3.6	Factor immobility and inflexible factor prices	50
4.1	Derivation of the offer curve	55
4.2	A country that can affect its terms-of-trade	57
4.3	The optimum tariff	58
4.4	Externalities in the production of agricultural goods	61
4.5	Export of the 'wrong' commodity when there are externalities in the production of agricultural goods	61
4.6	A tariff that reduces welfare when there are externalities in the production of agricultural goods	62
4.7	The mark-up on the import good	63
4.8	Derivation of the production possibility curve when factor prices differ between the sectors	64
4.9	Higher wages in manufacturing than in agriculture	67
4.10	The effect on the factor market of factor-generated externalities	70
4.11	Production and comsumption with factor-generated externalities	71
5.1	Tariff production in agriculture	75
5.2	An import restriction	78

5.3 A relative production goal 80
5.4 Detail from Figure 5.3 80
5.5 An absolute production goal 82
5.6 The contingency goal as a capital restriction 84
5.7 Inflexible techniques and market failures 87
6.1 The infant industry argument 94
6.2 Import substitution in practice 97
6.3 Import substitution policy and capacity utilized 100
7.1 Urban bias 109
7.2 Urban bias in public investment 112
7.3 The rise of the black market 117
7.4 Distorted commodity and factor prices 120
8.1 The labour market in the 'European' economy 134
8.2 The 'civilized labour market policy' 137
8.3 Resource allocation with influx control and
     reservation of skilled jobs for whites 140
8.4 The labour market in the homelands 141
9.1 Resource allocation in a planned economy 160
10.1 Optimal lobbying 167
10.2 The optimal tariff from the point of view of the
      protectionist party 168
10.3 The tariff-seeking process 169
10.4 The optimal level of a collective good 173
10.5 Suboptimal production of collective goods 174
11.1 The costs of theft 185
11.2 Production capacity and directly unproductive
      profit-seeking activities 186
11.3 Different categories of unproductive activities 187
11.4 Revenue seeking 188
11.5 Revenue seeking when the entire revenue is not sought 191
11.6 Premium seeking 192
11.7 Premium seeking when the entire revenue
      is competed away 194
11.8 Lobbying that eliminates a tariff and increases welfare 195
11.9 Tariff seeking 196
11.10 Tariff seeking that yields no result 197
12.1 Optimal clique size regarding income and security 210
12.2 Optimal size of the public sector 218
12.3 The revenue-maximizing bureaucracy 219
13.1 The ruler's costs and revenues as functions of the clique size 229
13.2 The Haitain rulers' choice between income and security 230
13.3 The effects of a conspiracy 231

Preface

This book is the result of a long process. The origin of the work was lecture notes for a course on international trade policy and political economy at the Stockholm School of Economics, where both authors were involved. No suitable textbook was available for this purpose, so a selection of suitable readings had to be used.

The Distorted Economy covers topics across many traditional economic subdisciplines, as the purpose was to illuminate the problem of distortions from different points of view. The main emphasis, however, is on international trade, development economics and political economy.

The questions dealt with often require a rather advanced analytical apparatus to be used. A good foundation in economic theory is therefore a precondition for a full understanding of the text. We have tried to make the book as easy to read as possible, however. Therefore graphical analysis is used to a great extent and we have also tried to provide intuitive explanations for the phenomena described. Hence we believe that the book is comprehensible to a broader audience, even if all analytical details may not be fully digested. In particular, we hope that economic and political decision-makers will find it useful.

We are grateful to several batches of students who had to be objects for our attempts at finding out how the text works out in practice and thus helped us eliminating errors and awkward arguments. A slightly simplified version of Chapter 12 was published in Swedish in the *Journal of the Economic Society in Finland* (vol. 50, 3rd series, 1997). We are grateful to the publishers for the permission to use the text in this book. We are also obliged to Hans Hed for his technical advice on editing the figures.

Helsinki and Stockholm

HANS C. BLOMQVIST
MATS LUNDAHL

1
Welfare, Government Intervention and Political Economy

In all economic reasoning the fundamental questions are, on the one hand, how the allocation of resources is made – how the factors of production of the economy are employed in different activities – and, on the other hand, how the resulting output is distributed among the citizens and what the welfare consequences of a given allocation are. As far as the resource allocation is concerned, there are in principle two possibilities: either the allocation is handled impersonally by the 'market forces', or administrative processes are used. In the latter case resources are allocated with the aid of more or less central planning. In practice the economic system virtually always represents a mix of the two ways of organizing an economy. In a market economy the public sector usually plays a reallocating role, and in addition resources are usually allocated *inside* both firms and the public sector by administrative processes, not by markets. The branch of economics that deals with *how well* the allocation of resources functions is welfare economics. When you pass judgements with respect to the impact of different characteristics of markets or of policy interventions you are after the welfare effects.

In all welfare discussions two concepts are central. One is the *efficiency* of the resource allocation (i.e., whether a society gets a maximum out of its scarce resources) and the other is the *equity* aspect of allocation. Are resources allocated in an equitable way between the numbers of society? In the present book, which analyses different types of *distortions* in the economy, it is of course these two questions that are in the foreground. In addition, we will discuss the reasons why distorting interventions are made at all. Often the explanation is found in what is known as the *political economy*, (i.e., in the struggle between different groups in society that attempt to change the allocation of resources and the distribution of incomes in their own favour). Distortions, however, may also be the unintended consequences of policy interventions that are intended to achieve equilibrium in the economy at the full employment level.

1

This introductory chapter provides an analytical framework for the rest of the work. We will both define a norm for comparison (the 'optimal' allocation of resources) and discuss, in general terms, what reasons there may be for the actual allocation to differ from the optimal one. Let us, however, begin with a discussion of the two basic concepts, equity and efficiency, both of which are highly relevant for what we mean by welfare.

Equity

The equity concept may be taken to mean two completely different things. On the one hand we may speak of *horizontal* equity, which means that everybody should have equal pay for equal work, regardless of, for example, skin colour or sex. From this point of view equity simply means absence of discrimination. *Vertical* equity, in turn, has to do with the distribution of income between individuals making different efforts or having different abilities (e.g., in terms of intelligence or education). Horizontal equity is endorsed by most people, whereas vertical equity is often questioned. Even though extreme poverty must always be avoided, it is far from clear to what extent an equalization of incomes is desirable. Political parties have different ambitions. If income inequalities may be clearly linked with different identifiable (e.g., ethnic) groups in society, or with geographical regions or professions, they will constitute the basis for attempts to change the distribution via the political decision-making process, through lobbying or by the foundation of parties based on group membership.

Efficiency

Economic efficiency has to do with the ability of the economy to make use of given resources. Efficiency on the production side refers to maximizing the value of the output that may be obtained with a given factor endowment. On the consumption side it means that the resulting output is distributed among the citizens in such a way that no single individual may be better off without someone else simultaneously being worse off. Efficiency defined in this way is referred to as *Pareto optimality*. It is, however, not a question of an unequivocal definition of the 'best' allocation as there is an infinite number of combinations that comply with this prerequisite. The notion of Pareto optimality only provides a partial ranking.

The definition of efficiency in terms of Pareto optimality is central in economic theory. It is attractive because it avoids interpersonal utility comparisons and hence avoids equity questions for which objective measures are difficult to construct. Distortions of the economy, the main theme of the present work, refer precisely to deviations from Pareto optimality.

Central to our theme is the question of whether a given intervention moves the economy towards Pareto optimality or instead creates a distortion. As we will demonstrate later, under certain conditions Pareto optimality will result if *all markets in the economy are characterized by perfect competition*. This is nothing but Adam Smith's idea about the 'invisible hand'. When the individual actors in the economy try to maximize their own utility, as a by-product utility for society as a whole will also be maximized. The ability of the market to coordinate the economic activities, however, has its limitations. In such cases there are reasons for the government to interfere. Sometimes, however, the state also intervenes when there are no problems with the functioning of the market. Behind the latter type of interventions different kinds of special interests are often to be found. Interventions may also be made in order to increase national welfare at the expense of the rest of the world.

Distortions and government interventions

If the market system handles the allocation of resources efficiently, should the government not avoid getting involved and instead concentrate on redistributions of income and wealth that are perceived as 'fair'? The answer is not given. There are two problems in this context. In the first place it is in practice difficult to redistribute income and wealth without affecting the resource allocation. Second, the operation of the market system is optimal only if there is perfect competition, including the absence of externalities (cf. below) and economies of scale. If not, distortions have already been built into the functioning of the markets, which in turn provides a rationale for government intervention. In addition, perfect competition is a necessary, but not a sufficient condition for Pareto optimality. This optimum can – at least theoretically – be achieved also in other ways (e.g., through central planning). We will start by looking at the 'second-best' problem: the question of what the optimal policy with respect to the other markets is when there is a distortion in some market.

The second-best problem

Assume that we have two goods: necessities and luxuries. The government wants to affect the distribution of income by transfer payments to the poor. Since both poor and rich buy necessities, but almost nobody except the rich buys luxuries, the transfers may be financed through a tax on luxuries. This is shown in Figure 1.1.

D is the demand curve and S is the supply curve for the good (which also shows the marginal cost, MC, of producing it). If no taxation takes place the quantity Q_1 is produced at price P_1. The market is in equilibrium in point A. Let us now introduce a tax of t dollars per unit produced. For producers to receive as much as before at an output of Q_1 units it is necessary that consumers pay the price P_2. We would then end up at point B. This point, however, is to the right of the demand curve. At price P_2 consumers are only

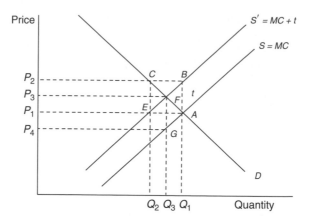

Figure 1.1   A tax on luxuries

willing to purchase Q_2 units. We move from B to C in the diagram. The producers would still receive P_1 (point E).

As we can see, the tax makes the consumers pay more for the good than the the producers receive. Points C and E, however, are not equilibrium points. At point E the price received by the producers exceeds their marginal cost of producing the good. It then pays for them to increase their production. They would like to produce at point A. However, the producers can sell a larger quantity only if the price that the consumers have to pay falls. The new equilibrium point will be F, where the demand curve intersects the S' curve. The latter curve shows the marginal cost of producing the good when the tax on production is included. Q_3 units are produced. Consumers pay a price of P_3 (point F) and producers receive a price of P_4 (point G). It does not pay to produce more since to the right of F and G the sum of the marginal cost of producing the good and the tax amounts to more than the consumers are willing to pay.

Taxation makes consumers of luxuries pay more for the good than producers receive (the difference is the tax). The consumers buy so much that their marginal utility is equal to the new, higher price, while the producers want to sell the quantity that equals their marginal cost to the new, lower, price. The marginal utility for the consumers is now higher than the marginal social cost of producing the good. From the point of view of society it would hence pay to produce more, but from the private point of view it does not. The tax has introduced a distortion into the system. Only so-called lump-sum taxes and transfers, the size of which are independent of the behaviour of the individuals and hence do not affect it, are neutral from the point of view of allocation. The problem is that, for reasons of equity, lump-sum taxation is seldom used.

It is, however, possible that there are already distortions in the system before the government has to make its decision to tax the luxury industry. What policy will then be optimal? If the only concern is that of optimal resource allocation, the best, *first-best*, solution is simply to attack the distortion 'at the source' (i.e., to remove the tax on necessities). If this, however, is impossible (say, for fiscal reasons) one might imagine that it would be optimal to make sure that the luxury goods industry would at least be free from distortions.

However, this reasoning is not valid. The reason is that a distortion in one market in principle has repercussions in all other markets because goods and factors are either substitutes for each other or complements. A tax on necessities, for example, lowers the private opportunity cost of producing luxuries (what the production factors might have earned if employed elsewhere). This will make producers produce too much of the luxuries (and too little of the necessities). The distortion in the market for necessities, however, remains (i.e., we have a *second-best* solution).

Market failures

When do distortions arise then, if they are not introduced by the public sector? Market failure is a term that refers to all situations where free, unregulated markets do not achieve a socially optimal allocation of resources. There are various reasons for this, notably imperfect competition, externalities and non-existing markets.

The first of these cases is the simplest one. If the competitive situation deviates from perfect competition firms will produce 'too little' (i.e., the marginal utility of the consumers exceeds the marginal cost for society of increasing production). Society traditionally reacts to distortions introduced by monopolies by introducing legislation to regulate competition. Since it is possible to attack the problem 'at the source', second-best solutions seldom arise in this case. The formation of cartels (collusion between firms in the same branch in order to keep prices up) and mergers may, for example, in certain cases be prohibited and monopolies may perhaps be ordered to subdivide into several, independent, companies. (This is, however, not instrumental in the case of so-called natural monopolies where one large company can produce more cheaply than several small ones because of economies of scale.) Legislation with respect to competition, however, varies greatly from country to country. Small, open economies are often more tolerant than large ones since, on the one hand, it is possible to argue that there is not room for many efficient firms in a small market and, on the other hand, foreign competition in practice eliminates the market power of domestic firms. In the following we will deal almost exclusively with small, open economies and will therefore, with few exceptions, disregard the case of imperfect competition.

Externalities or external effects mean that the production of a commodity or service creates costs or benefits for third parties which producers do not take into account in their calculations. Since all social costs or benefits are not taken into account producer decisions result in a misallocation from the social point of view, even though they may be optimal from the private perspective. Examples of negative externalities are the contamination of air and water and the noise that usually accompanies industrial production, but these are not taken into account when producers calculate how much they should produce. Positive externalities are, for example, the opportunities for recreation and fishing that result from the construction of a dam. The problem with externalities is that markets are lacking for the 'products' under consideration, and therefore the optimal quantities must be determined by the state in some other manner. Here there are in principle two possibilities. One is direct legislation about what is allowed and not allowed with respect to polluting production, and so on; the other is 'pricing' of the environment through taxes and/or subsidies. In this way an artificial 'market' for pollution is created.

Let us take an example. An industry producing pulp emits contaminated water into nature. Since it is cheaper to emit unclean water than to clean it this is what firms will do in spite of the fact that other users of the water incur costs in the form of cleaning, deterioration of fishing and negative effects of artificial irrigation of nearby fields with contaminated water. Hence the social cost exceeds the private one. Figure 1.2 illustrates the problem. *MPC* stands for the private marginal cost (which for reasons of simplicity is assumed to be constant) and *MSC* is the marginal social cost. *D* represents the demand for pulp.

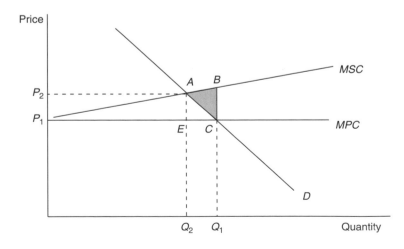

Figure 1.2   Welfare loss from an externality

With no regulation the pulp industry will produce Q_1 at price P_1. The socially optimal quantity, however, is Q_2 and the optimal price P_2. (Since society also values pulp the production of the latter, and hence pollution, will not be reduced to zero even when the social cost is taken into account.) Firms will, however, not produce the socially optimal quantity unless they are forced to do so. On the other hand it is often difficult to prohibit the polluting activity categorically since this – as we just noted – also has positive welfare effects. Instead the problem is how to make firms produce the socially optimal quantity.

How large will the welfare loss resulting from the misallocation be? At Q_1 the marginal social cost is BQ_1 while the marginal utility is CQ_1. A reduction of production hence reduces the cost more than it reduces the benefit, which means that it is socially profitable. The social cost of producing Q_1 instead of Q_2 equals ABQ_1Q_2 and the addition to utility is ACQ_1Q_2. The marginal cost exceeds the marginal utility with the shaded triangle ABC.

In order to eliminate the misallocation the government may tax the production of pulp with P_1P_2 per unit. This makes it advantageous for the industry to produce only Q_2. It is also possible to use licences (say) to force firms to produce Q_2. The difference is that the state in the former case obtains tax revenue – which could be used to clean up the pollution – whereas in the latter case the industry gets a supernormal profit of AEP_1P_2 (unless the licences are auctioned away by the state). In the latter case there are no incentives for firms to invest in techniques that inflict less damage on the environment either. (A more complicated procedure is that of regulating the amount of pollution, not output. This has the advantage that it creates incentives to invest in environment-friendly techniques, provided that the revenue from increased sales covers the cost of investment.) In addition, the method of direct regulation is often more complicated from the administrative point of view.

The third main cause of market failure is the lack of markets for certain types of production. Often this has to do with the fact that information with respect to the future is deficient. One such important defect is the lack of futures markets for most commodities (i.e., markets for purchases and sales that take place in the future). By choosing how much they consume today and how much they save households choose to postpone some of their lifetime consumption. Firms that invest create a readiness to supply their goods and services in the future. The present and the future are connected, but since there are seldom any markets for future transactions the behaviour of the economic agents today is not necessarily optimal. There are, however, exceptions. Futures markets exist for foreign currency and many important raw materials, among other things. In these cases the organization of futures markets is simple since the commodity to be dealt with is known with certainty. When it comes to, for example, cars there are no futures markets, however, since it is impossible to know what next year's models will look like.

In the same way there are defects in the market for insurance. The economic actors usually avoid risky activities, other things being equal. There should thus be a market for insurance (i.e., contracts which at a certain price eliminate the risk for the insured party). The problem is that the market system will not create insurance markets for each and every situation. One such case is that of so-called moral hazard. This means that having insurance changes the behaviour of the buyer of the insurance in such a way as to make it more probable that the incident against which the insurance is issued actually takes place. If firms, for example, could insure themselves against losses the incentives to avoid these would disappear. Probably all insurance companies would then make losses. Regardless of the size of the premiums the result would be the same. Nobody will therefore offer such insurance.

Another case is that of so-called adverse selection of buyers of insurance policies. If, for example, the premiums for life insurances have been calculated on the basis of the life expectancy of the entire population they will be much more attractive for individuals who incur large risks (e.g., mountain climbers) than for those whose behaviour tends towards the average. The same is true for people suffering from a chronic illness (which the insurance company does not know about). The customers of the insurance company will then on average represent high risk in comparison with the population in general. This, in turn, forces the insurance company to increase its premiums which makes it unattractive for those individuals who constitute 'low' risks. A possible solution in some cases is price discrimination (e.g., so that non-smokers may pay lower life insurance premiums than smokers). However, the possibility of control becomes low in this case, and, as a consequence, the possibility of cheating is high. In both the foregoing cases the market will be missing altogether – since the supply side is absent – if those who supply the commodities cannot control the customers and detect and punish abuse.

Distortions as policy: an overview

Government interventions in the price system are common even in cases where there are no obvious market failures or second-best problems. Since such interventions are difficult to justify with the aid of traditional economic theory the question then is why they arise. The answer to this question most often is to be found in the so-called political economy (i.e., the issue is one of intending to manipulate markets so as to benefit the home country, your own group or the firm where you work). Frequently the state itself – that is, the elite making decisions in the name of the state – is the most important interest group. The present book to a large extent deals with distortions that are introduced without being triggered by allocation problems.

Many of the most common policy distortions are to be found in the *international division of labour*. After presenting our analytical tools we look at the proposal that free trade will result in an optimal division of labour, and how different interventions, such as tariffs, quotas and subsidies, will affect the situation. Chapter 5 uses as an example Swedish agricultural policy, where the politicians have gone a long way towards meeting a special interest, with large economic losses as a consequence. (The same problems appear in the other Nordic countries and in the European Union.) Thereafter, import-substitution policy in developing countries is examined. In both these cases the actual motives behind the distortions are not necessarily the official ones, and in both cases the misallocation and the social cost often become substantial.

Distortions may also take the form of 'incorrect' factor prices. In many developing countries, typically, the cost of capital is far too low, relatively speaking. This leads to the use of an unnecessarily capital-intensive technique, while at the same time the possibilities of employing the generally most abundant resource – the labour force – are lower than they could be. Often this distortion is the direct result of an import-substituting policy, above all an overvalued currency, which as a rule is a consequence of this policy. That, however, is not the only reason. Often the use of capital is subsidized by generous tax rules or regulated interest rates. At the same time, the wage level in the formal sector may be relatively high as a consequence of union activity and the fact that multinational corporations often constitute an important part of the modern sector. Here, we will study how distortions in factor markets interact with distortions that are caused by import substitution policies.

There are, however, also plenty of purely *domestic* distortions. An example of this is the case of 'urban bias' that will be studied in Chapter 7. The term refers to the situation where the state in different ways favours urban areas at the expense of rural areas and agriculture. This may take place in various ways. Relative prices may be distorted in favour of the urban sector, taxation may favour this sector, or public investment may be concentrated to cities, and so on.

Another type of distortion arises when different social classes and/or ethnic groups squeeze out economic advantages for their own groups. An extreme system for favouring certain ethnic groups over others is found in the South African apartheid policy. To begin with, racial discrimination was based simply on the alienation of agricultural land from the Africans. Later it worked, on the one hand, via a race-based regulation of the access to certain categories of jobs, and, on the other hand, through a race-based regulation of educational possibilities. This systematically made it difficult for Africans to establish themselves in 'middle class positions', while at the same time the free flow of labour between the sectors was hampered and the division of income was distorted in favour of the whites. As a result of the regulations an excess demand for skilled workers arose which could be satisfied only through immigration. A combination of decreasing immigration and increasing demand for skills, however, led to increasing scarcity of trained workers from the 1970s onwards. With time, the system became untenable. The apartheid problem is analysed in Chapter 8.

Chapter 9 deals with the distortions found in countries with a pure planned economy. In this case the price mechanism has been put completely out of order and the allocation of resources takes place with the aid of administrative planning routines. Since both prices and the quantities to be produced are determined 'outside' the system there is, however, nothing to guarantee that supply will equal demand. The difficulties are multiplied by the fact that the individual markets cannot be dealt with one by one. All are interrelated since the different sectors deliver inputs to each other. Simultaneously a heavy and powerful bureaucracy is created which often looks more to its own interests than to those of society in general.

So far we have above all looked at the *effects* of different types of distortion for social welfare. Since these effects are virtually always negative from the point of view of society as a whole it is essential to proceed with the analysis and ask the question why they are introduced at all. We have already seen that special interests are often behind distorting interventions. It therefore remains to examine the logic behind the actions of these groups. Chapters 10–13 deal with this.

Which distortions will materialize is determined in a 'political market' where interventions are carried out by politicians in exchange for support (e.g., in the form of votes) from the special interest groups. To what extent this will succeed depends on how well the special interests manage to organize. This is normally easier for small groups than for large. With time the economy may be bound up more and more in a network of interests, with negative consequences for growth and structural change. These questions are examined in Chapter 10. In order to succeed, however, the lobby groups must devote real resources to work on politicians and public officials. These resources cannot then be employed in the production of the goods and services that the citizens demand. Lobbying may therefore be characterized as socially 'directly unproductive' activities. These activities are analysed in Chapter 11.

An extreme case of special interests and socially directly unproductive activities is when the state itself turns into a special interest group. When analysing this case it is not enough to see the state as a benevolent but 'exogenous' actor in the economic system. Instead, one has to look at the economic incentives for the political elite, the one making decisions on behalf of the state. It then becomes evident that the selfish interests of the power holders may influence the decisions. Abuse of this kind is found in all states. Sometimes, however, the special interest degenerates to the point where a so-called *predatory state* will arise, such that the only goal of the public administration is that of enriching the politicians and civil servants involved. Chapter 12 offers a theoretical overview of this problem while Chapter 13 examines two typical cases of predatory states: Haiti and the Dominican Republic. Chapter 14 briefly summarizes the logical development from the perfect market economy without distortions to the thoroughly corrupt predatory state.

Literature

Works dealing with efficiency and (to some extent) equity problems in general and discuss market failure:

Bator, Francis M. (1958), 'The Anatomy of Market Failure', *Quarterly Journal of Economics*, Vol. 72.

Begg, David; Fischer, Stanley and Dornbusch, Rudiger (2000), *Economics* (6th edn). McGraw-Hill, New York.

Bohm, Peter (1987), *Social Efficiency: A Concise Introduction to Welfare Economics* (2nd edn). Macmillan Education, London.

Johansson, Per-Olov (1991), *An Introduction to Modern Welfare Economics*. Cambridge University Press, Cambridge.

Koplin, H. T. (1971), *Microeconomic Analysis. Welfare and Efficiency in Private and Public Sectors*. Harper & Row, New York.

Nath, S. K. (1969), *A Reappraisal of Welfare Economics*. Routledge & Kegan Paul, London.

Literature dealing with the principles of the international division of labour:

Caves, Richard E., Frankel, Jeffrey A. and Jones, Ronald W. (1999), *World Trade and Payments: An Introduction* (8th edn). Addison-Wesley, Reading, MA.

Krugman, Paul R and Obstfeld, Maurice (2000), *International Economics: Theory and Policy* (5th edn). Addison-Wesley, Reading, MA.

Salvatore, Dominick (2001), *International Economics* (7th edn). Wiley, New York.

Södersten, Bo and Reed, Geoffrey (1994), *International Economics* (3rd edn). Macmillan, London.

A discussion of Swedish agricultural policy is found in:

Hedlund, Stefan and Lundahl, Mats (1986), 'Emergency Considerations in Swedish Agriculture: A Retrospective Look', *European Journal of Agricultural Economics*, Vol. 13.

Hedlund, Stefan and Lundahl, Mats (1998), Emergency Policies for Swedish Agriculture', in Lundahl, Mats, *Themes in International Economics*. Ashgate, Aldershot.

Import substitution policy in developing countries is discussed in:

Krueger, Anne O. (1978), 'Alternative Strategies and Employment in LDCs', *American Economic Review*, Vol. 68.

Krueger, Anne O. (1984), 'Trade Policies in Developing Countries', in: Jones, Ronald W. and Kenen, Peter B. (eds), *Handbook of International Economics*, Vol. 1. North-Holland, Amsterdam.

Little, Ian, Scitovsky, Tibor and Scott, Maurice (1970), *Industry and Trade in Some Developing Countries: A Comparative Study.* Oxford University Press, London.
Papageorgiou, Demetrios, Michaely, Michael and Choksi, Armeane (1991), *Liberalizing Foreign Trade,* Vol. 7. Basil Blackwell, Cambridge, MA.

The classic work on urban bias is:
Lipton, Michael (1977), *Why Poor People Stay Poor: A Study of Urban Bias in World Development.* Temple Smith, London.

The principles behind distortions in the labour market are analysed in:
Lundahl, Mats and Wadensjö, Eskil (1984), *Unequal Treatment. A Study in the Neo-Classical Theory of Discrimination.* Croom Helm, London and Sydney.

The distorting effects of the apartheid system are dealt with in:
Lundahl, Mats (1992), *Apartheid in Theory and Practice. An Economic Analysis.* Westview Press, Boulder, CO.

The problem of distortion in a planned economy is discussed in:
Halm, George N. (1970), *Economic Systems. A Comparative Analysis* (3rd edn). Holt, Rinehart & Winston, London.
Kornai, János (1992), *The Socialist System: The Political Economy of Communism.* Clarendon Press, Oxford.
Winiecki, Jan (1988), *The Distorted World of Soviet-Type Economies.* Routledge, London.

The behaviour and consequences of special interest groups are dealt with in:
Olson, Mancur (1965), *The Logic of Collective Action: Public Goods and the Theory of Groups.* Harvard University Press, Cambridge, MA.
Olson, Mancur (1982), *The Rise and Decline of Nations. Economic Growth, Stagflation, and Social Rigidities.* Yale University Press, New Haven, CT.

The theory of directly unproductive, profit-seeking activities is presented in:
Bhagwati, Jagdish (1982), 'Directly Unproductive, Profit-seeking Activities', *Journal of Political Economy,* Vol. 90.
Krueger, Anne O. (1974), 'The Political Economy of Rent-Seeking', *American Economic Review,* Vol. 64.

The state as a special interest group is dealt with in:
Brennan, Geoffrey and Buchanan, James M. (1983), 'Predictive Power and the Choice of Regimes', *Economic Journal,* Vol. 107.
Gunnarsson, Christer and Lundahl, Mats (1996), 'The Good, the Bad and the Wobbly. State Forms and Third World Economic Performance', in: Lundahl, Mats and Ndulu, Benno J. (eds), *New Directions in Development Economics. Growth, Environmental Concerns and Government in the 1990s.* Routledge, London and New York.
Levi, Margaret (1988), *Of Rule and Revenue.* University of California Press, Berkeley, CA.

Examples of how the predatory state works are given in:
Lundahl, Mats (1992), *Politics or Markets? Essays on Haitian Underdevelopment.* Routledge, London and New York.

2
Some Analytical Tools

The welfare problem is complicated and in order to carry out a more pro-found analysis we need to master some technical refinements, 'tools', that may be used in the study of the allocation affects of different distortions. The present chapter provides a set of such tools. We begin with a look at the characteristics of linearly homogeneous production functions (which are often preferred to a more general formulation because they are easier to handle). Thereafter we move on to a specific graphic technique of present-ing the production function, the so-called factor diagram. With the aid of this, another graphic tool, the box diagram, can be constructed, which allows us to take both commodity and factor markets into account simul-taneously. From the box diagram the production possibility curve may be derived, and this shows all the combinations of (two) goods that an econ-omy can produce with given resources. If this is combined with social indifference curves (showing the preferences of society) and relative com-modity prices we may shed light on the interaction between production (supply) and demand.

The box diagram with relative factor prices and the combination of the production possibility curve, indifference curves and relative commodity prices together constitute a simple general equilibrium model that may be employed for studies of how different interventions or market conditions affect social welfare. We also demonstrate that, under certain conditions, there is a one-to-one correspondence between commodity prices, factor prices and production techniques. This simplifies the analysis of what happens with respect to resource allocation and income distribution after a government intervention, for example.

Linearly homogeneous production functions

The production function expresses the amount of input needed in order to produce a given quantity of a certain commodity:

$$Q = Q(K, L) \tag{2.1}$$

where Q is the quantity produced and K and L stand for the inputs of capital and labour, respectively. Economic theory frequently employs linearly homogeneous production functions, since these display a number of analytically attractive features. A linearly homogeneous production function possesses the characteristic that

$$\lambda Q = Q(\lambda K, \lambda L) \tag{2.2}$$

where $\lambda > 0$: that is, if the inputs of capital and labour increase in the same proportion (e.g., are doubled), so will output. Thus production does not display any economies of scale (constant returns to scale).

The production function is also assumed to meet the following conditions:

$$Q_K \equiv \frac{\partial Q}{\partial K} > 0$$

$$Q_L \equiv \frac{\partial Q}{\partial L} > 0$$

$$Q_{KK} \equiv \frac{\partial^2 Q}{\partial K^2} < 0$$

$$Q_{LL} \equiv \frac{\partial^2 Q}{\partial L^2} < 0$$

$$Q_{KL} \equiv \frac{\partial^2 Q}{\partial L \partial K} > 0$$

$$Q_{LK} \equiv \frac{\partial^2 Q}{\partial K \partial L} > 0$$

The conditions state the following: the marginal products of the two factors of production are positive, but decreasing. If the input of only one of the factors increases so will output, but the additions will become successively smaller. Both factors of production hence display *diminishing returns*. On the other hand, if, for example, the input of capital is increased the marginal product of *labour* will increase, and vice versa. This means that when labour is combined with more capital its capacity to produce increases and, likewise, a unit of capital becomes more productive as more workers are added.

The size of the marginal products in the case of linearly homogeneous production functions depends only on the proportions in which capital and labour are employed: that is, on the quotient between the inputs (the *factor proportions*). In order to see this we may modify (2.2) by setting $\lambda = 1/L$. We may then write the production function (2.2) as

$$q = \frac{Q}{L} = Q\left(\frac{K}{L}, 1\right) = q(k) \tag{2.3}$$

that is, simply as a function of the capital–labour ratio, or

$$Q = LQ\left(\frac{K}{L}, 1\right) = Lq(k) \tag{2.4}$$

where $k = K/L$.

We may then write the marginal products as

$$Q_K = \frac{\partial Q}{\partial K} = \frac{\partial(Lq)}{\partial K} = Lq_k \frac{\partial k}{\partial K} = q_k > 0 \tag{2.5}$$

and

$$Q_L = \frac{\partial Q}{\partial L} = \frac{\partial(Lq)}{\partial L} = q + Lq_k \frac{\partial k}{\partial L} = q + Lq_k \frac{-K}{L^2} = q - kq_k > 0 \tag{2.6}$$

where

$$q \equiv q(k) \text{ and } q_k \equiv q_k(k) \equiv \frac{\partial q}{\partial k}$$

Thus the marginal products depend only on the capital intensity, K/L. But what does this dependence look like? To see this we must move on to the *changes* of the marginal products:

$$Q_{KK} - \frac{\partial q_k}{\partial K} - q_{kk} \frac{\partial k}{\partial K} = \frac{q_{kk}}{L} < 0 \tag{2.7}$$

and

$$Q_{LL} = \frac{\partial(q - kq_k)}{\partial L} = q_k \frac{\partial k}{\partial L} - kq_{kk} \frac{\partial k}{\partial L} - q_k \frac{\partial k}{\partial L} = -kq_{kk} \frac{-K}{L^2} = \frac{k^2}{L} q_{kk} < 0 \tag{2.8}$$

We have assumed that Q_{KK} and Q_{LL} are both negative. Hence

$$\frac{\partial Q_K}{\partial k} = \frac{\partial q_k}{\partial k} = q_{kk} < 0$$

If the capital intensity increases the marginal product of capital will decrease. We may also determine the sign of

$$\frac{\partial Q_L}{\partial k} = \frac{\partial (q - kq_k)}{\partial k} = q_k - q_k - kq_{kk} = -kq_{kk} > 0 \tag{2.9}$$

The marginal product of labour will increase when the capital intensity increases.

The factor diagram

Production functions may be expressed graphically with the aid of the so-called factor diagram shown in Figure 2.1. In the figure we measure the factor use on the two axes (e.g., capital on the horizontal and labour on the vertical one). The two curves, *II* and *JJ*, are production isoquants for the two commodities, which we may call manufactures and agricultural goods. The isoquants show the different combinations of capital and labour required to produce given quantities of the commodities. (For each of the commodities there is a series of isoquants, extending from the southwest to the northeast, where an isoquant further to the northeast indicates a larger output than one further to the southwest.) If in the following we assume that the production functions are linearly homogeneous the isoquant for two units must be exactly twice as far away from the origin as the isoquant for one unit. The isoquants are continuous curves whose properties are determined by the assumptions made at the beginning of the present chapter, since it is assumed that it is possible to substitute labour for capital and vice versa in the production of both goods.

If we move along a given isoquant from the northwest to the southeast the input of labour is reduced with *dL* while the input of capital increases with

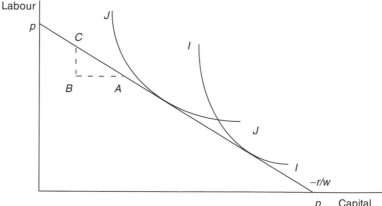

Figure 2.1   Production isoquants

dK. If we take the total differential of the production function (2.1) and put it equal to zero we can see what happens on the factor side when output is held constant (i.e., as we move along the isoquant):

$$dQ = Q_K dK + Q_L dL = 0 \tag{2.10}$$

and

$$\frac{dL}{dK} = -\frac{Q_K}{Q_L} \tag{2.11}$$

The slope of the isoquant is given by the ratio of the marginal products of the two factors.

The factor diagram also shows the marginal products of the different factors. If, as before, we assume that the marginal product of labour increases with the amount of capital available (and vice versa), a movement from the northwest to the southeast along an isoquant implies that the marginal product of labour increases (while that of capital decreases) since the labour/capital ratio decreases.

Throughout the present work we will assume that the production isoquants of the two commodities intersect each other *only* once. This assumption implies that we always know which of the two goods is the (most) capital-intensive and which the labour-intensive one, respectively. (Should the isoquants intersect twice, the relative factor prices will decide which good is capital-intensive and which is labour-intensive.)

The slope of the straight *pp* line indicates the relative factor prices in the economy (i.e., how many units of labour may be traded for a given amount of capital). *AB* units of capital, for example, cost *BC* units of labour. The relative price of capital, *r/w* (where *r* denotes the cost of capital and *w* the wage rate), thus is *BC/AB*. The flatter the slope of *pp*, the more expensive is labour, relatively speaking, and the more units of capital are needed to 'buy' a given amount of labour.

A line such as *pp* is also known as a *budget line*. The budget line is an *isocost line* that may be expressed by the equation

$$C = wL + rK \tag{2.12}$$

The equation shows the different combinations of labour and capital that give rise to the same cost. If we differentiate (2.12) and put the differential equal to zero, at given factor prices, we obtain:

$$dC = wdL + rdK = 0 \tag{2.13}$$

or

$$\frac{dL}{dK} = -\frac{r}{w} \tag{2.14}$$

that is, the slope of the factor price line. The total cost, C, does not affect the slope but determines the distance between the budget line and the origin.

Each point on an isoquant denotes a given factor combination and different factor combinations can be used to produce the same quantity of the commodity. Which production technique will be chosen is given by the relative factor prices of the economy. (As we will soon see, how much we want to produce does not matter.) For each given cost level it pays to produce as much as is technically possible. The maximum point is found where the isocost line is tangent to an isoquant. (It is also possible to produce at any other point on the isocost line, but all other points lie on lower isoquants than does the point of tangency.) If, on the other hand, the goal is to produce a given quantity, the cheapest way of doing this is given by the point of tangency between the corresponding isoquant and an isocost line.

In the above reasoning producers are assumed to maximize their profits (i.e., they raise production factors up to the point where the value of their marginal products equals what they are paid):

$$w = PQ_L \tag{2.15}$$

$$r = PQ_K \tag{2.16}$$

where P is the price of the commodities. If P is eliminated from (2.15) and (2.16) we find that

$$\frac{r}{w} = \frac{Q_K}{Q_L} \tag{2.17}$$

that is, the slope of the factor price line (budget line) must coincide with that of the isoquant. (This is of course the tangency condition.)

Thus, if one knows the relative factor prices it is possible to determine the relation between the marginal products of the factors. Then we also know the proportions in which the production factors are used. Since we have already shown that the marginal products are functions only of the factor intensities, the latter must also remain unchanged as long as relative factor prices are constant. This means that the optimal factor intensity is independent of the output volume. If we shift the isocost line outwards from the origin without changing its slope, the optimal production points will lie on a straight line that goes through the origin.

The box diagram

By combining two isoquant diagrams (assuming that the economy produces only two goods) we may construct a *box diagram*, as shown in Figure 2.2. The box diagram shows the production of commodities and the factor use simultaneously. It is hence a powerful tool for analyses that have to take into account the interdependence between markets. Exactly as in Figure 2.1 the use of labour is measured on the vertical axis and the use of capital on the horizontal axis. The isoquants for manufactures extend from the southwest to the northeast, precisely as in Figure 2.1. The sides of the box show the total factor endowment of the economy and the slope of the diagonal *OO'* the relative factor supply.

The finesse with the box diagram is that we may introduce a second commodity: agricultural goods. The production of the latter is measured from the northeast to the southwest, with *O'* as the origin, while the factor use in agriculture is measured downwards (labour) and leftwards (capital). The figure displays a number of points where the *I* and *J* isoquants are tangents to each other. All these points are interesting because from such a point it is not possible to increase the production of one of the goods without reducing the production of the other. All such points are hence *efficient*. No other points have this feature. If we take, for example, point *A* as the point of departure we see that it is possible to increase the production of manufactures without having to reduce the production of agricultural goods. What is needed is a reallocation of production factors between the two sectors. If we join all the efficient points we obtain the so-called *contract curve*. In our figure this happens to lie below the diagonal. That means that the production of manufactures is relatively capital-intensive and the

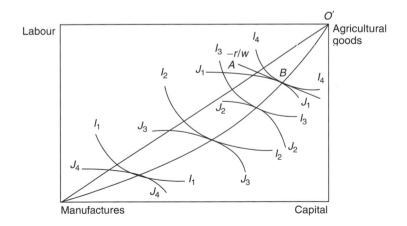

Figure 2.2 The box diagram

production of agricultural goods relatively labour-intensive. This must be true for all factor and commodity prices since the tangency points of the isoquants are determined exclusively by the technologies of the two sectors.

If the common tangents through all efficient production points are drawn, the relative factor prices that result precisely in this production are obtained. As we move from the southwest to the northeast along the contract curve ever more manufactures are produced in relation to agricultural goods. This increases the demand for capital in relation to the demand for labour since the production of manufactures is capital-intensive, relatively speaking. The price line gets steeper and steeper (i.e., the relative price of capital increases).

At the same time, however, factor substitution takes place. Labour is substituted for capital in both sectors. This can be seen by drawing straight lines from O to points that lie further and further to the northeast on the contract curve. These lines get steeper and steeper (in relation to the lower horizontal axis). Lines from O' to the contract curve, on the other hand, form an ever narrower angle with the right-hand vertical axis. The labour intensity thus increases also in the agricultural sector.

The production possibility curve

The box diagram indirectly contains information about relative commodity prices. The more expensive labour gets in terms of capital, the more expensive the labour-intensive good – the agricultural good – will get in terms of the capital-intensive good, manufactures. (We will prove this formally later.) If, however, we want to find out how the structure of production changes when commodity prices change, or what will happen if the relative factor endowment changes or technological progress takes place it is often practical to use the *production possibility curve* (transformation curve). This curve can be derived from the box diagram. The derivation is shown in Figure 2.3. We start from the contract curve and the production isoquants that have common points of tangency on this curve. Three such pairs of isoquants have been put into the figure.

In order to derive the production possibility curve we use the points where the isoquants cut the diagonal. Since we are working with linearly homogeneous production functions the diagonal may be used as a yardstick for the production of the two goods. (Each point on the diagonal corresponds to a given combination of labour and capital, and output changes in the same proportion as factor use.) From the diagonal we project the output of agricultural goods on the horizontal axis and the output of manufactures on the vertical. In order to arrive at the production possibility curve we now simply need to extend the vertical projection lines upwards and the horizontal ones leftwards until they intersect each other. The point of intersection indicates the maximum quantity of agricultural goods that the economy can produce

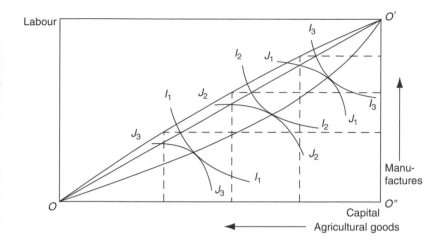

Figure 2.3   Derivation of the production possibility curve

given the output of manufactures, and vice versa. We have hence derived a point on the production possibility curve. In the figure three points have been derived. In principle of course an infinite number of points can be derived in the same way. If we connect these with each other we obtain the complete production possibility curve.

In Figure 2.4 we have taken the production possibility curve out of the box diagram and turned it through 90 degrees. On the horizontal axis we now measure the production of manufactures and on the vertical axis the production of agricultural goods. Point A is a (technically) *efficient* production point. Given an industrial output of I_1 the economy can produce a maximum of J_1 agricultural goods.

All points on the production possibility curve are efficient. Given the factor endowment of the economy (labour, capital) and given the prevailing technology they show the *maximum* combinations of the two commodities that may be produced. A point such as C, on the other hand, is inefficient. The resources of the economy are not fully used, but it is possible to increase the production of one good without reducing the production of the other good.

We are also interested in a measure of the slope of the production possibility curve. For this, we need the two production functions:

$$I = I(K_I, \ L_I) \tag{2.18}$$

$$J = J(K_J, \ L_J) \tag{2.19}$$

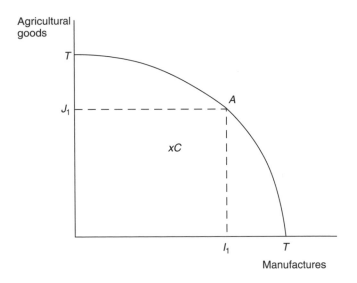

Figure 2.4   The production possibility curve

The production possibility curve is defined for a given capital stock and a given labour force:

$$\overline{K} = K_I + K_J \tag{2.20}$$

$$\overline{L} = L_I + L_J \tag{2.21}$$

If we differentiate (2.18)–(2.21) we obtain the changes of output and factor use as we move along the production possibility curve:

$$dI = I_K dK_I + I_L dL_I \tag{2.22}$$

$$dJ = J_K dK_J + J_L dL_J \tag{2.23}$$

$$0 = dK_I + dK_J \tag{2.24}$$

$$0 = dL_I + dL_J \tag{2.25}$$

We may thereafter solve for

$$dK_J = -dK_I \tag{2.26}$$

$$dL_J = -dL_I \tag{2.27}$$

and substitute into (2.23). This yields

$$dJ = -J_K dK_I - J_L dL_I \tag{2.28}$$

If we combine (2.28) with (2.23) we get the slope of the production possibility curve in terms of the changes in factor use:

$$\frac{dJ}{dI} = -\frac{J_K dK_I + J_L dL_I}{I_K dK_I + I_L dL_I} \tag{2.29}$$

This expression may in turn be simplified. We know that if producers maximize their profits they will pay the two production factors the value of their marginal products:

$$r = P_J J_K = P_I I_K \tag{2.30}$$

and

$$w = P_J J_L = P_I I_L \tag{2.31}$$

where P_J and P_I are the prices of agricultural goods and manufactures, respectively. These expressions may be solved for the marginal products:

$$J_K = \frac{r}{P_J} \tag{2.32}$$

$$I_K = \frac{r}{P_I} \tag{2.33}$$

$$J_L = \frac{w}{P_J} \tag{2.34}$$

$$I_L = \frac{w}{P_I} \tag{2.35}$$

These expressions may thereafter be substituted into the expression for the slope of the production possibility curve (2.29):

$$\frac{dJ}{dI} = -\frac{\frac{r}{P_J} dK_I + \frac{w}{P_J} dL_I}{\frac{r}{P_I} dK_I + \frac{w}{P_I} dL_I} \tag{2.36}$$

After simplification, this can be shown as:

$$\frac{dJ}{dI} = -\frac{P_I}{P_J} \tag{2.37}$$

The slope of the production possibility curve coincides with the relative commodity prices when profits are maximized.

The shape of the production possibility curve

The slope of the TT curve provides a measure (in real terms) of the opportunity cost of producing the two goods (the marginal rate of transformation). This opportunity cost increases with the output volume. If we move towards the southeast from point A in Figure 2.4 along the production possibility curve, all the time making equal reductions of the output of agricultural goods, we find that the additions to the production of manufactures get smaller and smaller. This means that, at the margin, the production of manufactures gets even more expensive in terms of agricultural goods. Conversely, of course, a given reduction of the production of manufactures results in smaller and smaller increases of agricultural output (a movement towards the northwest along TT). The increasing opportunity cost makes for the characteristic outward-bending (convex) shape of the production possibility curve. (In the borderline case of constant opportunity cost the transformation curve becomes a straight line. The additional output of one good when the production of the other good is reduced is then always the same.)

It is easily demonstrated that the opportunity cost, as given by the production possibility curve, can be interpreted in terms of marginal cost. We have already derived the opportunity cost in terms of J of increasing the production of I as the relation between the commodity prices (the relative price of I or the price of I in terms of J: see equation 2.37). However, under perfect competition we know that the price of a good is equal to its marginal cost,

$$P_I = MC_I \tag{2.38}$$

$$P_J = MC_J \tag{2.39}$$

so that

$$\frac{dJ}{dI} = -\frac{P_I}{P_J} = -\frac{MC_I}{MC_J} \tag{2.40}$$

There may be different reasons for the outward-bending slope of the production possibility curve. A simple case is when some factor, such as capital, is *sector-specific* (i.e., immobile between sectors). In that case the diminishing returns in both sectors will lead directly to a convex production possibility curve. Another possibility is when the production factors display skill differences. The workers most productive in manufacturing are hired first in that sector. If the production of industrial goods is to expand fewer and fewer skilled workers have to be hired (i.e., workers who contribute less and less to output).

In the foregoing we have, however, worked with *homogeneous* production factors (i.e., all workers have equal skills and all capital is of equal value in terms of productivity), and we have not put any restrictions on the mobility of capital between sectors. In spite of this, given that the production functions are linearly homogeneous, it can be demonstrated that the production possibility curve – except for certain special cases – must be outward-bending. This can be done, for example using Figures 2.5 and 2.6.

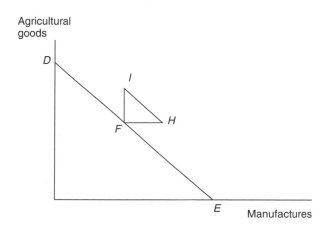

Figure 2.5 The convexity of the production possibility curve, I

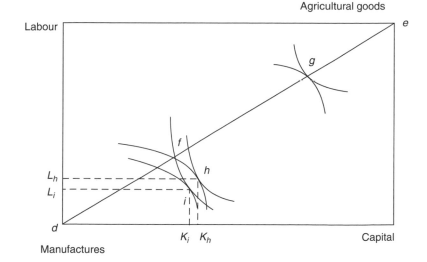

Figure 2.6 The convexity of the production possibility curve, II

At point D in Figure 2.5 only agricultural goods are produced and at point E only manufactures. These points correspond to points d and e in the box diagram of Figure 2.6. The economy may, however, also produce at any point on the diagonal of the box, such as f, by using the same techniques as at e and d (i.e., the techniques that are given by the capital intensity K/L, the capital intensity of the economy as a whole).

To point f corresponds point F in Figure 2.5. The DFE line must be straight because a given increase of the production of manufacturers anywhere on the line requires a constant decrease of agricultural output. (This follows from the assumption of linear homogeneity.) For production to be efficient, so that we are on the contract and production possibility curves, two production isoquants must be tangential to each other in the box, *which in turn implies that the ratios of the marginal products of the two factors are equal in the two lines of production.* Assume that this is the case in some point on the diagonal, such as g. Then the same is true for all points on the diagonal, since with linearly homogeneous production functions the slopes of the isoquants are equal along a ray from the origin (e or d). The production possibility curve then is the straight line DE.

This, however, is a special case, implying that the economy uses the same technique in both lines of production, which is hardly probable. If instead two production isoquants cut each other at point f the efficient production points lie outside the diagonal, for example at h and i, which correspond to H and I in Figure 2.5. Thus, the production possibility curve must contain points such as H and I, northwest of the straight line DE. We may therefore repeat the reasoning. In point i in the box diagram (point I in Figure 2.5) L_i units of labour and K_i units of capital are used in manufacturing. If we increase the production of manufactures, moving to point h (H) (i.e., with FH) we must increase the factor use in the manufacturing sector with L_iL_h and K_iK_h. But the same factors could have been employed to produce IF agricultural goods. We may draw another box with sides L_iL_h and K_iK_h with the end points i and h and the diagonal ih. Thereafter we may repeat the reasoning above and demonstrate that the efficient production points between I and H must lie to the northeast of IH if the factor intensity differs between the sectors.

Finally the question arises whether, for example, IH may not constitute a linear segment on a production possibility curve that otherwise is outward-bending. The answer is no. Both I and H correspond to points in the box where the techniques employed differ. When you move from I to H along the straight line IH, production factors are shifted from agriculture to manufacturing in fixed proportions: $(K_iK_h)/(L_iL_h)$. By coincidence the agricultural sector may use precisely these factor proportions, but as we already know the manufacturing sector is using a different technique. For the movement along IH, which corresponds to the diagonal in the new box, to be a movement along the contract curve, factor proportions have to remain constant in both lines of production so that the slopes of the isoquants in the points of tangency are not altered. This, however, is impossible. The factor proportions in agriculture do not change when you move from *i* to *h*, but those of manufacturing must do so, since this sector at the outset had a capital intensity K_h/L_h which did not correspond to $(K_iK_h)/(L_iL_h)$. Hence the isoquants must intersect each other along the diagonal *ih*.

Social indifference curves

The production possibility curve describes the supply since of the economy. To describe the demand side we use *social indifference curves*. Indifference curves are shown in Figure 2.7.

Indifference curves are easiest to describe when they portray the preferences of a single individual. A given indifference curve, such as U_1, shows the combinations of manufactured goods and agricultural goods that give the individual the same utility. U_2 lies to the northeast of U_1 and hence represents a higher utility level than U_1. This is easily seen if we take an arbitrary point on U_1 (e.g., *A*). All points on the segment *CB* are preferred to *A* because they represent more of at least one of the goods than *A*. The same reasoning may be applied to all points on U_1. U_2 hence represents a higher utility level altogether than U_1.

The slope of the indifference curve is negative. In order to give up a fixed quantity of one of the goods individuals require more of the other and, if the marginal utility of the good in question is diminishing, people will require larger and larger additions of, say, agricultural goods to successively give up a fixed quantity of manufactures, and vice versa. As a result of this the

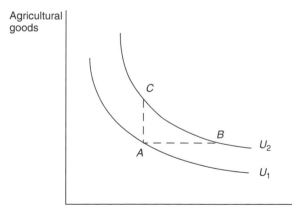

Figure 2.7 Indifference curves

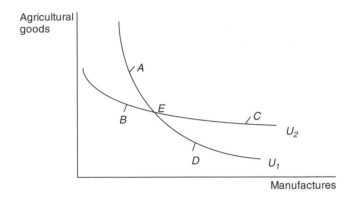

Figure 2.8   Intransitivity of preferences

indifference curves bulge inwards. They are *convex to the origin*. The slope of a curve, which indicates how many agricultural goods the consumer is prepared to abstain from at the margin in order to get more manufactured goods, *the marginal rate of substitution in consumption*, thus diminishes as we move towards the southeast along a given curve. (The same is true for manufactures as we move towards the northwest.) The indifference curves of an individual cannot intersect each other. This is shown with the aid of Figure 2.8. In this figure the two 'indifference curves' cut each other. This, however, leads to *intransitivity* in the preferences of the individual (i.e., to a sequence where alternative *B*, which is as good as alternative *C*, is preferred to alternative *D* which in turn is as good as alternative *A*). Simultaneously, however, *A* is preferred to *B* in a direct comparison of these two points. In order to rule out this type of inconsistency (*intransitivity*) in the behaviour of the individual, the indifference curves must not intersect each other.

Indifference curves are, however, used also on an aggregate level to express the preferences of 'the entire society'. This variety of indifference curves is considerably more complicated even though the social indifference curves on the surface look exactly like individual curves. A social indifference curve may be defined as all the combinations of the two goods that put every citizen in society on predetermined arbitrary utility levels. ('Society' is indifferent between the different commodity combinations precisely because the utility level does not change for any citizen.)

How such a curve may be derived is illustrated in Figure 2.9 for the simple two-person case. Society is taken to consist of two individuals: *H*-son and *T*-son. The total endowment of goods in society is given by the axes of the box in the figure. *H*-son's utility level is measured towards the northwest from *O*, and *T*-son's towards the southwest from *O'*. At point *C* the individuals have divided the entire output between themselves. Point *C* in addition

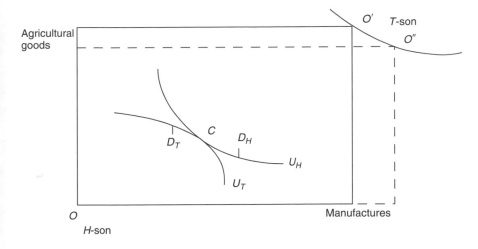

Figure 2.9   Social indifference curves

is Pareto optimal. The indifference curves are tangents to each other. Nobody can be better off (obtain more of at least one good) unless the other one becomes worse off (obtains less of at least one good).

In order to obtain the first point on the social indifference curve we need the smallest total quantity of each the two goods that place *H*-son and *T*-son on the utility levels given by point *C*. If we measure from point *O* this combination obviously is the one given by point *O*' (i.e., the total outputs of manufactures and agricultural goods). The individuals have divided these between themselves in the proportions given by point *C*.

It is, however, not enough with *O*'. We need more points to be able to construct a curve. The definition of the social indifference curve required that neither *H*-son's nor *T*-son's utility level be changed. This can be achieved by letting *T*-son's indifference curve 'slide' along *H*-son's so that the two curves continue to have a point of tangency. A possible point is D_H on U_H which would then be tangential to point D_T on U_T. *T*-son's utility will remain unchanged if in D_H he can consume as many manufactures and as many agricultural goods as in *C*. Then, however, we can no longer measure *T*-son's utility level from *O*', as *T*-son's origin must be shifted rightwards to the corresponding extent. He must get as many manufactures as are indicated by the distance between D_H (as it has been drawn) and the right-hand vertical axis in the box. To this we must add *H*-son's consumption of manufactures. Altogether more manufactures are required than before. *T*-son's new origin must lie on the broken vertical line, which has been obtained by adding *H*-son's and *T*-son's consumption from left to right. (Alternatively we may begin in D_H, with *H*-son's new consumption of manufactures, and to this add *T*-son's unchanged quantity, which is the distance between *C* and the vertical axis through *O'*.)

We may thereafter add also *H*-son's and *T*-son's consumption of agricultural goods in D_H and D_T, respectively, and measure total consumption from the bottom of the box. This tells us that *T*-son's new origin must also lie on the broken *horizontal* line. This new origin thus is *O''*. To compensate *H*-son and *T*-son for the reduction of the total consumption of agricultural goods their combined consumption of manufactures must increase. (We have assumed that *T*-son's consumption in *C* is the same as in D_H.) Point *O''* indicates exactly how much is required to compensate for the given total reduction. *O''* hence lies on the new social indifference curve.

In this way it is possible in principle to construct a social indifference curve, say U_1 in Figure 2.8, also for several individuals; so far, so good. We took as our point of departure a given distribution of income between *H*-son and *T*-son (the one given by point *C*). The problem with social indifference curves, however, is that when the distribution of income changes (which it typically does over time) this will lead to intransitivity (the indifference curves intersect each other). This may be seen by choosing another efficient consumption point in the original box (Figure 2.9), for example, somewhere northeast of point *C*. In the new point of tangency *H*-son has more resources and *T*-son fewer. The distribution of income has changed to the detriment of *T*-son. At this point as well, however, *T*-son remains at his point of origin, *O'*. If we want to construct a new social indifference curve, given the new income distribution, this will also thus pass through *O'*. It will, however, not pass through *O''*. The additional manufactures required by the two individuals in order to compensate for the given reduction of the total consumption of agricultural goods will hardly be the same as at point *C*, since the distribution of income has changed. The new social indifference curve will intersect the old one.

We arrive at the situation depicted in Figure 2.8. In the former situation, for example, points *B* and *C* are as good as *E*. The new distribution of income will generate, for example, points *A* and *D* as equivalent to *E*. This naturally creates problems when it comes to using social indifference curves. When the distribution of income changes, so will the preferences of 'society'. This means that the very yardstick used for measuring the welfare effects of changes is itself subject to change. In order to use social indifference curves, strictly speaking the distribution of income must be kept constant. The problem is that policy measures virtually always have an impact on the distribution of income. To neutralize this in principle a system of lump-sum taxes and transfers is required which restores the original income distribution (and does not influence how resources are allocated in the system).

We may also derive the slope of the indifference curve algebraically. The utility of society is a function of the total consumption of manufactures and agricultural goods:

$$U = U(C_I, C_J) \tag{2.41}$$

(Here, we assume that the distribution of income is kept constant through lump-sum taxes and transfers.)

The indifference curve shows the various combinations of the two goods that yield the same social utility. We may hence differentiate the utility function totally to arrive at a measure of the change of utility when the consumption of the two commodities changes, and put the differential equal to zero (which keeps the sum of the utility changes constant):

$$dU = U_I dC_I + U_J dC_J = 0 \tag{2.42}$$

From this we may derive the slope as

$$\frac{dC_J}{dC_I} = -\frac{U_I}{U_J} \tag{2.43}$$

that is, as the ratio of the marginal utilities (the marginal rate of substitution in consumption).

The commodity price line

The production possibility curve and the indifference curve are not by themselves sufficient to determine which point on the indifference curve and the production possibility curve, respectively, the consumers and the producers choose. You also have to know the relative prices prevailing in the economy. If the prices of manufactures and agricultural goods are denoted by P_I and P_J and the total budget of the consumer by R (provided that the entire income is consumed) we have

$$R = P_I C_I + P_J C_J \tag{2.44}$$

Equation (2.44) yields the price or budget line. (Each price line is simultaneously an *isobudget* line: i.e., it shows the combinations of the two goods that may be purchased for a given budget.)

The slope of the budget line is obtained by differentiating (2.44) totally and putting the result equal to zero:

$$dR = P_I dC_I + P_J dC_J = 0 \tag{2.45}$$

or

$$\frac{dC_J}{dC_I} = -\frac{P_I}{P_J} \tag{2.46}$$

Thus, the slope is given by the relative commodity prices. The distance between the lines and the origin is determined by the size of the budget, given these prices.

The above reasoning is illustrated in Figure 2.10, where the slope of the price line, *pp*, indicates how much of one commodity is required to obtain a given quantity of the other commodity in the market. Thus, *AB* manufactures are required to get *BC* agricultural goods, and vice versa. The steeper the slope, the more agricultural goods are required to purchase a given quantity of manufactures (i.e., the more expensive are the latter). The figure also shows a price line, *p'p'*, which is parallel to *pp*. This represents a higher income level (budget) in society, which means that it is possible to buy more of both goods.

We have in the foregoing demonstrated how profit maximization among producers results in a slope of the transformation curve at the optimum point that coincides with the slope of the commodity price line. It then remains to investigate the consumption side in the corresponding way. For this we must maximize the social welfare function with the national income (the value of what the country produces) as the budget restriction. It is assumed that the entire national income is consumed:

Maximize

$$U(C_I,\ C_J)$$

when

$$R = P_I C_I + P_J C_J \tag{2.44}$$

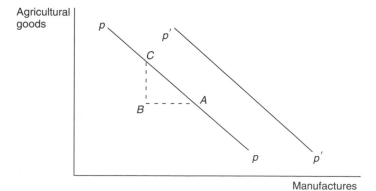

Figure 2.10   Relative commodity prices

This yields the Lagrangean

$$\varphi = U(C_I,\ C_J) - \mu[R - (P_IC_I + P_JC_J)] \qquad (2.47)$$

and the maximum is obtained when

$$U_I + \mu P_I = 0 \qquad (2.48)$$

$$U_J + \mu P_J = 0 \qquad (2.49)$$

or when

$$\frac{dC_J}{dC_I} = -\frac{P_I}{P_J} \qquad (2.50)$$

that is, when the slope of the social indifference curve coincides with that of the budget line.

Equilibrium in the commodity market

In Figure 2.11 we depict the equilibrium in a closed economy (an economy without foreign trade), which is what we just derived. The marginal rate of substitution in consumption coincides with the relative commodity prices, provided that consumers maximize their utility, as well as with the marginal rate of transformation (the opportunity cost) in production, given that producers maximize their profits.

The choice of the consumers ('society') is determined by the relative prices, given the preferences and the income. The combination chosen is the one given by the point of tangency, A, between the price line that corresponds

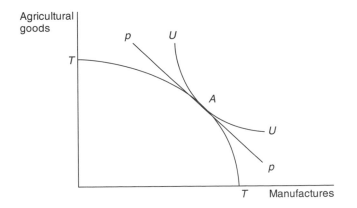

Figure 2.11 Equilibrium in the commodity market

to the income level in society and an indifference curve. All other indifference curves cut the price line and lie to the southwest of the curve that is tangent to the line. Hence they represent a lower social utility.

On the production side the price line determines where on the production possibility curve production will take place. Even though all points on the curve are *technically* efficient, only one point is *economically* efficient. At the economically efficient point the *opportunity cost* of producing coincides with the prevailing relative prices. At all other points the income of the producers is lower, since these points lie to the southwest of the budget line.

Commodity prices and factor prices

We have already demonstrated that there is a one-to-one correspondence between relative factor prices and production techniques (capital intensity). This relation can be extended to encompass relative commodity prices as well.

In order to prove this we need *Euler's theorem*. This theorem states that if we have linearly homogeneous production functions

$$Q \equiv Q_K K + Q_L L \tag{2.51}$$

which means that the resulting output is divided among the two factors if these are rewarded with their marginal products. The marginal products are given by (2.5) and (2.6) as $Q_K = q_k$ and $Q_L = q - kq_k$.

The right-hand side of (2.51) may now be written as

$$q_k K + (q - kq_k)L = q_k K + qL - kq_k L = qL = Q \tag{2.52}$$

We also know that when profits are maximized

$$PQ_K = r \tag{2.53}$$

and

$$PQ_L = w \tag{2.54}$$

The production factors receive the value of their respective marginal products. We may denote the use of capital and labour per unit of output with

$$a_{KQ} = K/Q \tag{2.55}$$

and

$$a_{LQ} = L/Q \tag{2.56}$$

If we have two products, manufactures and agricultural goods (I and J), with the aid of Euler's theorem (using P_I and I as well as P_J and J, for the prices and quantities of manufactures and agricultural goods, respectively) we obtain expressions such as

$$P_I I = P_I I_K K_I + P_I I_L L_I$$

K_I and L_I represent the use of capital and labour, respectively, in the industrial sector. Since we have a corresponding expression for the agricultural sector, with the use of (2.53–2.56) we may write the relative commodity price as

$$\frac{P_I}{P_J} = \frac{r a_{KI} + w a_{LI}}{r a_{KJ} + w a_{LJ}} \tag{2.57}$$

or, dividing both the numerator and the denominator on the right-hand side by w in order to get the relative factor price r/w:

$$\frac{P_I}{P_J} = \frac{(r/w) a_{KI} + a_{LI}}{(r/w) a_{KJ} + a_{LJ}} \tag{2.58}$$

We are interested in the sign of $d(P_I/P_J)/d(r/w)$. With the aid of the formula for the derivative of a quotient we get

$$\frac{d(P_I/P_J)}{d(r/w)} = \frac{1}{[(r/w) a_{KJ} + a_{LJ}]^2} \left[\left(\frac{r}{w} a_{KJ} + a_{LJ} \right) \left(a_{KI} + \frac{r}{w} a'_{KI} + a'_{LI} \right) \right.$$
$$\left. - \left(\frac{r}{w} a_{KI} + a_{LI} \right) \left(a_{KJ} + \frac{r}{w} a'_{KJ} + a'_{LJ} \right) \right] \tag{2.59}$$

where the prime sign indicates a change in the factor use per produced unit:

$$a'_{KI} = \frac{d a_{KI}}{d(r/w)},$$

and so on.

The expression (2.59) may be simplified by using the profit-maximization condition that the relative factor price has to coincide with the slope of the production isoquant:

$$\frac{r}{w} = -\frac{dL_i}{dK_I} = -\frac{d(a_{LI} I)}{d(a_{KI} I)} = -\frac{a'_{LI}}{a'_{KI}} \tag{2.60}$$

(where we make use of the definitions $a_{LI} = L_I/I$ and $a_{KI} = K_I/I$). In the same way we obtain

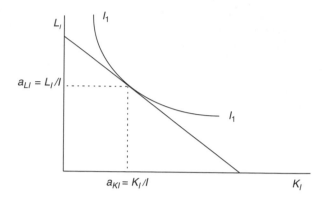

Figure 2.12 Cost minimization per unit of output

$$\frac{r}{w} = -\frac{a'_{LJ}}{a'_{KJ}} \tag{2.61}$$

This may be illustrated by Figure 2.12.

The last two equations may be rewritten as

$$\frac{r}{w}a'_{KI} + a'_{LI} = 0 \tag{2.62}$$

and

$$\frac{r}{w}a'_{KJ} + a'_{LJ} = 0 \tag{2.63}$$

which we can then put into the expression for the price changes (2.59) and obtain

$$\frac{d(P_I/P_J)}{d(r/w)} = \frac{a_{KI}\left(\frac{r}{w}a_{KJ} + a_{LJ}\right) - a_{KJ}\left(\frac{r}{w}a_{KI} + a_{LI}\right)}{\left[(r/w)a_{KJ} + a_{LJ}\right]^2} =$$

$$= \frac{a_{KI}a_{LJ} - a_{KJ}a_{LI}}{\left[(r/w)a_{KJ} + a_{LJ}\right]^2} = \frac{\left(\frac{a_{KI}}{a_{LI}} - \frac{a_{KJ}}{a_{LJ}}\right)a_{LI}a_{LJ}}{\left[(r/w)\frac{a_{KJ}}{a_{LJ}} + 1\right]^2 a_{LJ}^2} = \frac{a_{LI}}{a_{LJ}}\frac{(k_I - k_J)}{\left[(r/w)k_J + 1\right]^2} \tag{2.64}$$

into which the symbols for the capital intensities of the two branches of production

$$k_I = \frac{a_{KI}}{a_{LI}} \text{ and } k_J = \frac{a_{KJ}}{a_{LJ}}$$

have been substituted.

Expression (2.64) is greater than zero if $k_I > k_J$ (i.e., if manufacturing is the capital-intensive sector). This leads to the intuitively plausible conclusion that an increase in the relative price of capital leads to an increase in the price of the capital-intensive goods, and vice versa. We have thus shown that there is a one-to-one correspondence between commodity prices, factor prices and production techniques (capital intensities) in the case of linearly homogeneous production functions, provided that manufactures always – at any factor prices – are more capital-intensive than agricultural goods (i.e., no factor reversals take place).

Conclusions

This chapter has been devoted to the construction of an analytical 'tool box' which, in spite of its simplicity, is a very useful instrument for analysing the allocation effects of different government interventions. The remainder of the present work will to a large extent deal with how this apparatus may be used in different concrete situations. Before that, however, in Chapters 3 and 4 we will go into a fundamental, general, application. There, we will demonstrate when and why the fundamental thesis of the theory of international trade is valid – that welfare is maximized through free trade – and what will happen when the conditions that have to be fulfilled for free trade under *laissez-faire* to maximize welfare are no longer met.

Literature

Linearly homogenous production functions are dealt with in:
Chacholiades, Miltiades (1978), *International Trade Theory and Policy*. McGraw-Hill, Kogakusha, Tokyo, ch. 4.

The factor diagram is treated in all basic microeconomic works, including:
Kogiku, K. C. (1971), *Microeconomic Models*. Harper & Row, New York, ch. 2.
Lerner, Abba P. (1932), 'The Diagrammatical Representation of Cost Conditions in International Trade', *Economica*, Vol. 12.
Varian, Hal R. (1996), *Intermediate Microeconomics. A Modern Approach* (4th edn). Norton, New York and London, ch. 19.

The box diagram is discussed in:
Chacholiades, *International Trade Theory and Policy*, ch. 4.
Södersten, Bo and Reed, Geoffrey (1994), *International Economics* (3rd edn). Macmillan, London, ch. 3.

The production possibility curve and its derivation from the box diagram are found in:
Chacholiades, *International Trade Theory and Policy*, ch. 4.
Savosnick, Kurt Martin (1958), 'The Box Diagram and the Production Possibility Curve', *Ekonomisk Tidskrift*, Vol. 60.
Södersten and Reed, *International Economics* (3rd edn). Macmillan, London, ch. 3.

The convexity of the production possibility curve is discussed in:

Black, J. (1957), 'A Formal Proof of the Concavity of the Production Possibility Function', *Economic Journal*, Vol. 67.
Chacholiades, *International Trade Theory and Policy*, ch. 4.
Worswick, G. D. N. (1957), 'The Convexity of the Production Possibility Function', *Economic Journal*, Vol. 67.

Basic consumption theory can be found in:

Green, H. A. John (1971), *Consumer Theory*. Penguin, Harmondsworth.
Kogiku, *Microeconomic Models*, ch. 1.

Social indifference curves are dealt with in:

Chacholiades, *International Trade Theory and Policy*, ch. 4.
Leontief, Wassily W. (1933), 'The Use of Indifference Curves in the Analysis of Foreign Trade', *Quarterly Journal of Economics*, Vol. 47.
Lerner, Abba P. (1934), 'The Diagrammatical Representation of Demand Conditions in International Trade', *Economica*, N. S., Vol. 1.
Samuelson, Paul A. (1956), 'Social Indifference Curves', *Quarterly Journal of Economics*, Vol. 70.
Scitovszky, Tibor de (1942), 'A Reconsideration of the Theory of Tariffs', *Review of Economic Studies*, Vol. 9.

For the relationship between commodity prices and factor prices, see the classic:

Stolper, Wolfgang F. and Samuelson, Paul A. (1941), 'Protection and Real Wages', *Review of Economic Studies*, Vol. 9.

And for the algebraic proof, see:

Chacholiades, *International Trade Theory and Policy*, ch. 9.

Works that bring up the functioning of the neoclassical system as a whole include:

Bator, Francis M. (1957), 'The Simple Analytics of Welfare Maximization', *American Economic Review*, Vol. 47.
Friedman, Lee S. (1984), *Microeconomic Policy Analysis*. McGraw-Hill, New York, especially ch. 10.
Johansson, Per-Olov (1991), *An Introduction to Modern Welfare Economics*. Cambridge University Press, Cambridge.
Kogiku, *Microeconomic Models*, ch. 1.

3
The Gains from Foreign Trade: The Fundamental Theorem

An old truth, but still one of the cornerstones in the theory of international trade, is that free trade under *laissez-faire* constitutes the optimal trade policy, provided that prices are flexible, production factors domestically mobile, the country cannot influence its terms-of-trade and all markets operate under conditions of perfect competition. However, free trade under *laissez-faire* is not the best policy in situations where some kind of distortions exist in the commodity or factor markets. (We will provide examples in next chapter.) In such cases better results are obtained with the aid of policy interventions of different kinds. Before we examine how these interventions work, we will investigate the condition that must be met if we are to achieve the highest possible welfare level in the open economy.

The formal model

Assume that we have a small open economy that cannot affect its terms-of-trade. This economy has a social welfare function, defined over two commodities (manufactures and agricultural goods) which is to be maximized. The country exports manufactures and imports agricultural goods. Since it is the *consumption* of the commodities that is assumed to generate welfare we obtain the following social welfare function:

$$U = U(C_I, C_J) \tag{3.1}$$

which is to be maximized subject to the following restrictions:

$$J = f(I) \tag{3.2}$$

The domestic production possibility curve (the production of agricultural goods depends on how much the manufacturing sector produces),

$$M_J = g(X_I) \tag{3.3}$$

which represents the terms on which the economy may trade in the international market:

$$C_I = I - X_I \tag{3.4}$$

The consumption of manufactures is given by domestic production minus exports:

$$C_J = J + M_J \tag{3.5}$$

and the consumption of agricultural goods is given by the domestic production plus imports.

In order to arrive at the first-order conditions for a maximum we form the Lagrangean

$$\Phi = U(C_I, C_J) - \lambda_1[J - f(I)] - \lambda_2[M_J - g(X_I)] - \lambda_3[C_I - I + X_I] \\ - \lambda_4[C_J - J - M_J]$$

and take the derivatives of this with respect to C_I, C_J, I, J, X_I and M_J. This yields

$$\Phi_{C_I} = U_{C_I} - \lambda_3 = 0 \tag{3.6}$$

$$\Phi_{C_J} = U_{C_J} - \lambda_4 = 0 \tag{3.7}$$

$$\Phi_I = \lambda_1 f' + \lambda_3 = 0 \tag{3.8}$$

$$\Phi_J = -\lambda_1 + \lambda_4 = 0 \tag{3.9}$$

$$\Phi_{X_I} = \lambda_2 g' - \lambda_3 = 0 \tag{3.10}$$

$$\Phi_{M_J} = -\lambda_2 + \lambda_4 = 0 \tag{3.11}$$

We may now define three rates: (1) the domestic rate of transformation (*DRT*), which is the slope of the domestic production possibility curve (the opportunity cost of domestic production): how much the production of one of the goods must be reduced if the output of the second commodity is to increase; (2) the foreign rate of transformation (*FRT*), which is the terms-of-trade the country faces in the international market; and (3) the domestic rate of substitution (*DRS*) in consumption, which is how much of one of the goods the economy is willing to sacrifice, on a given welfare level, to increase consumption of the second commodity. Define:

$$DRT \equiv -f'$$

$$FRT \equiv g'$$

Note that the latter is equal to dM_J/dX_I: that is, *FRT* expresses the import increase made possible by increasing exports. *FRT* thus gives us the marginal terms-of-trade.

$$DRS \equiv -\frac{dC_J}{dC_I}$$

Equations (3.6) and (3.7) yield

$$\frac{\lambda_3}{\lambda_4} = \frac{U_{C_I}}{U_{C_J}} = -\frac{dC_J}{dC_I} = DRS \tag{3.12}$$

From (3.8) and (3.9) we obtain

$$\frac{\lambda_3}{\lambda_4} = -f' = DRT \tag{3.13}$$

and, from (3.10) and (3.11),

$$\frac{\lambda_3}{\lambda_4} = g' = FRT \tag{3.14}$$

In optimum thus

$$DRT = FRT = DRS \tag{3.15}$$

For a small, open economy that cannot affect its terms-of-trade, $FRT = p_V = P_I/P_J$, the given (relative) world market price, and free trade makes $p_V = p_H$ (the domestic price). p_H in turn is equal to *DRT* and *DRS*. Graphically, we have the situation depicted in Figure 3.1.

At world market prices, p_V, the economy produces at point *B* and consumes at point *C*. Exports are equal to *DB* and imports to *DC*. In equilibrium the slopes of the indifference curve, the production possibility curve and the budget line (whose slope gives the terms-of-trade) are equal, which means that $DRT = FRT = DRS$.

The fundamental theorem of foreign trade

The fundamental theorem of the theory of foreign trade states that when both commodity and factor markets are characterized by perfect competition and world market prices may be taken as given from the point of view of the individual economy, foreign trade under *laissez-faire* leads to potentially

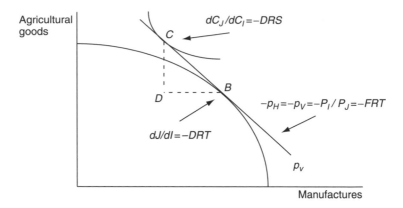

Figure 3.1   Welfare maximization in a small, open economy operating under perfect competition

higher welfare than autarky (absence of trade). This may be seen with the aid of Figure 3.2.

If no foreign trade takes place the domestically determined prices are p_H. The economy both produces and consumes at point A. Nothing is exported or imported. If the economy is opened to foreign trade, commodity transactions will no longer take place at autarky prices but world market prices, p_V, are valid. (Here we disregard transportation costs.) Consumption is no longer restricted by domestic production and the output may also be

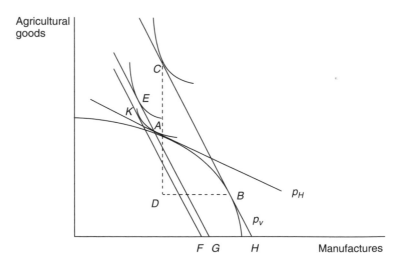

Figure 3.2   The gains from foreign trade

exported. This allows for specialization in production. More is then produced of one of the commodities than domestic consumption requires, but the surplus is exported while simultaneously the commodity whose production has been reduced may be imported. The economy produces at point B and consumes at point C, on a higher social indifference curve than the one going through A. BD manufactures are exported and DC agricultural goods are imported.

Note, however, that these gains from foreign trade are 'conditional'. If no further interventions are made, certain groups will make a loss. When trade is opened the production of manufactures increases while the production of agricultural goods decreases, as a result of the increase in the relative price of manufactures. Under perfect competition no profits exist at the outset and, when the relative price of agricultural goods decreases, agricultural producers make a loss. Resources move into the manufacturing sector. Agriculture is the labour-intensive sector and will release more labour in relation to capital than the manufacturing sector is willing to receive at given factor prices. The wage must hence fall and the workers will be worse off than before. At the same time the return to capital will increase since production techniques will grow more labour-intensive in both sectors. If the worker group is not to be worse off than before it must be compensated by the winners/capital owners.

Some kind of redistribution is thus required. In economic theory it is normally assumed that the income redistribution needed for restoring the original distribution of income takes place via different lump-sum taxes and transfers (i.e., transfers which do not depend on any variables in the economic system and which hence do not affect the allocation of resources). In practice, however, this type of intervention is difficult to employ for equity reasons. Instead, commodity and factor taxes (or subsidies) of the type actually used in most economies may be employed. The argument is as follows.

Since we are working with linearly homogeneous production factors the output value under autarky (A) is divided exactly between the two factors. (This follows from Euler's theorem: see Chapter 2.) If, in addition, we assume that no saving takes place, the factor owners will consume their entire income:

$$P_{IA}I_A + P_{JA}J_A = r_A\overline{K} + w_A\overline{L} = P_{IA}C_{IA} + P_{JA}C_{JA} \tag{3.16}$$

Trade is opened at international prices, p_V, and the production value is still divided between the factor owners:

$$P_{IV}I_V + P_{JV}J_V = r_V\overline{K} + w_V\overline{L} \tag{3.17}$$

Next, let the state tax and subsidize consumption and factor use so that the consumers still pay P_{IA} and P_{JA} and the factor owners still receive r_A and w_A. When trade was opened the relative price of manufactures increased and with that the relative price of capital, since manufacturing is capital-intensive. Consumers pay more for manufactures and less for agricultural goods than under autarky. The former should hence be subsidized and the latter should be taxed. Likewise, the capital owners have increased their incomes while those of the wage earners have decreased. Capital income should then be taxed while the wage earners will receive a subsidy. In summary, this means that the consumers will continue to consume C_{IA} and C_{JA}. (The factor supply is assumed to be given.) The welfare of consumers and factor owners hence is unchanged.

At given world market prices, r_V and w_V, producers maximize their profits by selling an output, I_V and J_V whose value exceeds the value of autarky production (and consumption) measured in terms of world market prices:

$$P_{IV}I_V + P_{JV}J_V > P_{IV}I_A + P_{JV}J_A = P_{IV}C_{IA} + P_{JV}C_{JA} \qquad (3.18)$$

(This can easily be verified in Figure 3.2, where the value of production in A, at world market prices, is lower than the value in B. The price line through B lies outside the price line through A.) Via its tax and subsidy policy the state does the following. It 'buys' C_{IA} and C_{JA} from the producers at P_{IV} and P_{JV} and 'sells' the same quantities to the consumers at P_{IA} and P_{JA}. Furthermore the state 'buys' factor quantities K and L from the factor owners at r_A and w_A and 'sells' them to the producers at r_V and w_V. The difference constitutes the net revenue of the state:

$$\left(P_{IA}C_{IA} - P_{IV}C_{IA}\right) + \left(P_{JA}C_{JA} - P_{JV}C_{JA}\right) + \left(r_V\overline{K} - r_A\overline{K}\right) + \left(w_V\overline{L} - w_A\overline{L}\right)$$

It now remains to show that the government revenue is positive. Since the entire income is consumed under autarky (3.16) may be used. All terms containing autarky prices cancel. The revenue expression is than reduced to

$$\left(r_V\overline{K} + w_V\overline{L}\right) - \left(P_{IV}C_{IA} + P_{JV}C_{JA}\right)$$

Since, when trade is allowed, the total output value is distributed between the production factors we may write

$$\left(P_{IV}I_V + P_{JV}J_V\right) - \left(P_{IV}C_{IA} + P_{JV}C_{JA}\right)$$

which, according to the inequality (3.18), is positive.

Thus the state obtains a positive net revenue through its tax and subsidy policy, while at the same time the welfare of the citizens remains unchanged. It may then reduce the tax level and/or increase the subsidy level, which will increase the welfare of the citizens since it allows them to increase their consumption. The shift to free trade is Pareto sanctioned. The gains from trade become unequivocal without resort to lump-sum taxes or subsidies.

In principle, the gains made through foreign trade are of two types. Let us for a moment assume that production is fixed at point A in Figure 3.2. This means that the economy cannot reallocate production factors from agriculture to manufacturing when trade is opened. The welfare level then is given by the indifference curve going through point A where the economy consumes at autarky prices, p_H. If instead world market prices are used, consumption must take place at point K if the same welfare level is to be reached.

Even though a reallocation of production factors between the sectors is not possible, the welfare level can be increased by allowing trade. The country may trade at international prices and may hence exchange manufactures for agricultural goods in the proportions given by p_V. The optimal consumption will then be given by point E, which lies on a higher indifference curve than K. This movement represents the *consumption gain* from trade. The logic in this is that manufactures, relatively speaking, have a higher value at world market prices than at autarky prices. (We may measure the gains in terms of either good: e.g., as FG manufactures.) If, finally, we relax the assumption of a given structure of production the economy may move to point C, which lies on an even higher indifference curve. This represents a *specialization gain* of GH in terms of manufactures.

Tariffs and free trade

Free trade thus potentially leads to a higher welfare level than autarky. It may also be shown that tariffs result in lower welfare than free trade, with the aid of a graphic model of the same type as the one used above. In Figure 3.3 free trade is compared to what will happen if a tariff is imposed on the agricultural good.

As before, the economy would produce at B and consume at C with free trade (the 'trade triangle' has not been drawn). If a tariff is imposed on agricultural imports, *domestic* prices will change (e.g., to p_T), while we may still trade at world market prices, p_V, in the international market. More agricultural and fewer manufactured goods are produced compared to the case of free trade (point E). The trade volumes shrink. FG agricultural goods are imported and EG manufactures are exported. The welfare level is reduced (point F) since consumers have to pay p_T and not the world market price, p_V. We may also compare with the autarky point A. Interpreted in terms of tariffs this point represents what will happen if we introduce a prohibitive tariff on agricultural goods (a tariff that strangles foreign trade completely). We may furthermore study the effect of abolishing the tariff. This effect, as before, may be divided into a consumption gain (from F to J) and a specialization gain (from J to C).

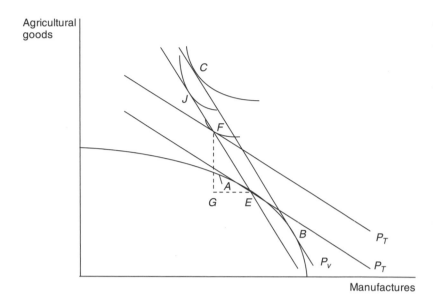

Figure 3.3   Tariffs and free trade

Dynamic effects of free trade

The traditional argument for free trade that we have presented here is *static* in the sense that it is valid at a given point in time. Trade may, however, also have *dynamic* effects: that is, the capacity of the economy to produce goods and services may increase over time as a result of foreign trade. This is illustrated in Figure 3.4.

At the outset the economy produces at *B* and consumes at *C*, exactly as before. There is free trade. As a result of dynamic effects of trade, however, the production possibility curve moves outwards over time, from *TT* to *T'T'*. If we assume that world market prices are not affected by this ('our' economy is small in relation to the world market with respect to both commodities), the new production point will be *H* and the new consumption point *I*, on a higher social indifference curve than the one that goes through *C*.

What do the 'dynamic' effects behind the shift of the production possibility curve consist of? In the first place, *savings* may increase. International trade increases the supply of goods in the economy, but the entire increase does not have to be consumed, and savings and capital formation may rise. This increases the production capacity.

Second, trade may result in the introduction of new *production techniques* so that the production possibility curve shifts outwards, with given factor endowments. Technology may be imported from abroad and free trade may

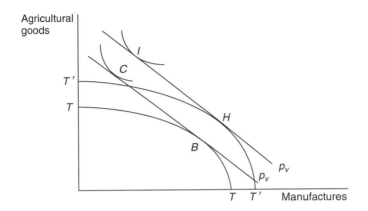

Figure 3.4   Dynamic effects of free trade

check domestic monopoly tendencies, which in turn forces domestic producers to become more efficient and renew their techniques at the same pace as their competitors. Competition also forces firms to utilize the new technology as efficiently as possible. For this a 'training process' is often required for the employees, who must learn to handle new techniques in the most efficient way. This phenomenon is known as 'learning-by-doing'. (The search for new techniques is encouraged also by the widening of the market and the establishment of contact networks that may facilitate the borrowing of new techniques.)

Third, international trade may stimulate factor movements. Immigration and capital movements shift the production possibility curve outwards. Countries trading with other nations obtain loans more easily from the latter that may be used to finance capital formation, because they have export revenue to pay with.

The above arguments can be interpreted more or less strictly in our model. In addition there are other arguments that can be presented here only on an intuitive level: trade thus makes possible the importation of goods not produced domestically. These may, for example, be *investment goods* used in the production of agricultural and manufactures goods, if we stick to our two-commodity example.

A fifth possible mechanism is the 'demonstration effect'. When the possibility of trade is introduced and new commodities are imported, this acts as a stimulus to increased labour efforts in order to make it possible to buy the import good. In that case the production possibility curve, which is defined for a given number of work hours, shifts outwards. Possibly, in the two-good case, the demonstration effect may be interpreted as an adaptation of the consumption habits to the international patterns when trade is opened.

Sixth, the wider market that arises when trade is introduced may be a necessary condition for investment to take place in sectors displaying economies of scale. The mere domestic market may be insufficient. (Note, however, that in the present work we are employing linearly homogeneous production functions, *without* scale economies.)

Possible objections

The fundamental theorem of the theory of international trade is that free trade is to be preferred to both autarky and tariff protection. Against this, however, a number of objections are often raised. Let us look at two such objections.

Inflexibilities in the resource allocation

The analysis carried out so far assumes flexibility in the resource allocation. We have assumed that capital and labour may be moved freely between agriculture and manufacturing. In practice, however, this does not always have to be the case.

In Figure 3.5 a situation is shown where no change in production from the autarky point A is possible. The production possibility curve then shrinks to a rectangle. Nevertheless, free trade also in this case leads to a welfare gain. AK manufactures are exported and JK agricultural goods are imported. The explanation of the welfare gain, as before, is that the gains from trade in

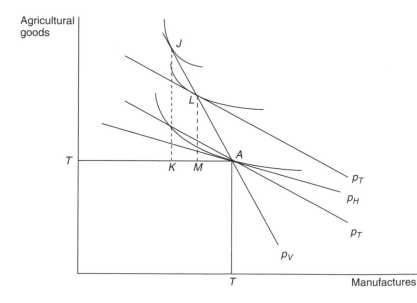

Figure 3.5   Factor immobility

principle may be divided into two parts: a specialization gain which arises when production factors can be reallocated as commodity and factor prices change, from p_H to p_V, and a consumption gain, the movement from A to J, by trading export goods for imports so as to increase the amount of goods available for consumption. In the case of immobile production factors the former gain disappears while the latter remains, and this is large enough to make it possible for the winners to compensate the losers.

A corresponding argument is valid in the tariff case. Consumption now takes place at L (at a non-prohibitive tariff), at domestic prices, p_T, and the volume of trade has shrunk in comparison with the free trade case. All manufactures are exported and LM agricultural goods are imported. The superiority of free trade is shown by the welfare gains, measured as the distance between the indifference curves containing L and J, respectively.

It should be noted that the inflexibility of the resource allocation is mainly a short-run phenomenon. Different sectors impose different educational requirements and education may require time. The capital stocks within agriculture and manufacturing are not identical and may for the most part not be moved freely between sectors. If a reallocation is to take place disinvestment is required in one of the sectors and investment in the other one, over a long period (mainly through the new investment in the latter of resources freed by depreciation in the former).

Inflexibility of factor prices

One of the reasons why a consumption gain arises also when resources are not reallocated is that factor prices change with commodity prices when the economy switches from autarky to free trade. Thus the remaining producers avoid making losses after the opening of trade.

Another complication may, however, arise: inflexibility in the formation of factor prices. Assume, for example, that the agricultural labour force refuses to accept a falling wage as the relative price of agricultural goods falls when trade is opened. Such a situation is shown in Figure 3.6. The agricultural workers cannot move into manufacturing, exactly as in Figure 3.5. Under autarky the economy consumes and produces in A. Had the agricultural wage been flexible, free trade would have increased welfare by allowing consumption to take place at point J. When this is no longer possible free trade may instead lead to a welfare loss.

This (somewhat surprising) result is derived from the following reasoning: When trade is opened the relative price of agricultural goods falls. This in turn means that the amount of manufactures that may be bought for a wage that is given in terms of agricultural goods also shrinks. This, however, is not accepted by the agricultural workers, who demand that the wage be preserved in terms of manufactures. This can only be achieved if the marginal productivity of labour increases in agriculture and this in turn takes place

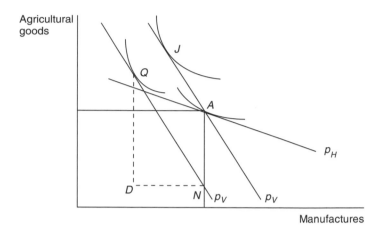

Figure 3.6   Factor immobility and inflexible factor prices

only if the use of labour in the agricultural sector is reduced. (There are decreasing returns to labour.)

Let us, for the sake of simplicity, assume that the wage rate originally was the same in both sectors:

$$w = w_I = w_J \tag{3.19}$$

or, taking into account that the wage has to equal the value of the marginal product,

$$w = P_I I_L = P_J J_L \tag{3.20}$$

The wage in terms of manufactures is

$$\frac{w_I}{P_I} = \frac{w_J}{P_I} = \frac{P_J J_L}{P_I} \tag{3.21}$$

When trade is opened P_J/P_I, the relative price of agricultural goods falls. If the wage rate in agriculture is not to fall in terms of manufactures (constant w_J/P_I), J_L has to increase enough to compensate for the reduction of P_J/P_I. When production factors are not mobile between sectors this must result in unemployment in agriculture. The capital stock in the sector will still be fully employed, since the return to capital will adjust to the new commodity prices. When labour leaves the sector and becomes unemployed the marginal product of labour will increase and, with that, at commodity prices which are given (by the world market), the wage rate also increases. Agricultural production contracts until the marginal cost of producing agricultural goods coincides with the import price (e.g., at point *N*). *DQ* agricultural goods will be imported.

At point *N* as many manufactured goods as before are produced but, since the domestic consumption of these is lower than before, *DN* is exported. As the figure shows, welfare is lower than in pure autarky, since point *Q* lies on a lower indifference curve than point *A*. The relative price of manufactures does not improve enough to make the consumption gain outweigh the loss that is being made when agricultural production decreases without any increase of manufacturing output. This is, however, not a necessary conclusion. Everything depends on how large the difference in relative prices is between the autarky and free trade situations. When trade is opened the relative price of agricultural goods is reduced and, if the reduction is large enough (i.e., if the slope of the p_V line is steep enough), trade may still pay. This is because the country is allowed to trade manufactures for agricultural goods on conditions that are favourable enough to outweigh the production loss in agriculture.

Conclusions

The present chapter has laid the foundations for the discussion that will be conducted in the remaining chapters. We have presented the fundamental theorem in the theory of international trade, that free trade under *laissez-faire* potentially leads to the best result in terms of social welfare. The result is, however, only valid given some strictly defined conditions that are not always met. Some examples of this were produced in the chapter. We will take a closer look at different distortions in the commodity and factor markets and their effects in the next chapters.

Literature

The optimality conditions for a small, open economy are derived in:
Bhagwati, Jagdish N., Panagariya, Arvind and Srinivasan, T. N. (1998), *Lectures on International Trade* (2nd edn). MIT Press, Cambridge, MA and London, ch. 18.

The fundamental theorem of foreign trade can be found in all standard texts:
Baldwin, Robert E. (1952), 'The New Welfare Economics and Gains in International Trade', *Quarterly Journal of Economics*, Vol. 66.
Batra, Raveendra N. (1973), *Studies in the Pure Theory of International Trade*. Macmillan, London.
Bhagwati, Panagariya and Srinivasan, *Lectures on International Trade*, ch. 18.
Caves, Richard E., Frankel, Jeffrey A. and Jones, Ronald W. (1999), *World Trade and Payments: An Introduction* (8th edn). Addison Wesley, Reading, MA, ch. 2.
Chacholiades, Miltiades (1978), *International Trade Theory and Policy*. McGraw-Hill Kogakusha, Tokyo, ch. 16.

Samuelson, Paul A. (1962), 'The Gains from International Trade Once Again', *Economic Journal*, Vol. 72.
Södersten, Bo and Reed, Geoffrey (1994), *International Economics* (3rd edn). Macmillan, London, ch. 1.

The argument about the gains from factor trade and commodity and factor taxes is presented in:
Bhagwati, Panagaryia and Srinivasan, *Lectures on International Trade*, ch. 18.
Dixit, Avinash K. and Norman, Victor D. (1980), *Theory of International Trade*. James Nisbeth/Cambridge University Press, Cambridge, ch. 6.

The measure of the welfare gains from trade can be found in:
Bhagwati, Panagaryia and Srinivasan, *Lectures on International Trade*, ch. 19.
Chacholiades, *International Trade Theory and Policy*, ch. 5.
Greenaway, David and Milner, Chris (1993), *Trade and Industrial Policy in Developing Countries*. Macmillan, London, ch. 3.

The welfare effects of tariffs are dealt with in practically all standard texts, such as:
Caves Frenkel and Jones, *World Trade and Payments: An Introduction*, ch. 10.
Chacholiades *International Trade Theory and Policy*, ch. 17.
Södersten and Reed, *International Economics*, ch. 11.

See also:
Jones, Ronald W. (1969), 'Tariffs and Trade in General Equilibrium: Comment', *American Economic Review*, Vol. 59.

Dynamic effects of free trade are dealt with in:
Burenstam Linder, Staffan (1971), 'Trade and Technical Efficiency', in Bhagwati, Jagdish N. *et al.* (eds), *Trade, Balance of Payments and Growth: Papers in International Economics in Honor of Charles P. Kindleberger*. North-Holland, Amsterdam.
Greenaway and Milner, *Trade and Industrial Policy in Developing Countries* ch. 3.
Haberler, Gottfried (1959), *International Trade and Economic Development*. National Bank of Egypt, Fiftieth Anniversary Commemoration Lectures, NBE Printing Press, Cairo.

For a discussion of 'learning by doing', see also:
Arrow, Kenneth J. (1962), 'The Economic Implications of Learning by Doing', *Review of Economic Studies*, Vol. 29.

The objections to free trade are discussed in:
Haberler, Gottfried (1950), 'Some Problems in the Pure Theory of International Trade', *Economic Journal*, Vol. 60.
Johnson, Harry G. (1965), 'Optimal Trade Intervention in the Presence of Domestic Distortions', in Baldwin, Robert E. *et al.* (eds), *Trade, Growth and the Balance of Payments. Essays in Honor of Gottfried Haberler*. Rand McNally, Chicago, IL.

4
Trade, Distortions and Welfare

In the foregoing chapter we derived the conditions for an optimal allocation of resources in an open economy. We could conclude that free trade potentially establishes the welfare-maximizing result, provided that a number of conditions are met: prices are flexible, production factors are mobile, the country cannot influence its terms-of-trade and perfect competition prevails in all markets. We also analysed a number of cases where all optimality conditions are not met. We looked at the effects of tariffs, at what will happen if the production factors are not completely mobile, and at the consequences when factor prices fail to adjust to conditions in other markets.

In the present chapter we will continue on the same road. The purpose is to examine systematically the distortions that arise as a result of different deviations from the optimum conditions. The common denominator is that *laissez-faire* is no longer the optimal policy.

A classification of distortions

The optimal relation between the domestic rate of transformation, the foreign rate of transformation and the domestic rate of substitution in consumption, $DRT = FRT = DRS$, may be disturbed in different ways. In addition the domestic rates of technical substitution in the factor markets ($DRTS$) – that is, the slopes of the production isoquants – may differ from the relative factor prices. We will presently deal with the following four cases:

1 $FRT \neq DRT = DRS$.
2 $DRT \neq DRS = FRT$.
3 $DRS \neq DRT = FRT$.
4 The economy does not operate on the production possibility curve.

These distortions may in turn in principle be of three different kinds:

- endogenous
- autonomous, 'side effects' of economic policy
- instrumental, consciously caused by economic policy

Let us take a closer look at what these three types of distortions imply. *Endogenous* distortions may arise when there are market imperfections and the economy is characterized by *laissez-faire*. If the country can affect its terms-of-trade (i.e., has market power in the international markets), distortion 1 will arise. Externalities in production will lead to distortion 2. Distortion 3 will arise when those selling imported goods charge a uniform mark-up over the world market price on both imported and import-competing goods. Distortion 4 arises when a production factor obtains different remuneration in different sectors. This distortion may also occur when externalities are caused by the factor use of some sector.

Distortions may, however, also arise as a result of the economic policy pursued in the country even though no market imperfections exist. Distortion 1 arises when tariffs are introduced in a situation where the country cannot affect its terms-of-trade, or if the tariff in question diverges from the optimal one when the export price can be influenced (cf. below). Distortion 2 arises if the country pursues a policy that subsidizes production in one sector and taxes production in another. Distortion 3 arises in a corresponding way if the consumption of certain goods is subsidized while the consumption of other goods is taxed. Distortion 4, finally, arises when production factors are subsidized and taxed.

The distortions caused by policy interventions may be either *autonomous* (i.e., the by-products of a policy measure whose purpose is not the creation of the distortion, say, to change the distribution of income), or *instrumental*, when the purpose of the intervention is to create the distortion, as when a tariff leading to a distortion is introduced to reduce imports and increase the degree of self-sufficiency. In the latter case the distortion is the 'price' that has to be paid for increased self-sufficiency.

The fundamental principle when the purpose is (1) to correct distortions and (2) to introduce distortions when the goal is not that of maximizing welfare in society is to use, if possible, a combination of taxes and subsidies (on production, consumption, foreign trade or production factors) that affects the distortion or goal that the policy-maker has in mind directly. If not, secondary effects arise which in turn are welfare-reducing. For each type of distortion it is possible to rank different types of interventions with respect to efficiency. The same is true for situations where the purpose is to introduce a distortion to reach some non-economic goal.

Let us see how this works for different distortions. Which is the optimal policy in each case? We will concentrate on endogenous distortions in the present chapter. In Chapters 5–8 we will discuss how distortions may be used instrumentally to reach certain (often non-economic) goals.

The country can affect its terms-of-trade

When a country can affect its terms-of-trade the marginal foreign rate of transformation differs from the domestic rate of transformation (i.e., $FRT \neq DRT = DRS$). Before we go into a detailed analysis of this case we will introduce a graphic technique needed to illustrate this problem: offer curves.

Offer curves

From our previous analysis it may be deduced that the quantities exported and imported by a country depend on the relative price of the commodities. This relation may also be expressed in a different way, with the aid of *offer curves*. Offer curves are a useful tool, in particular when the analysis deals with the relations between a single economy and the rest of the world.

In order to derive the offer curve of a country we take the production possibility curve in Figure 4.1 as our point of departure. Note that we have chosen to draw the mirror image of this curve. Under autarky the country produces at A, at the relative price, p. This price line may be extended until it intersects the horizontal axis. If we draw a new vertical axis from this point the price line may thereafter be 'turned' leftwards in the diagram: that is, projected on the left-hand side with the same angle towards the new vertical axis, but with a positive leftward slope. If we assume that when the relative price of agricultural goods exceeds p the country has a comparative advantage in the production of agricultural goods (i.e., it can produce those goods relatively cheaper than other countries), it will export agricultural products and import manufactures. One such price is p'. The country then produces at

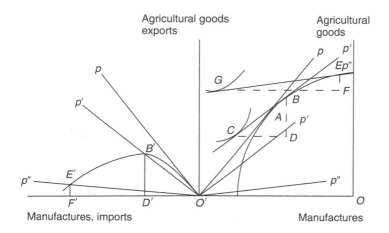

Figure 4.1 Derivation of the offer curve

point *B* and consumes at point *C*, where a social indifference curve is tangent to the price line, exports *BD* agricultural goods and imports *DC* manufactures.

We may now make a downward parallel shift of the price line in the diagram until the line cuts the new origin, *O'*. Thereafter we may make a parallel move of the entire trade triangle *BCD* so that *O'* corresponds to *C* and *CD* is projected along the horizontal axis. Finally we may 'turn' the new trade triangle leftwards like a page in a book and project it in the left-hand part of the diagram. We now have a measure of how much agricultural goods the country offers (*B'D'*) and how much manufactures it demands (*O'D'*) at the relative price *p'*. (At price *p* the country prefers autarky. Both exports and imports are equal to zero. The trade triangle is reduced to the point of origin *O'*.)

In the next step we choose a new relative price (e.g., *p''*), which gives us a new trade triangle *EFG*, with production at *E* and consumption at *G*. This is also projected along the horizontal axis, with *G* at *O'*, and is turned leftwards, to give us agricultural exports of *E'F'* and manufactured imports of *O'F'* at world market price *p''*. This procedure may thereafter be repeated for all prices implying a higher relative price of agricultural goods than is the case with *p*. The result is a number of points corresponding to *B'* and *E'* and, if all these points are joined, we get the offer curve of the country. This shows how much of the two goods the country supplies and demands, respectively, *in the world market* at different relative prices.

The optimum tariff

When a country is in the position where it can affect its terms-of-trade the best policy is a tariff: the optimum tariff. This case is shown in Figure 4.2.

Assume that the world market prices are given by the p_V line. With free trade the economy will then produce at point *A*. *BA* manufactures will be exported and *BC* agricultural goods will be imported or, rather, *given* that *BA* manufactures are supplied in the world market, the country will receive *BC* agricultural goods in exchange.

The world market prices are not given, however. Assume that we choose to fix production in point *A* and instead choose to supply a smaller quantity of manufactures (say, *AD*). This would give the country 'better' terms-of-trade: say, p'_V. (The export good is relatively more expensive in p'_V than in p_V.) *DA* manufactures could be exchanged for *DE* agricultural goods. The country is large enough to affect international commodity prices. The less of the manufactured good it supplies the better terms-of-trade it will face. By varying the supplied quantity we may derive the different terms-of-trade that correspond to the different quantities supplied. Joining the apexes of the different trade triangles yields the offer curve of 'the rest of the world' (with the origin at point *A*). This shows how the supply of the rest of the

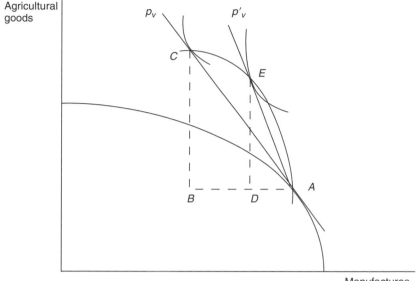

Figure 4.2 A country that can affect its terms-of-trade

world (i.e., 'our' country's imports of agricultural goods) changes when 'our' country's supply of manufactures in the world market changes.

From the above it also follows that *FRT*, which is defined as $-dM_J/dX_I$, will *not* coincide with the world market price, since the offer curve intersects the price line at point *E*. The difference between the two consists in that *FRT* is a relation between *marginal* entities while p_V denotes the *average* relative price. As we move along the offer curve, *AC*, our terms-of-trade will worsen. The first exported units, so to speak, fetch a better relative price than the last ones and what the terms-of-trade line, AC, indicates is the average for all transactions. The world market price p_V, however, coincides with *DRT* and *DRS*, which hence continue to be equal.

The optimal policy when a country can affect its terms-of-trade is a tariff. This is shown in Figure 4.3. Assume that the world market price is p_{VF}. With free trade the economy produced at *R* and consumed at *S*. If then a tariff is levied on the agricultural good, not only the domestic relative price changes (to p_{HT}) but also the world market price (to p_{VT}). The relative price of agricultural goods *rises* in the domestic market and *falls* in the world market, since 'our' country's supply of manufactures is reduced so that the country's terms-of-trade improve. The new production point is *U* and the new consumption point is *V*, on a higher indifference curve than *S*.

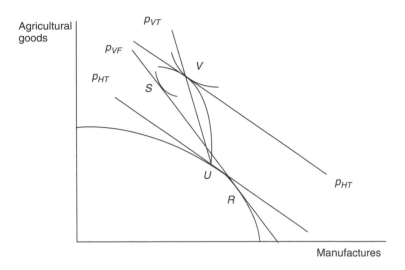

Figure 4.3   The optimum tariff

The tariff which maximizes the welfare of the country is the optimum tariff. To arrive at this we may 'slide' the (given) offer curve of the rest of the world along the production possibility curve (the lower end point of the curve moves along the production possibility curve) until we find a point where the domestic price line has the same slope as the production possibility curve (production in U), a social indifference curve and the foreign offer curve (consumption in point V). The slope of the latter is nothing but FRT (i.e., $-dM_J/dX_I$). Thus we have restored the equality $DRT = FRT = DRS$ with the aid of an optimum tariff.

External effects in production

External effects in production make $DRT \neq DRS = FRT$. When the activities of a firm affect those of other firms, positively or negatively, the social cost of producing a commodity will differ from the private cost. This complicates the analysis. Now the relative prices (domestic and international: the same as with free trade) will no longer coincide with the (social) opportunity cost (i.e., the price lines will *intersect* the production possibility curve).

When externalities are present production of one of the commodities is affected by the production of the other commodity. Suppose that agricultural production affects the production of manufactures, say, by polluting a river from which the manufacturing sector obtains its water which then must be purified before it can be used. The production functions for agricultural goods and manufactures then become

$$J = J(K_J, \ L_J) \tag{4.1}$$

$$I = I(K_I, \ L_I, \ J) \tag{4.2}$$

where I_J is larger or smaller than zero depending on whether the externality is positive or negative. When we differentiate (4.1) and (4.2) we get

$$dJ = J_K dK_J + J_L dL_J \tag{4.3}$$

and

$$dI = I_K dK_I + I_L dL_I + I_J \left(J_K dK_J + J_L dL_J \right) \tag{4.4}$$

where we have used (4.3). From thus we get the slope of the production possibility curve as

$$\frac{dJ}{dI} = \frac{J_K dK_J + J_L dL_J}{I_K dK_I + I_L dL_I + I_J \left(J_K dK_J + J_L dL_J \right)} \tag{4.5}$$

The factor endowments of the economy are given:

$$\overline{K} = K_J + K_I \tag{4.6}$$

$$\overline{L} = L_J + L_I \tag{4.7}$$

The change in factor use between the sectors is

$$dK_J = -dK_I \tag{4.8}$$

$$dL_J = -dL_I \tag{4.9}$$

which may be substituted into the expression for the slope of the production possibility curve. The slope then is

$$\frac{dJ}{dI} = -\frac{J_K dK_I + J_L dL_I}{(I_K - I_J J_K) dK_I + (I_L - I_J J_L) dL_I} \tag{4.10}$$

Profit-maximizing producers employ factors up to the point where these are rewarded with the value of their marginal products:

$$r = P_I I_K = P_J J_K \tag{4.11}$$

$$w = P_I I_L = P_J J_L \tag{4.12}$$

When we solve for the marginal products we obtain

$$I_K = \frac{r}{P_I} \tag{4.13}$$

$$J_K = \frac{r}{P_J} \tag{4.14}$$

$$I_L = \frac{w}{P_I} \tag{4.15}$$

$$J_L = \frac{w}{P_J} \tag{4.16}$$

The marginal products may in turn be substituted into the expression for the slope of the production possibility curve (4.10):

$$\frac{dJ}{dI} = \frac{-(r/P_J)dK_I - (w/P_J)dL_I}{[r/P_I - I_J(r/P_J)]dK_I + [w/P_I - I_J(w/P_J)]dL_I} \tag{4.17}$$

We may factor out $(rdK_I + wdL_I)$ and simplify:

$$\frac{dJ}{dI} = -\frac{1}{P_J(1/P_I - I_J/P_J)} = -\frac{1}{(P_J/P_I - I_J)} \tag{4.18}$$

After multiplying both the numerator and the denominator by P_I we finally obtain:

$$\frac{dJ}{dI} = -\frac{P_I}{P_J - P_I I_J} \tag{4.19}$$

The slope of the price line, however, is $-P_I/P_J$. As long as the externality is present (i.e., as long as $I_J \neq 0$, the slopes of the production possibility curve and the price line differ. If, for example, the externality is *negative* (i.e., $I_J < 0$) the slope of the production possibility curve is less steep than that of the price line. This case is illustrated in Figure 4.4.

The real (social) opportunity cost for producing *manufactures* is given by the slope of the production possibility curve (DRT). Since producers do not take the externality into account, however, they mistake the cost for the slope of the price line, p_V (this is the *private* cost). The cost of producing agricultural goods is underestimated and hence too much of these are produced and not enough manufactured goods (point B).

Free trade takes place at point C. If the producers had perceived the costs correctly production would instead have taken place at D and consumption at E, still at world market prices. In order to arrive at this result the production of manufactures may be subsidized and the production of agricultural goods taxed until the private costs coincide with the social ones. This is the

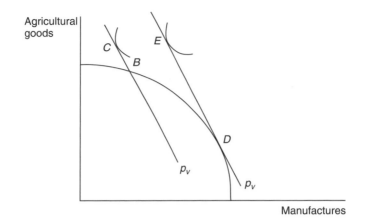

Figure 4.4 Externalities in the production of agricultural goods

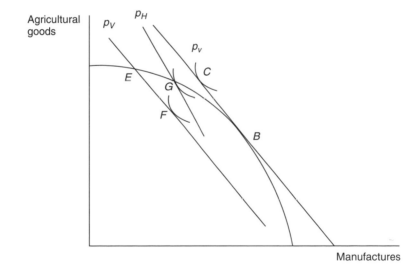

Figure 4.5 Export of the 'wrong' commodity when there are externalities in the production of agricultural goods

best policy and also an example of the existence of an optimal tax cum subsidy policy in the case of domestic distortions, in the same way as there is an optimal tariff capable of correcting for foreign distortions.

When there are externalities in production there is a risk that the economy exports the 'wrong' commodity. Figure 4.5 shows this result. The optimal situation is production at *B* and consumption at *C*. It may, however, very well be the case that production takes place, say, at *E* and consumption at *F*. Agricultural goods are exported because the producers do not perceive all the social costs of agricultural production.

If we employ a tariff on manufactures the best we can do is to reach autarky with production and consumption at point *G*. (Tariffs cannot reverse the direction of the trade flows.) The optimal policy, however, is still that of subsidization of manufacturing production and taxation of agricultural production. This intervention eliminates a distortion without introducing any new ones, which is the case with tariffs. It is by no means certain that a tariff will improve welfare. Such a case is shown in Figure 4.6.

Here point *F* is on a higher indifference curve than point *G*. The *production* or *specialization gain* that arises through the tariff does not suffice to compensate for the *consumption loss* that arises when the relative price of manufactures rises. (The production gain arises when the structure of production shifts towards the optimal mix. Then a world market price line going through point *G* lies outside a line with the same slope through point *E*. The point of tangency between the indifference curve through *G* and a world market price line, however, lies on a lower indifference curve than point *F*. The consumption effect, in other words, is negative.)

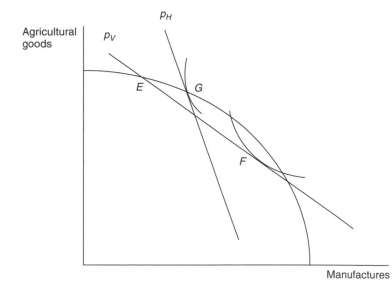

Figure 4.6 A tariff that reduces welfare when there are externalities in the production of agricultural goods

Mark-ups by the intermediaries

The third case of distortions is when $DRS \neq DRT = FRT$. This case arises, for example, when both import-competing and imported goods are marked up with the same percentage by those selling the products in the domestic market. This affects the prices paid by the consumers while producer prices are not affected. We then get a distortion of *consumption* consisting of a divergence of the domestic rate of substitution in consumption from the domestic and foreign rates of transformation. The situation is illustrated in Figure 4.7.

Here the economy can produce at world market prices in point A. The highest possible welfare level is given by point B, but since a mark-up is made on the import commodity, agricultural goods, the price of this commodity for the consumer increases to p_C, and the optimal consumption point is C, on a lower welfare level than B. To solve the problem the state can subsidize the consumption of agricultural goods and tax the consumption of manufactures, thus changing the relative price until reaching point B.

The economy does not produce on the efficient production possibility curve

If factor prices diverge between the two sectors of the economy the result will be that production takes place inside the efficient production possibility curve. This may happen, for example, when the labour force in manufacturing is unionized while that in agriculture is not. A similar case arises if there are so-called factor generated externalities in the economy. This means

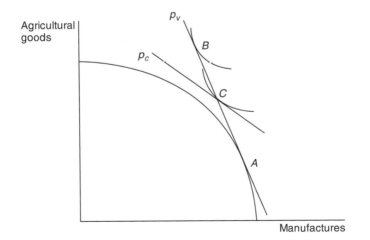

Figure 4.7 The mark-up on the import good

that production in one of the sectors is a function of the factor use of the other sector. We will start with the former case.

The difference in factor prices makes the actual production possibility curve lie inside the efficient one. This result is derived in the same way as we derived the production possibility curve in Chapter 2. In the latter case we depart from points where two isoquants have a common point of tangency and where the slope of a line running through the point of tangency indicates the relative factor price. If factor prices differ production must take place at a point where the isoquants cut each other. The slopes of the isoquants at the intersection point correspond to the relative factor prices in manufacturing and agriculture respectively. The argument is illustrated in Figure 4.8.

In the figure labour is measured on the vertical and capital on the horizontal axis. At the same time we measure agricultural and manufacturing production on the horizontal and vertical axes, respectively, with the south-eastern corner of the box diagram as the origin. First we derive points a and b on the efficient production possibility curve, as in Chapter 2 (all other points may be derived in the same way). If, however, relative factor prices differ between the sectors – but all factors continue to be used in production – production will have to take place at points where the isoquants intersect each other: for example, points such as q and r. If, as before, we use the

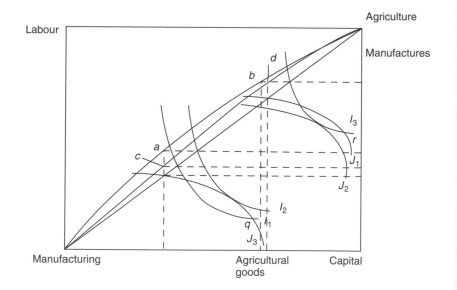

Figure 4.8 Derivation of the production possibility curve when factor prices differ between the sectors

diagonal as our yardstick and project the produced quantities on the sides of the box we obtain points *c* and *d*, which represent a smaller output of manufacturing than point *a* and also fewer agricultural goods (than at point *b*). (The same quantity as before is produced of one of the goods, but less of the other, using all the available production factors.) The new production possibility curve may also be located on the 'other' side of the diagonal. It may then be wholly or partially *concave*. The former phenomenon will occur if the distortion leads to reversal of the factor intensities in both sectors (i.e., the contract curve 'shifts' to the other side). If this does not take place the transformation curve may still be locally concave.

Second, the slopes of the price line and the production possibility curve do not coincide. The proof of this is analogous to the proof in the case of externalities.

Differentiate the two production functions:

$$J = J(K_J, L_J) \tag{4.1}$$

$$I = I(K_I, L_I) \tag{4.20}$$

This yields

$$dJ = J_K dK_J + J_L dL_J \tag{4.3}$$

$$dI = I_K dK_I + I_L dL_I \tag{4.21}$$

The slope of the production possibility curve is given by

$$\frac{dJ}{dI} = \frac{J_K dK_J + J_L dL_J}{I_K dK_I + I_L dL_I} \tag{4.22}$$

The factor use in the two sectors is given by

$$\overline{K} = K_J + K_I \tag{4.6}$$

$$\overline{L} = L_J + L_I \tag{4.7}$$

Differentiate these:

$$dK_J = -dK_I \tag{4.8}$$

$$dL_J = -dL_I \tag{4.9}$$

The remunerations of the production factors equal the values of the marginal products when producers maximize their profits

$$r_J = P_J J_K \tag{4.23}$$

$$w_J = P_J J_L \tag{4.24}$$

in agriculture, and

$$r_I = P_I I_K \tag{4.25}$$

$$w_I = P_I I_L \tag{4.26}$$

in manufacturing.

Solve for the marginal products in (4.23)–(4.26) and substitute these together with (4.8) and (4.9) into the expression for the slope of the production possibility curve (4.22):

$$\frac{dJ}{dI} = -\frac{P_I}{P_J}\left(\frac{r_J dK_I + w_J dL_I}{r_I dK_I + w_I dL_I}\right) \tag{4.27}$$

If $r_J = r_I$ and $w_J = w_I$ the expression with parenthesis reduces to one and (4.27) to

$$\frac{dJ}{dI} = -\frac{P_I}{P_J} \tag{4.28}$$

(i.e., the 'normal' case). The price line is here tangent to the production possibility curve.

If, on the other hand, $w_J < w_I (r_J = r_I = r)$ the production possibility curve will have a negative slope which is less steep than that of the price line (i.e., the expression within parentheses is less than one). The price line then cuts the production possibility curve 'from above'.

The problem with different factor prices in different sectors is summarized in Figure 4.9. Free trade in this case yields a production point such as B (where the production possibility curve has a less steep slope than the price line) and the consumption point C. The optimal policy in this case must bring the economy back to the undistorted production possibility curve. This, for example, tariff policy can never do since it does not attack the root of the evil: the distortion in the factor market. Neither will taxes and/or subsidies in the commodity markets help. They may, however, be used to bring about a second-best solution where $FRT = DRT^* = DRS$, where DRT^* is the slope of the inner transformation curve. The economy then produces at point F and consumes at point G on a higher welfare level than with *laissez-faire*. The *undistorted*, efficient, transformation curve, however, cannot be reached without changing the relative factor prices.

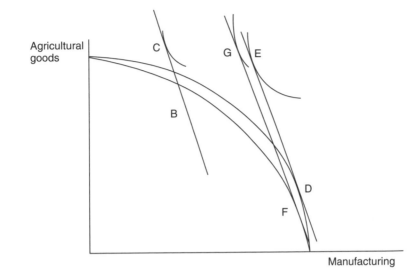

Figure 4.9 Higher wages in manufacturing than in agriculture

What is needed is, first, that factor prices are equal (here, $w_J = w_I$) in both sectors, which means that production takes place on the contract curve (where the isoquants are tangents to each other).

Second, the slope of the price line must coincide with the slope of the undistorted production possibility curve, which, according to (4.33), will take place when $w_J = w_I$. The result can be obtained via subsidization of the use of labour in manufacturing and/or taxation of the use of labour in agriculture. The economy can then be made to produce at point *D* and consume at point *E* (the highest possible welfare level).

Finally, different factor prices in different sectors may also make a change in relative commodity prices increase the supply of the commodity whose price has become relatively *lower*. This may happen if the capital-intensive sector pays higher wages than the labour-intensive sector. In this case the physically more capital-intensive sector (here manufactures) is the most labour-intensive one in value terms. If the relative price of agricultural goods now increases it can be shown that the wage rates will also fall in relation to the return on capital, given that the relative capital intensities in value terms are opposite to those in physical terms. Relatively cheaper labour will then be substituted for capital in both sectors. We get an excess supply of capital. It is possible to demonstrate (with the aid of the so-called Rybczynski theorem) that an increased supply of capital will make the physically capital-intensive sector (i.e., manufactures) expand and the physically labour-intensive sector (agriculture) contract. A higher price on manufactures will hence make manufacturing output contract. To what extent the case of perverse supply reactions is to be considered a realistic empirical possibility is unclear. Some researchers contend that this type of supply reactions will lead to equilibria that are unstable and that they should hence be regarded as theoretical curiosities.

Factor-generated externalities

When factor-generated externalities exist in the economy the production in one of the sectors is affected by the factor use in the other sector. If, for example, the labour use in manufacturing leads to emissions that reduce production in agriculture we obtain the following production functions:

$$I = I(K_I, L_I) \tag{4.29}$$

$$J = J(K_J, L_J, L_I) \tag{4.30}$$

With these production functions production will be inefficient. The economy will produce at a point which is not on the contract curve in the box diagram.

To obtain the slopes of the two production isoquants we differentiate the production functions and keep the production of the two commodities constant:

$$dI = I_K dK_I + I_L dL_I = 0 \tag{4.31}$$

$$dJ = J_K dK_J + J_L dL_J + J_{LI} dL_I = 0 \tag{4.32}$$

We also use the fact that

$$\bar{L} = L_J + L_I \tag{4.7}$$

so that

$$dL_I = -dL_J \tag{4.33}$$

$$dJ = J_K dK_J + (J_L - J_{LI}) dL_J = 0 \tag{4.34}$$

This yields:

$$DRTS_I = -\frac{dL_I}{dK_I} = \frac{I_K}{I_L} \tag{4.35}$$

$$DRTS_J = -\frac{dL_J}{dK_J} = \frac{J_K}{J_L - J_{LI}} \tag{4.36}$$

(the marginal domestic rates of technical substitution).

In the factor markets we have perfect competition, so the production factors will be remunerated with the value of their respective marginal products:

$$r = P_I I_K = P_J J_K \tag{4.11}$$

$$w = P_I I_L = P_J J_L \tag{4.12}$$

which yields

$$\frac{I_K}{I_L} = \frac{r}{w} \tag{4.37}$$

$$\frac{J_K}{J_L} = \frac{r}{w} \tag{4.38}$$

These may be substituted into the expressions for the rates of substitution:

$$DRTS_I = \frac{r}{w} \tag{4.39}$$

$$DRTS_J = \frac{r/P_J}{w/P_J - J_{LI}} = \frac{r}{w - P_J J_{LI}} \tag{4.40}$$

We find that the slope of the production isoquant in agriculture does not coincide with that of the factor price line. Since $J_{LI} < 0$

$$DRTS_J < \frac{r}{w} \tag{4.41}$$

The production isoquants of manufacturing and agriculture must hence intersect each other at a point where

$$DRTS_J < DRTS_I \tag{4.42}$$

that is, where the agricultural isoquant has a flatter slope than the manufacturing isoquant (e.g., point *a* in Figure 4.10).

We then know that we can derive a production possibility curve that lies inside the efficient one. Factor-generated externalities will also make the price line cut the production possibility curve.

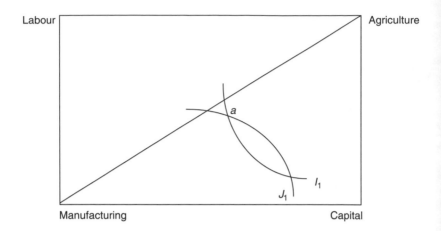

Figure 4.10   The effect on the factor market of factor-generated externalities

We have already derived expressions for how production in agriculture and manufacturing will change when the factor use changes. If, in addition, we make use of

$$dK_J = -dK_I \tag{4.8}$$

and

$$dL_J = -dL_I \tag{4.9}$$

we may write the slope of the production possibility curve as

$$\frac{dJ}{dI} = -\frac{J_K dK_I + (J_L - J_{LI})dL_I}{I_K dK_I + I_L dL_I} \tag{4.43}$$

If we substitute the expressions for the marginal products (from the profit maximizing conditions 4.11 and 4.12) we finally obtain

$$\frac{dJ}{dI} = -\frac{P_I}{P_J} + \frac{P_I J_{LI} dL_I}{r dK_I + w dL_I} \tag{4.44}$$

The last term is negative. Hence, the slope of the production possibility curve is *steeper* than that of the price line. This is illustrated in Figure 4.11.

The economy will produce at B on the inner production possibility curve and consume at C; to get back to production in A and consumption in D we must attack the source of the two distortions. The manufacturing sector

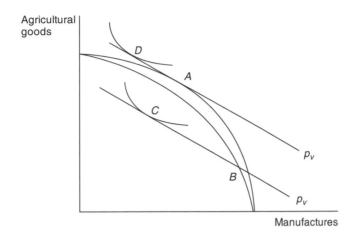

Figure 4.11 Production and consumption with factor-generated externalities

must be made to use less labour (and more capital). The use of labour in the sector must be taxed. Alternatively the use of labour in agriculture may be subsidized. We want to have $DRTS_I = DRTS_J$. If we denote the wage rates *inclusive* of taxes and subsidies with w_I and w_J we see from the expressions for $DRTS_I$ and $DRTS_J$ that this requires either that

$$w_I = w_J - P_J J_{LI} \tag{4.45}$$

(taxation of the labour use in manufacturing) where $J_{LI} < 0$, or

$$w_J = w_I + P_J J_{LI} \tag{4.46}$$

(subsidization of the labour use in agriculture). We see that the size of the tax or the subsidy will amount exactly to the value of the externality. The same tax/subsidy re-establishes the equality between DRT and p_V (*FRT*).

Conclusions

In the present chapter we have analysed the consequences of non-fulfilment of all the optimum conditions that we have derived. In all the cases, distortions (i.e., violation of some optimality condition) produce an outcome which is inferior to the ideal case (free trade and no distortions). The distortions may, however, always be attacked with economic policy measures. Depending on which distortion we are dealing with, tariffs, taxes or subsidies (or combinations of these) are optimal.

In the case of different factor prices in different sectors, however, intervention in the commodity markets will not help. The distortion must be attacked at the source if we are to obtain the optimal result: that is, taxation and subsidization must take place in the factor markets. In the next chapter we will examine some cases where the distortions have been caused by policy interventions (i.e., they are either autonomous or instrumental).

Literature

The systematization of distortions and the instruments for elimination of them are based on:

Bhagwati, Jagdish N. (1983), *The Theory of Commercial Policy. Essays in International Economic Theory.* MIT Press, Cambridge, MA, ch. 2.

The principle that a distortion should be attacked 'at the source' is dealt with in this work and also in:

Corden, W. Max (1974), *Trade Policy and Economic Welfare.* Clarendon Press, Oxford.
Greenaway, David and Milner, Chris (1993), *Trade and Industrial Policy in Developing Countries.* Macmillan, London, ch. 2.

The classic formal derivation of offer curves is found in:

Meade, James E. (1952), *A Geometry of International Trade.* George Allen & Unwin, London, chs 1–4.

Offer curves are also dealt with in:

Findlay, Ronald (1970), *Trade and Specialization.* Penguin, Harmondsworth, ch. 2.
Salvatore, Dominick (2001), *International Economics* (7th edn). John Wiley, New York, ch. 4.
Södersten, Bo and Reed, Geoffrey (1994), *International Economics* (3rd edn). Macmillan, London, ch. 11.

The optimum tariff is discussed, for example, in:

Baldwin, Robert E. (1952), 'The New Welfare Economics and Gains in International Trade', *Quarterly Journal of Economics*, Vol. 66.
Bhagwati, Jagdish N., Ramaswami, V. K. and Srinivasan, T. N. (1963), 'Domestic Distortions, Tariffs, and the Theory of Optimum Subsidy', *Journal of Political Economy*, Vol. 71.
Bhagwati, Jagdish N., Ramaswami, V. K. and Srinivasan, T. N. (1969), 'Domestic Distortions, Tariffs, and the Theory of Optimum Subsidy: Some Further Results', *Journal of Political Economy*, Vol. 77.
Bhagwati, Jagdish N., Panagaryia, Arvind and Srinivasan, T. N. (1998), *Lectures on International Trade* (2nd edn). MIT Press, Cambridge, MA and London, ch. 21.
Johnson, Harry G. (1968), 'The Gain from Exploiting Monopoly and Monopsony Power in International Trade', *Economica*, NS, Vol. 35.
Kemp, Murray C. (1967), 'Notes on the Theory of Optimal Tariffs', *Economic Record*, Vol. 43.

Externalities in production and other domestic distortions as well as consequences of these are discussed in:

Bhagwati, Panagaryia and Srinivasan, *Lectures on International Trade*, ch. 22.

Haberler, Gottfried (1950), 'Some Problems in the Pure Theory of International Trade', *Economic Journal*, Vol. 6.

Johnson, Harry G. (1965), 'Optimal Trade Intervention in the Presence of Domestic Distortions', in Baldwin, Robert E. *et al.* (eds), *Trade Growth and the Balance of Payments: Essays in Honor of Gottfried Haberler.* Rand-McNally, Chicago, IL.

Kemp, Murray and Negishi, Takashi (1969), 'Domestic Distortions, Tariffs, and the Theory of Optimum Subsidy', *Journal of Political Economy*, Vol. 77.

Distortions in factor markets are discussed in:

Bhagwati, J. and Srinivasan, T. N. (1971), 'The Theory of Wage Differentials: Production Response and Factor Price Equalisation', *Journal of International Economics*, Vol. 1.

Hagen, Everett E. (1958), 'An Economic Justification for Protectionism', *Quarterly Journal of Economics*, Vol. 72.

Hazari, Bharat R. (1978), *The Pure Theory of International Trade and Distortions.* Croom Helm, London.

Herberg, Horst and Kemp, Murray C. (1971), 'Factor Market Distortions, the Shape of the Locus of Competitive Outputs, and the Relation Between Product Prices and Equilibrium Outputs', in Bhagwati, Jagdish N. *et al.* (eds), *Trade, Balance of Payments and Growth: Papers in International Economics in Honor of Charles P. Kindleberger.* North-Holland, Amsterdam.

Johnson, Harry G. (1965), 'Factor Market Distortions and the Shape of the Transformation Curve', *Econometrica*, Vol. 34.

Jones, Ronald W. (1971), 'Distortion in Factor Markets and the General Equilibrium Model of Production', *Journal of Political Economy*, Vol. 77.

Magee, Stephen (1973), 'Factor Market Distortions, Production and Trade: A Survey', *Oxford Economic Papers*, NS, Vol. 25.

Magee, Stephen (1976), *International Trade and Distortions in Factor Markets.* Marcel Dekker, New York.

Neary, J. Peter (1978), Dynamic Stability and the Theory of Factor-Market Distortions', *American Economic Review*, Vol. 68.

The Rybczynski theorem is proved in practically all international economics texts; see, for example:

Södersten and Reed, *International Economics*. Macmillan.

Factor-generated externalities are treated in:

Chacholiades, Miltiades (1978), *International Trade Theory and Policy.* McGraw-Hill, New York, ch. 7 (appendix).

Kemp, Murray C. (1964), *The Pure Theory of International Trade.* Prentice-Hall, Englewood Cliffs, NJ, ch. 8.

5
Instrumental Distortions: Swedish Agricultural Policy

During an international crisis securing the domestic supply of food is very important. Swedish agricultural policy during the postwar period provides a good example of how *instrumental* distortions (distortions that are deliberate policy measures) may be introduced into an economy to protect it against loss of the possibility of importing food. The reasoning developed presently is of relevance also for a number of other Western countries. The agricultural sector has for different reasons been sheltered from international competition (e.g., in order to secure the national provision of foodstuffs, to guarantee 'fair' incomes for the farmers or to reduce the exodus of workers from the primary sector when the rest of the economy cannot absorb them).

Swedish agriculture after the Second World War has been characterized by extensive overproduction in combination with minimum prices. Such surpluses may be placed on the world market only with the aid of subsidized exports. The system goes all the way back to the 1930s and ultimately to the First World War, which for the first time highlighted the problem of emergency considerations for a blockade (and demonstrated what the consequences of neglecting these considerations might be). Another relevant factor in this context is the large fall in the price of food that took place at the end of the 1920s. In order to secure the farmers' income level, protectionist regulations were then introduced which increased output considerably. This in combination with the existing apparatus of regulations made food provision easier during the Second World War. The system, however, became permanent. Marginal shifts of emphasis in the policy, which balanced producer and consumer interests against each other, have not been able to hide the fact that the extent of real reform was insignificant, and the central problems – high prices and protectionism – were barely attacked at all.

The fundamental problems arising from protection of agriculture are illustrated in Figure 5.1. Free trade at international prices (p_V) would have resulted in production at point B on the production possibility curve and consumption at point C. (Sweden exports 'manufactures' and imports 'agricultural goods'.) However, this policy has not been followed. Instead a

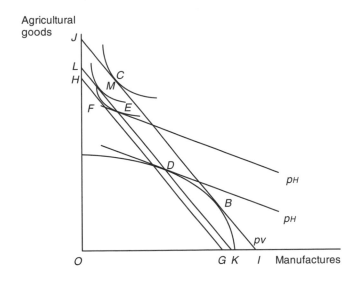

Figure 5.1   Tariff protection in agriculture

'high-price' policy has been pursued, with tariff protection for agriculture. This in Figure 5.1 amounts to production at D and consumption at E, at domestic prices (p_H). That policy has lowered welfare, E being on a lower social indifference curve than C.

To arrive at a (traditional) measure of the cost of protection we begin by looking at the consumption mix at world market prices that would yield the same welfare level as point E. This combination is indicated by point F, on the same indifference curve as E. In terms of manufacturing, this point represents a value equal to OG and, if we choose to measure in terms of agricultural goods, the value is OH. In the same way, we may obtain the value of the consumption bundle at international prices as OI and OJ, respectively. The total cost of protection then is GI, in terms of manufactures, or HJ, in terms of agricultural goods.

The total cost may be split into two components: a consumption cost and a production cost. The former is obtained by fixing production to point D. At world market prices, this yields a consumption cost of GK or HL, respectively, depending on whether the cost is measured in terms of manufactures or agricultural goods. The production cost is thereafter obtained by moving production to the free trade point B, as KI or LJ, respectively.

In the Swedish debate, a 'low-price' policy has also been discussed. Such a policy would build on the use of production subsidies instead of tariffs to move the point of production from B to D. This would change relative producer prices to p_H but consumption would then take place at world market prices, p_V, in point *M*. The consumption cost *GK* (*HL*) would disappear. Only the production cost, *KI* (*LJ*), would remain.

Finally, during certain periods, a 'middle-price' policy has been employed. Production has been protected by means of tariffs, meaning that it has taken place at point *D*, while consumption has been subsidized simultaneously. In terms of Figure 5.1, this would entail a steeper consumption price line than p_H, with a higher level of welfare than the one given by point *E* (however, it would not be as high as the one indicated by point *M*).

Emergency policy

It is obvious that Swedish postwar agricultural policy has not been optimal from the welfare point of view. The policy has had three main goals: a *production goal*, which above all is aimed at ensuring the food supply if the country is cut off from international trade; an *income goal*, which means that those who are employed in agriculture are to be guaranteed a standard of living which is as high as that of other, comparable, groups in society; and an *efficiency goal* which states that the supply of food is to be ensured at the lowest possible real cost to the economy. Of these three traditional goals, the first and the second have dominated the picture. In 1985, additional goals in terms of food quality were included on the agenda, namely environmental conservation and regional balance, but these have remained subordinate to the production and income goals. Clearly, the policy pursued builds on the above goals, but even so it is far from certain that the interventions which have taken place have been the optimal ones.

We will in the following concentrate on the production goal and try to determine what kind of policy is optimal for reaching this goal. In this process extensive use is made of the theory of distortions. The description of Swedish agricultural policy that was made above assumed that no production goal existed.

In order to analyse with some degree of precision what an optimal policy would look like, we must know something about the characteristics of the situation for which Swedish agriculture has to be prepared. The scenario that was accepted by most of the government commissions looking into the agricultural sector during the postwar period is a throwback to the Second World War: a three-year total cutoff from foreign trade. Thus, for the most part, agricultural policy has been tied to a single alternative. This is unfortunate, and sharp criticism as well as alternative scenarios have been presented. It is, however, difficult to have any definite opinion with respect to the value of these scenarios. The fundamental problem is that, *ex ante*, it is impossible to make reliable forecasts regarding what a future worldwide conflict situation would look like. Here, we have a very wide range of possibilities, from very small disturbances of Sweden's foreign trade to a country that has been completely destroyed by a nuclear war. Which situation should we plan for? The extreme cases are more or less trivial. In the first case, hardly any interventions will be needed. In the second, they will have no effect. The most realistic alternative lies somewhere between these extremes, but we do not know exactly where. The situation includes uncertainty as one of the most salient characteristics.

In decision theory, the distinction is often made between decisions under certainty, risk and genuine uncertainty. In the first case, the outcomes are known, in the case of risk the probabilities of different outcomes are known; but in the case of genuine uncertainty not even the probabilities are known. Unfortunately, Swedish agricultural policy has to be devised with an eye to uncertainty. We do not have any idea whatsoever regarding future contingencies.

To a certain extent, food policy can be handled via storage. On the one hand, cultivation may not always be possible (e.g., after a nuclear war), and on the other hand, Sweden may not be cut off long enough to call for a restructuring of the production pattern. (Even if this is necessary, storage may be required to handle the period that will elapse before the structure of agricultural production has been adapted to the isolation from international markets, if the latter exist at all.)

Given the above, it appears reasonable to employ some kind of maximin decision rule. (The term comes from game theory and means that the strategy is chosen which leads to the best of the possible worst outcomes.) How can we make the best out of the 'worst' possible situation, where foreign trade and import possibilities are non-existent while the entire population remains and has to eat? If this situation can be handled, so can, presumably, the 'less serious' cases. (If part of the population disappears as well, it may be difficult to handle production, but this cannot be planned for, other than by storage. We will thus pay no further attention to this case.)

How, then, should the emergency or contingency (production) goal be formulated? Unfortunately, official declarations have not been crystal clear and leave a lot to be desired. In fact, they leave plenty of room for interpretation. Accordingly, it is necessary to examine a number of possible options. Below we look at five different formulations of the emergency (production) goal:

- an import restriction
- a 'relative' production goal: a given share of consumption
- an 'absolute' production goal: a given minimum quantity
- a minimum capital stock in the agricultural sector
- a contingency target that assumes a lack of technical flexibility and a partial 'market failure'

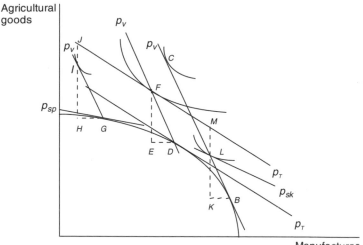

Figure 5.2   An import restriction

We will examine what kinds of measures are called for in each of the five cases. We will also comment on the realistic chances of each formulation arriving at a conclusion regarding the emergency to be planned for.

An import restriction

A simple formulation of the contingency target is in terms of import restrictions. Agricultural imports may then amount only to a certain maximum and the rest of the consumption must be covered by domestic production. This formulation is illustrated in Figure 5.2, where three different ways of keeping imports down are compared: a tariff, a low-price policy based on producer subsidies, and a tax on the consumption of agricultural goods.

Free trade would lead to production at point B and consumption at point C but, since the level of imports is to be kept down, free trade is out of the question. Instead, the problem is to find a policy that gives rise to a given import quantity, say, EF. Then, world market prices can no longer be employed. A tariff increasing the relative price of agricultural goods to p_T, on the other hand, brings about the desired result, with production at D and consumption at F. If a subsidy-based low-price policy is chosen instead, other prices are required. The relative price that yields an import level equal to EF is p_{sp}. The production of agricultural goods increases and consumption takes place at I on a lower indifference curve than the one through point F.

That *I* represents a lower welfare level than *F* can be demonstrated in the following way. The two trade triangles *EFD* and *HIG* are equal in size. Production point *G* is to the northwest of *D*. Then the consumption point *I* must also be to the northwest of *F*. If the p_T line through *F* is extended until it cuts the extension of *HI*, we end up at point *J*. This point must lie above *I* and is hence preferred to *I* from the welfare point of view. The two p_T lines are parallel. The slope of the production possibility curve in *G* is less steep than the slope at *D*. Thus, *G* is below the p_T line that goes through *D*, and *HI* consequently does not reach the p_T line through *F*. When we move from *F* to *J* we cross a number of indifference curves on the way, all of which have a steeper slope than p_T at the intersection points. (All the indifference curves are convex to the origin.) This is also true for the curve that goes through point *J* and for the curve through point *I*. Thus, the curve through *I* represents a lower welfare level than the curve through *F*. Tariffs are superior to production subsidies from the welfare point of view.

Are tariffs also superior to a tax on the consumption of agricultural goods? In the latter case, the economy produces at world market prices at *B* and the consumer prices that yield an import level of $KL = EF$ are given by P_{sk}. This policy is also inferior to tariffs. Point *B* is to the southeast of *D*. The two trade triangles are equally large. Then, point *L* is southeast of *F*. In the same way as before, we may prove that *M* is above *L*. Moving from *F* to *M* entails cutting ever lower indifference curves since p_T will have a steeper slope than the indifference curves in the intersection points. (The indifference curves continue to be convex to the origin.) Point *M* is superior to point *L* from the welfare point of view (more agricultural goods and as many manufactures), but inferior to point *F*. Thus, tariffs are preferable to consumption taxes.

The reason why tariffs (a high-price policy) are preferable to both the low-price policy and taxes on consumption is simply the fundamental principle of the theory of distortions. The tariff works *directly* on the size of imports since it constitutes a tax on foreign trade, and the contingency target in the present formulation is tied to the size of imports.

A 'relative' contingency target

A contingency target expressed as a pure import restriction is not well formulated. The problem at hand is not first and foremost to keep imports out but to see to it that domestic agriculture can produce enough during a period of isolation. It thus makes more sense to formulate a production target which states that domestic production under non-emergency conditions must amount to a certain minimum share of domestic consumption. This formulation is analysed in Figures 5.3 and 5.4.

As before, free trade, with production at *B*, is ruled out. The contingency target impedes that. Let us begin with how the contingency target may be expressed in terms of our diagram. We choose any point on the production

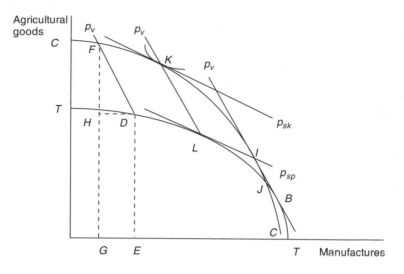

Figure 5.3   A relative production goal

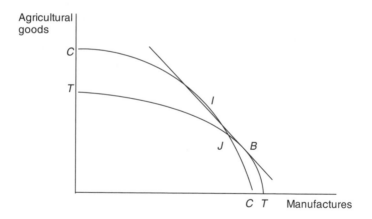

Figure 5.4   Detail from Figure 5.3

possibility curve, such as D. There, the domestic production of agricultural goods amounts to DE. In order to reach our target, DE must amount to a certain share of the total consumption of agricultural goods, such as X. If we know this share, we also know how much imports is allowed.

X = DE/FG and imports may not exceed FH. We may thereafter repeat the exercise, taking point after point on the production possibility curve, and derive new consumption points that meet the contingency restriction.

Joining all such points yields the *CC* curve. This ends just above the horizontal axis, a little above the trade triangle that would arise if infinitely small amounts of agricultural goods were produced domestically.

The points on this curve that lie to the southeast of *I*, which corresponds to point *B* on the production possibility curve – the production point with free trade – are of no interest. See Figure 5.4, which is a magnification of the southeast corner of Figure 5.3. First, we have the points on *CC* that lie to the southeast of the intersection point *J* between *CC* and *TT*. All these points imply that consumption takes place inside the transformation curve. For all these points pure autarky represents less waste of resources than consumption on *CC*. Instead of producing on the *TT* curve, trading at world market prices and consuming to the northwest of this curve, on the *CC* curve it is possible to produce and consume at a point on *TT* that lies immediately to the right of the *CC* curve. This yields the same consumption of agricultural goods and a higher consumption of manufactures in spite of the fact that the production of manufactures is lower than if the trade option had been chosen. In the limiting case, the intersection point between the two curves, the same consumption is obtained regardless of which strategy is chosen, but the production of manufactures is still lower in the autarky case.

The points between *I* and the point of intersection between the two curves, *J*, are not interesting either. It is always possible to produce at *B* and import a smaller quantity than is required to get to *I*, (i.e., ending up on the straight line *IB*, to the right of *CC*), obtaining as high a consumption of agricultural goods as on *CC*, but a higher consumption of manufactures. In order to end up on *CC* between *I* and the intersection point a larger production of manufactures is required than is given by *B*. However, it pays to produce at *B* instead and consume along *IB*. (Below *I*, the contingency target is overfulfilled, since the consumption of agricultural goods thereafter shrinks faster than production as we move towards the southwest; but, of course, there is no reason to do that.)

Thus it is only the part of the *CC* curve that lies northwest of *I* that is of interest to us. But what does the optimal policy look like? All points on *CC* meet the contingency restriction. What is required is to find the point that yields the highest welfare level, and this point is *K* in Figure 5.3: the point on *CC* that is also a point of tangency with an indifference curve. For this, consumer prices p_{sk} are required. The production point that corresponds to *K* is *L*, on *TT*, with producer prices p_{sp}.

Thus, we find that intervention is required both on the consumption and the production sides. (Free trade with *laissez-faire* is optimal only in the special case when the point of tangency between the *CC* curve and the indifference curve happens to be in point *I*.) What is needed is a subsidy to agricultural producers and a tax on the consumption of these same goods. The per unit subsidy must be larger than the tax. Domestic production of agricultural goods must always amount to the same share of consumption.

Moving northwestwards along *TT* increases domestic agricultural production but also agricultural imports (i.e., the height of the trade triangles
increases). This is possible only if the slope of consumption points such as
K is steeper than the slope of production points such as *L*.

Again, we have an example of a policy that attacks the target 'directly'.
The production of agricultural goods is stimulated and the consumption of
it is held back. It should be noted that the tax cum subsidy policy is
equivalent to a middle-price policy. Point *L* can be reached via a tariff that
makes domestic relative prices equal to p_{sp}, but then consumers pay too high
a price for agricultural goods. This calls for a subsidy on consumption which
makes the relative price of agricultural goods fall to p_{sk}.

A high-price policy will be optimal only in the case where the degree of
self-sufficiency is 100 per cent. Then the production and consumption
points coincide and the slopes of the producer and consumer price lines
will be equal. As soon as the economy aims at less than complete autarky
the *CC* and *TT* curves will differ, and the rate of taxation will be lower than
the rate of subsidization.

An 'absolute' contingency target

The contingency goal may also be formulated in 'absolute' terms. Frequently, it has been indicated that domestic production should amount to
a certain minimum share of the 'normal' consumption of foodstuffs. If the
latter is known, we also know the required absolute level of agricultural
production. This case is analysed in Figure 5.5.

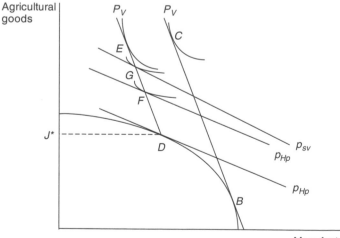

Figure 5.5   An absolute production goal

Let us assume that agricultural production must amount to at least J^*. This excludes pure free trade with production at B and consumption at C, since that would make for an insufficient level of agricultural production. Instead, the economy must produce at D, at the domestic relative prices indicated by p_{H_p}, and the highest possible welfare level is given by point E, where consumers are allowed to buy at world market prices. In other words, the optimal policy is a low-price one. Through subsidies to agricultural production, J^* is reached, at point D.

A high-price policy whereby producers are protected by tariffs and consumers have to pay the tariff-inclusive price yields a lower welfare level, with consumption in F. A middle-price policy, finally, where the consumer is subsidized, although not to the point of paying world market prices, would lead to consumption, say, at G, at consumer prices p_{SV}.

Capital use as a restriction

Production factors may not be reallocated without difficulty from manufacturing to agriculture if the economy is cut off from international trade. Presumably, labour is less of a problem, but the capital needed in agriculture differs considerably from that required for manufacturing. Then we may have to formulate the contingency target in such a way as to guarantee that a 'minimum' capital stock is available in agriculture so that the latter sector produces at least a given output quantity in case the economy is cut off from imports. In order to analyse what the optimal policy would look like when there is a restriction on the use of capital, we not only need the production possibility curve diagram but the box diagram as well (see Figures 5.6a and b).

In the box diagram we measure the employment of capital along the horizontal axis and the use of labour along the vertical one. Agricultural production is measured from northeast to southwest and the production of manufactures is measured from southwest to northeast. We furthermore assume that manufactured products are capital-intensive while agricultural goods are labour-intensive. (The agricultural sector also employs land, but that is of no consequence in the present context.)

If there had been no contingency restriction, the economy would have produced, say, at point b. There, production is efficient, since an agriculture isoquant is tangent to a manufacturing isoquant. The prevailing factor prices are r/w. In the free trade situation, point b corresponds to point B on the production possibility curve TT in Figure 5.6b. As before, this would yield the welfare level that corresponds to point C.

Let us, however, now assume that a restriction exists on the use of capital within agriculture. If autarky is forced upon the country, at least as much capital as is needed to produce J^* agricultural goods is required. This level is K^* in the agricultural sector. (The agricultural isoquant, J^*, becomes 'flat' at

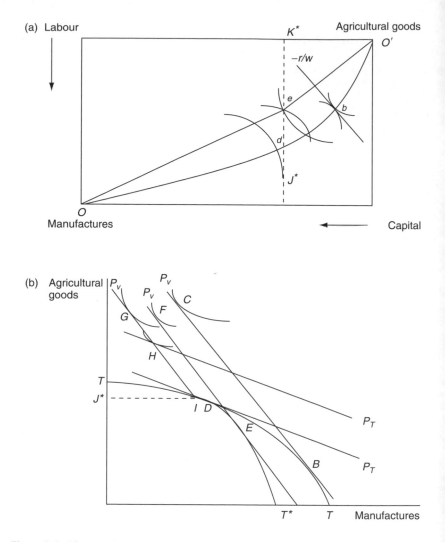

Figure 5.6   The contingency goal as a capital restriction

K^*. With less capital in the agricultural sector, producing J^* becomes impossible, regardless of how much labour is put in.)

This capital restriction means that the economy can produce only in the Od interval of the contract curve. In terms of the lower part of the diagram this means that the production possibility curve TT shifts inwards after point D, to DT^*. Capital can no longer be taken out of agriculture after this point. Only labour is mobile.

Let us then turn to the optimal policy. The highest indifference curve that we can reach is the one that goes through *F*. The economy produces at world market prices at *E* (*e* in the box) and consumes at the same prices at *F*. Since we intervene in the capital market the suspicion may arise that this may also make the price line cut the production possibility curve at the optimal production point. This is, however, not the case. To see this we must go back to expression (4.27):

$$\frac{dJ}{dI} = -\frac{P_I}{P_J}\left(\frac{r_J dK_I + w_J dL_I}{r_I dK_I + w_I dL_I}\right) \tag{4.27}$$

Since labour is freely mobile and is neither taxed nor subsidized, $w_I = w_J = w$. We, however, also know that we are on the dK^* capital restriction line in the box diagram when we produce on the DT segment of the production possibility curve. Thus $dK_I = 0$, and from this it follows that the slope of the production possibility curve equals the slope of the price line: that is

$$\frac{dJ}{dI} = -\frac{P_I}{P_J}$$

A low-price policy yields an inferior result. Assume that this policy is devised, for example, to yield exactly the desired volume of agricultural goods during the emergency, with production at *I*, at subsidized prices, p_T. This is conducive to a lower level of welfare, at point *G*. The high-price policy, according to which the consumers have to buy agricultural goods at the tariff-inclusive price, yields an even lower welfare level, at *H*. A middle-price policy, finally, would produce a result somewhere between these two points.

Free trade alone, however, is not sufficient to reach the welfare level *F*. Point *E* in the Figure 5.6b corresponds to point *e* in the box. The latter point must be on dK^* for the capital restriction to be met. Furthermore, less agricultural goods is produced there than at $D(d)$. The point *e* is not – as *d* – on the contract curve of the economy, since the capital stock has been fixed. Therefore, at *e* an agricultural isoquant must cut a manufacturing isoquant.

At the intersection point *e*, the slope of the manufacturing isoquant is steeper than the slope of the agricultural isoquant. This implies that the price of capital in terms of labour is higher in manufacturing than in agriculture. If we compare with point *b*, where no contingency constraint exists, we find that the labour intensity has increased within manufacturing but decreased in agriculture. (This is shown by the rays from the origins of the box to the production points.) Thus the optimal policy when the contingency constraint is formulated as a minimum capital stock in agriculture is a subsidy on capital use in that sector or a tax on capital use in manufacturing.

Limited flexibility of techniques: 'market failures'

In a situation where the economy is cut off from international trade and food scarcity arises, the market mechanism will naturally come into play. The relative price of agricultural goods will increase, and, in due course, so will the supply. The problem, however, is that such a shift may not come about fast enough, even though agricultural production is subsidized, once the emergency situation becomes a reality. The flexibility of the economy may be too low, thereby requiring other types of interventions as well. What form these interventions take depends on the way in which the economy lacks flexibility. In emergency situations we want the economy to produce at least a minimum quantity of agricultural goods *using efficient techniques* (i.e., the economy should produce on the contract curve). Thus we know the combination of labour and capital that the agricultural sector ought to employ in principle.

Three types of inflexibilities may arise: (1) the economy may fail to reach the production target in time, even though techniques are flexible and production factors are mobile; (2) the capital stock may be difficult to move between the sectors; (3) the production techniques employed by agriculture may be inflexible.

From the contingency point of view, the most realistic inflexibilities facing Swedish agriculture presumably consist of a combination of time lags in the increase of supply and limited flexibility of techniques. A restriction on the capital intensity appears to be the most realistic formulation. If part of the capital stock is rendered useless in an emergency, more labour-intensive techniques may be used, but it may be difficult to switch rapidly to these techniques if normal production is characterized by high capital intensity. Thus let us assume that there are two types of restrictions: a minimum labour intensity and a minimum output level, both in the agricultural sector. This is shown in Figures 5.7a and 5.7b.

The free trade situation is indicated by production at b in the box and at B on the production possibility curve, with consumption at C. In the emergency situation, we want an agricultural output level corresponding to isoquant J^*. During the emergency, however, the capital stock has shrunk (e.g., with OO_A), obliging us to measure the production of manufactures from O_A instead of from O. The economy gets a new contract curve, and we require production during the emergency to be efficient (i.e., the technique employed in agriculture must be the one given by the ray $O'd$, a technique that is more labour-intensive than the one used at b).

What does the optimal policy look like? If it is difficult to switch techniques in agriculture and it is difficult to rely on the market to increase

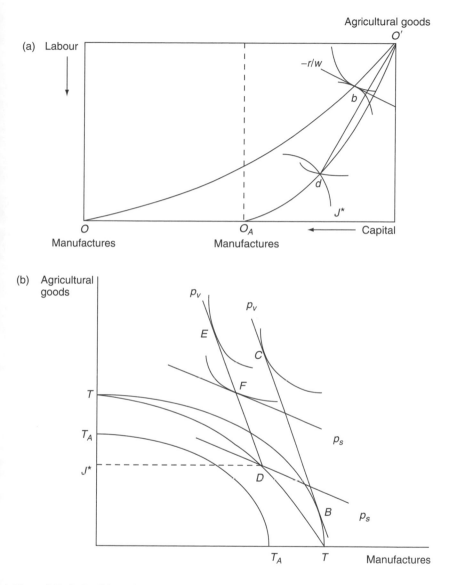

Figure 5.7 Inflexible techniques and market failures

the supply of agricultural goods spontaneously during the emergency, production under 'normal' circumstances should also take place at *d*. This
point is not on the normal contract curve *OO′*, but the *J** isoquant will cut
a manufacturing isoquant which is measured from *O*. As indicated by the
diagram, the relative price of capital at this point is higher in agriculture

than in manufacturing. Thus, the use of capital in agriculture should be taxed and the use of labour subsidized, in order to increase the labour intensity, as compared to the free trade situation.

In the commodity market, shown in Figure 5.7b, we find three production possibility curves: *TT*, the 'normal' one; $T_A T_A$, the one which is operative during an emergency; and the broken curve, *TDT*, which has the same endpoints as *TT* but which is below this curve. Under free trade and *laissez-faire*, the economy produces at *B* on *TT*. When we intervene in the factor market with subsidies and taxes, however, this curve shifts inwards, to the broken *TDT* line.

To arrive at an agricultural production level of *J**, above the free-trade level, a subsidy is needed that gives rise to the domestic price relations given by p_S. This yields a welfare level given by point *E*. With a high-price policy the economy ends up at *F*. The price line cuts the production possibility curve in the way indicated by the figure when the use of capital is taxed and the use of labour is subsidized in agriculture. This may be proved in the following way.

Again we take the expression for the slope of the production possibility curve (4.27) (here renumbered) as our point of departure:

$$\frac{dJ}{dI} = -\frac{P_I}{P_J}\left(\frac{r_J dK_I + w_J dL_I}{r_I dK_I + w_I dL_I}\right) \tag{5.1}$$

If the use of capital is taxed and the use of labour subsidized in agriculture we hence have:

$$r_J > r_I \text{ and } w_J < w_I$$

or

$$r_J = \alpha r_I; \alpha > 1 \tag{5.2}$$

and

$$w_J = \beta w_I; 0 < \beta < 1 \tag{5.3}$$

(5.1) may now be rewritten as

$$\frac{dJ}{dI} = -\frac{P_I}{P_J}\left(\frac{\alpha r_I I dK_I + \beta w_I dL_I}{r_I dK_I + w_I dL_I}\right)$$

$$\tag{5.4}$$

For the slope of the production possibility curve to be steeper than that of the price line the expression within parentheses must be greater than one. In other words, we must have:

$$\alpha r_I dK_I + \beta w_I dL_I > r_I dK_I + w_I dL_I \tag{5.5}$$

or

$$(\alpha - 1) r_I dK_I > (1 - \beta) w_I dL_I \tag{5.6}$$

which may in turn be written as:

$$\alpha - 1 > (1 - \beta)(w_I / r_I)(dL_I / dK_I) \tag{5.7}$$

But, as we have already shown, the slope of the manufacturing isoquant must equal the relation between the factor prices: that is,

$$\frac{dL_I}{dK_I} = - \frac{r_I}{w_I} \tag{5.8}$$

when (5.8) is substituted into (5.7), and the resulting expression is simplified, we obtain:

$$\alpha > \beta \tag{5.9}$$

Thus (5.9) is valid if the price line cuts the production possibility curve 'from below'. This, however, is always the case since $\alpha > 1$ and $\beta < 1$.

Thus, the optimal policy is a combination of a low-price policy – subsidization of labour in agriculture – and taxation of the use of capital in the sector. Such a policy, however, may be difficult to implement, since it could happen that 'perverse' supply responses may arise as a result of the interventions in the factor markets. However, it is possible to design a system in practice which builds on the principles that have been derived with the aid of Figure 5.7 and which avoids this potential problem. The problem is to master the technique given by the $O'd$ ray quickly. One way of making the adjustment process a smooth one is by subsidizing a number of farms that employ more labour-intensive techniques than is the case on average in Swedish agriculture. In this way a 'bank of knowledge' can be created and developed that may be useful in an emergency. This bank can be complemented by storing such capital goods as may be needed during the emergency (capital which has been adapted to technologically simpler production).

Conclusions

One of the most important goals of Swedish agricultural policy during the postwar period has been to ensure that the domestic agricultural sector can produce enough to feed the population in the event that the country is cut off from international trade. However, this goal has never been clearly formulated. Hence, it is difficult to discuss to what extent the actual policy pursued during most of the period – tariff protection for Swedish agriculture, the so-called high-price policy – has contributed to the attainment of this goal. In the present chapter we have presented five different possible formulations and derived the optimal policy interventions for each case. The conclusion to be drawn is that only in the unrealistic case where the emergency target is defined in terms of a maximum level of imports is a high-price policy optimal. When a 'relative' production target is chosen, a middle-price policy is required. Such a policy was in operation during the late 1970s and early 1980s. All other formulations call for a combination of subsidies and taxes, not for protection.

The most realistic formulation of the emergency target is the one which stresses three elements: (1) the agricultural sector must be able to produce a minimum quantity of food once the emergency becomes a reality; (2) part of the capital stock can no longer be employed (e.g., because of a lack of fuel); (3) the techniques employed in the emergency situation will be much more labour-intensive than today's techniques, but the transition from capital-intensive to labour-intensive production may take time. The theoretical solution derived for this case – subsidization of production in combination with subsidies to labour and taxes on capital use in agriculture – can be translated into relatively simple practical measures: subsidization of a number of labour-intensive farm units (on a marginal basis) to create a 'bank of knowledge' for alternative production methods, and storage of the relatively unsophisticated capital equipment that is needed for operations of this type.

Literature

The theory employed in the present chapter is presented in:
Batra, Raveendra N. (1973), *Studies in the Pure Theory of International Trade*. Macmillan, London.
Bhagwati, Jagdish N. Panagariya, A. and Srinivasan, T. N. (1998), *Lectures on International Trade* (2nd edn). MIT Press, Cambridge, MA, and London, ch. 28.
Chacholiades, Miltiades (1978), *International Trade and Policy*. McGraw-Hill, Kogakusha, Tokyo.
Magee, Stephen P. (1976), *International Trade and Distortions in Factor Markets*. Marcel Dekker, New York.

The historical background to Swedish agricultural policy is given in:
Hedlund, Stefan and Lundahl, Mats (1986), 'Emergency Considerations in Swedish Agriculture: A Retrospective Look', *European Review of Agricultural Economics*, Vol. 13.

Surveys of the principal problems of Swedish agriculture are available in:
Bolin, Olof, Meyerson, Per-Martin and Ståhl, Ingemar, with contributions by Brorsson, Kjell-Åke, Haraldsson, Ingemar and Rabinowicz, Ewa (1986), *The Political Economy of the Food Sector: The Case of Sweden*. SNS, Stockholm.
Rabinowicz, Ewa (1992), 'Agricultural Policy: Old Wine in New Bottles', in Bourdet, Yves (ed.), *Internationalization, Market Power and Consumer Welfare*. Routledge, London and New York.

6

Import Substitution in Developing Countries

In the previous chapter we dealt with Swedish agricultural policy as an example of how the theory of distortions can be applied. We showed how the tariff-based policy has led to welfare losses in comparison to the free trade situation, and we discussed how the optimal intervention policy is conditioned by the different formulations of the emergency restriction in agriculture. In the present chapter we will go into a similar application of the theory of distortions, which is a case that deals with increasing domestic production at the expense of imports, namely the trade policy of developing countries. This policy has often been based on import substitution behind tariff walls.

The background

The background to the import-substitution policy of developing countries can be found in two historical events in the theory of economic development of the 1950s and in the industrialization policy employed by the socialist bloc in Eastern Europe. The two historical events are the Depression of the 1930s and the Second World War. When the Depression arrived the developing countries were strongly dependent on raw material production and exports. The majority of Asian and African developing economies were still colonies where production patterns to a large extent focused on production for the needs of the European 'mother countries'. Latin America was also dependent on primary exports. Most of the manufactures consumed were imported.

Primary exports *per se* do not necessarily imply anything negative. On the contrary, it is quite possible for raw material exporting countries to obtain high growth rates in their economies with the aid of primary export. This, however, presupposes that the raw materials in question are *staples*, (i.e., goods in high and increasing demand in the world market). Primary exports have a direct effect on the national product and on the rate of growth. Even more important, however, is the fact that staple exports

91

may generate so-called linkage effects which stimulate growth indirectly. Forward linkage implies that the raw materials are used as inputs in the production of other sectors. Backward linkage consists of the spread of growth impulses from raw material production via the demand for other sectors' products to be used as inputs. Consumption linkages are also conceivable. The incomes generated by raw material production are used for buying the products of other sectors. Finally, raw material production will generate tax revenue for the government, and this revenue may be spent on increasing the production capacity and the infrastructure of the economy.

Raw materials are, however, not necessarily staples. Rather, the possibilities of growing along the lines of the staples model to a large extent depend on what happens in the industrialized economies that are the prime buyers of raw materials. The covariation between the growth of world trade in primary products and the growth of the manufacturing output of industrialized countries is high. According to Arthur Lewis, the trade in raw materials grew 0.87 times as quickly as the output of manufactures over both 1873–1913 and 1953–73.

For the developing countries the high correlation also implied that when the Depression of the 1930s arrived the prices of raw materials fell drastically. Hereby both export revenues and growth rates were reduced as well. Between 1929 and 1932 the average dollar price of raw materials was halved and export revenues fell further yet. Acute balance of payments problems arose, and this was exacerbated by the fact that many countries were net capital importers that had to manage their debt service at new, considerably lower, export prices.

The Second World War created another type of problem. The recovery after the Depression had in most countries been a slow affair, but when the war broke out the demand for raw materials increased in the industrialized economies. Export revenues were high, although the blockade, especially of Europe, made it difficult to use the entire export potential. A more important problem, however, was that of imports which consisted both of consumer goods and of important capital goods and inputs, since the production capacity in Europe and North America was employed primarily for the production of war material.

Hence, both the Depression and the war provided impulses for domestic industrial production. When the war came to an end the developing countries could also look for inspiration to the conscious industrialization drive that took place in the new East European bloc. There, the development of industry was given priority, often 'heavy' capital goods production. Foreign trade with countries outside the bloc was avoided whenever this was possible. Instead a meaningful division of labour within it was attempted.

During the first postwar years the attitude of economists to import substitution behind tariff wars was often positive. Several arguments were put forward in favour of an industrialization policy that was aimed at the domestic market and not at exports. Many development economists embraced an explicit *export pessimism*. It was contended that the demand in industrialized countries for raw materials from developing countries was characterized by a low income elasticity of demand. Foodstuffs account for a lower and lower share of the household budget when the income rises ('Engel's law'). Developed countries protect their markets against imports of raw materials they produce themselves. Synthetic products compete more and more with natural products. The export pessimism went hand in hand with the idea of *balanced growth*. According to this idea a less developed country cannot develop by concentrating on a limited number of industries, since the demand is not large enough when the income level is low. What is needed is instead a simultaneous advance across a broad range of industries.

Other economists pointed out that the linkage effects from primary production were often far weaker than was assumed by the staples theory. Many primary export sectors, especially mineral ones, tend to become enclaves in the economy without much contact with what takes place outside the export sector itself. The capital and the skilled labour used come from industrialized countries and the demand that is generated is to a large extent directed toward imports instead of towards domestically manufactured goods. Profits are repatriated instead of reinvested.

An export-based industrialization was considered difficult to carry out. Industrial goods, such as textiles (in which the developing countries possessed a distinct comparative advantage through their rich supplies of labour), were as a rule protected by tariffs in the industrialized countries. As a result of this many countries during the 1950s and 1960s opted for a development policy which built on industrial production for a protected domestic market.

The dynamic argument: 'infant industries'

Industrialization behind tariff walls and other obstacles to change was no new phenomenon. Historically, the method had been employed by many European countries (and Japan) and an explicit theoretical argument exists for this type of policy, known as the infant industry argument. This is illustrated in Figure 6.1.

At the outset the transformation curve of the economy is given by TT. If a free trade policy is pursued the economy produces at B and consumes at C, at world market prices p_v. Agricultural goods are exported and manufactures are imported. If we, however, put a tariff on manufactures, this changes the relative price of agricultural goods and manufactures to p_T. The optimum production point of the economy moves to D. Manufacturing output increases and agricultural output decreases. The consumers are forced to pay higher prices for manufactured goods. However, since the economy can still trade at world market prices the consumption point will be E, on a

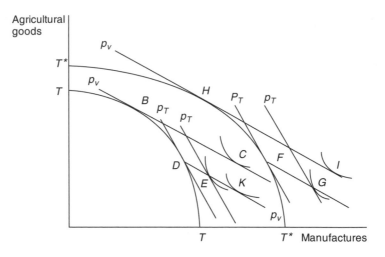

Figure 6.1   The infant industry argument

lower indifference curve than *C*. The tariff hence reduces the welfare level in the economy.

The idea behind protection of infant industries, however, is that the welfare-reducing effect of a tariff on manufactures should be temporary. The intention is to protect industries that with time may become competitive, in the sense that they are able to produce at world market prices without any tariff protection but which at the outset do not possess the necessary experience of production. Through learning-by-doing effects of various kinds it is hoped that the production capacity of the manufacturing sector will increase over time, given the factor supply. Hereby, the production possibility curve will expand to *T*T**.

On the new production possibility curve the economy produces at point *F* if tariffs are used and consumes at *G*, at the same prices. This is, however, not the best situation from the welfare point of view, even though the welfare level is higher than the original one. If the tariff protection is scrapped when the infant industry has 'grown up' and is able to compete at world market prices, the production point becomes *H* and the consumption point *I*. The welfare level has increased.

For temporary protection to increase welfare two criteria must be met. The first is known as *Mill's test* and states that the manufacturing sector must be able to produce at world market prices in the end. The second – *Bastable's test* – postulates that the accumulated production and consumption losses made by the economy during the period of protection must be outweighed by the eventual welfare gains.

The theoretical alternative

The infant industry argument provides a theoretical justification of the import-substitution policy. On closer inspection, however, the argument is not particularly convincing and it is at any rate weaker than claimed by its advocates, both on the theoretical and practical level. It is possible to find a policy which in principle has more favourable welfare effects than tariff protection, and the application of the protectionist policy has produced effects that have diverged considerably from the theoretical ones.

It is easy to provide a theoretical demonstration that a better policy than tariff protection exists if the purpose is to encourage the expansion of the domestic manufacturing section in the way indicated in Figure 6.1. This policy is based on subsidies. If the infant industry sector is subsidized, so as to make the relative producer price of manufactures increase, production at point *D* can be attained. Since the consumers may continue to buy manufactures at world market prices consumption will, however, take place at point *K* on a higher indifference curve than the one running through *E*. The losses made during the transition period will then be smaller.

Another criticism of the protectionist policy is based on the functioning of financial markets. If it is 'known' that the manufacturing sector after a breaking-in period can produce profitably at world market prices and financial markets can function, it should be easy to cover the initial losses with loans that are paid back when the learning period is over.

From the practical point of view the main objection against protection is that it is difficult to abolish. It tends to become a fixture, not least because firms do not have sufficient incentives to become more efficient. To this has to be added the fact that the original intervention in the market easily gives rise to problems which in turn are met by new interventions. The learning effect thus does not materialize and it becomes difficult to make the production possibility curve expand in the way indicated in Figure 6.1. A number of negative effects arise. Let us focus on which these effects may be.

The actual policy

The actual import-substitution policy has to a large extent been founded on a system of administrative controls instead of on the market mechanism. This may partly be explained by the way development economics evolved as an academic discipline. During the first postwar period an extensive discussion took place among development economists about the desirability and design of planning. This discussion took as its point of departure what were perceived as flaws in the traditional argument in favour of a market economy: the description of an economy working under conditions of perfect competition, where the selfish (profit and utility maximizing) behaviour of producers, consumers and factor owners leads both to technically efficient production and to a Pareto optimal allocation of resources in society.

The critics pointed out – correctly – that no perfect market economies exist. The real world is characterized by imperfect competition, indivisibilities and inflexibility. Resources are not allocated in the elegant way assumed by the model of perfect competition. In addition, according to the critics, it is highly doubtful whether a static model of resource allocation has any relevance for problems of growth and development.

The consequence of this reasoning was that many developing countries chose to base their development policy on administrative procedures and central planning instead of on the market mechanism. Planning and control were combined with import substitution. Tariffs, import quotas and currency regulations went hand in hand with interventions in the factor markets and licensing of raw material and capital.

At the same time the macroeconomic policy chosen was often inflationary. Expansive fiscal policy in a situation where the state had difficulties financing expenditures with taxes produced deficits in the government budget that had to be financed either via an inflow of foreign capital, leading to increased indebtedness, or via an increase of the money supply.

Consequently, inflation was fuelled. The domestic rate of price increases became higher than the international one. As a result the domestic currency appreciated in real terms. (If the real exchange rate is to remain unchanged, the currency must depreciate in nominal terms at the rate determined by the difference between the domestic and international rates of inflation.) Exporter costs increased faster than the costs of the international competitors and the amount of foreign currency obtained was worth less in terms of domestic goods than before. Imports, on the other hand, became more attractive since a given amount of domestic currency over time bought more and more foreign goods in relation to domestic goods. The balance of trade was thus threatened both by shrinking export revenue and by increasing imports.

The situation could of course have been changed by a devaluation, but that solution was often not the one chosen. Instead tariffs, import quotas and other direct restrictions on imports were used, with severe distortions as a consequence. In terms of the graphic analysis that we have hitherto applied the situation resembled the one depicted in Figure 6.2.

Let us begin in the box diagram. A free trade situation with no interference with market prices would lead to production, say, at point *b* where a manufacturing isoquant is tangential to an agricultural isoquant. Relatively more agricultural goods and relatively fewer manufactured goods are produced. This point corresponds to point *B* in the lower diagram. The economy would consume in point *C*, at world market prices.

The import-substitution policy gave rise to a completely different allocation. The factor markets were characterized by two types of distortions. In the

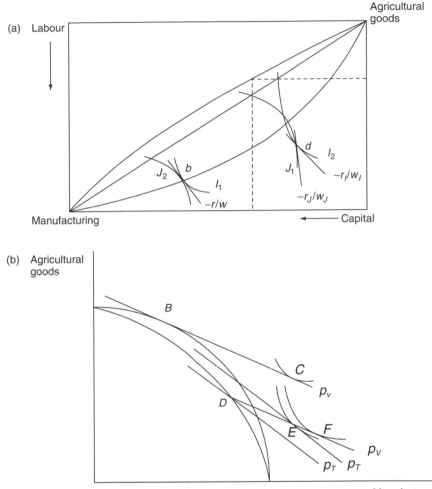

Figure 6.2 Import substitution in practice

first place the manufacturing sector was often forced to pay a wage above the value of the marginal product of labour in the agricultural sector (the social marginal cost of labour). This was partly, but only partly, motivated by a higher cost of living in urban areas. To this had to be added an element of distortion. Many developing countries had introduced minimum wage legislation. The latter, however, encompassed only the formal urban sector while traditional unregulated activities such as agriculture and the informal sector in the cities were not touched. In other cases strong trade unions pushed up the wage level in manufacturing, often with political support from the government. In this case, the informal activities were not touched.

In the market for capital as a rule the opposite situation prevailed. The manufacturing sector was favoured via the banking system, the system of import licensing and also the tax system. Subsidized credits, or at least credits on 'normal' banking conditions, were channelled to manufacturing, and the sector could often import rationed capital goods at a favourable rate of exchange. Simultaneously depreciation rules were often liberal. Agriculture, on the other hand (notably the small-scale traditional segment), usually had to rely on the informal credit markets where loans could be obtained only at considerably higher interest rates as a consequence of high risk and/or monopolistic supply conditions.

As a consequence of these distortions the economy produced off the contract curve in the box diagram, at a point such as *d*, where an agricultural isoquant cuts a manufacturing isoquant. As indicated by the slopes of the isoquants the ratio of interest to wages is higher in agriculture than in manufacturing. That the isoquants intersect in turn means that the production possibility curve of the economy has shifted inwards, as demonstrated by the derivation in the box diagram (the efficient production possibility curve is not shown in the box) with production at point *d*, which corresponds to *D* in Figure 6.2b. In *D*, as a result of tariff protection, more manufactured goods in relation to agricultural goods are produced than in the free trade situation.

The distortions in the factor markets also make the price line cut the production possibility curve at point *D*. Since capital, relatively speaking, is more expensive in agriculture than in manufacturing the price line intersects the production possibility curve 'from below', as demonstrated in Chapter 5. Consumption takes place at point *E*, on a lower indifference curve than the one going through point *C*.

The consequences of import substitution

In practice the import substitution policy has produced a far more complicated web of interventions and regulations than it is possible to illustrate with the aid of our simple model. Let us be more concrete with respect to what 'point *D*' and 'point *E*' entail in practice. We may begin with the administrative controls. From the discussion of the formerly centrally planned economies in Eastern Europe it is well known that extensive intervention into an economy with a large number of goods creates information and handling problems for the bureaucracy. (We will discuss this in Chapter 9.) Above all there will be delays of decisions that have to be made at the central level; these decisions are often of a routine character. In the meantime the wheels of the economy grind to a halt. Raw materials and spare parts are lacking. Alternatively, firms are forced to keep large stocks of inputs.

Non-routine decisions are delayed as well – in the firms. The ability of an economy to grow and develop is to a large extent dependent on decisions with respect to investment and technological innovation. If the production possibility curve is to shift outwards in the manner postulated by the infant industry argument the decision process within manufacturing must not be arrested, but that is precisely what often happens in a situation where firms become dependent on bureaucratic decisions. Such decisions often tend to acquire random or, in the worst case, systematically distorting characteristics. The lack of information with respect to local conditions which always exists in a centralized bureaucracy, in combination with the large number of decisions that the bureaucrats must handle, necessarily leads to the use of relatively simple rules of thumb, and these rules are usually not based on economic criteria. Instead, for example, the distribution of licences is based on the principle that 'the early bird gets the worm', already installed production capacity, historical production figures, 'fair shares', and so on. This contributes to the conservation of the existing industrial structure and to the creation of obstacles to entry and innovations. Small and medium-sized firms are discriminated against and large firms are favoured. Quite probably the result will be that the production possibility curve fails to shift outwards.

The infant industries tend never to grow up. The firms producing manufactures produce inefficiently, and if they survive they do so mainly because of the protection they obtain by high tariffs on their outputs and low tariffs on the imported inputs they use (the effective rate of protection is high: see below). As a result of the trade and current account problems the protectionist policy gives rise to there is often a shortage of inputs even though these goods are cheap. Only a fraction of the installed capacity is therefore utilized. The capital–output ratio of the economy increases. Figure 6.3 illustrates the argument.

Due to the lack of inputs the manufacturing sector produces less than the amount corresponding to point d (e.g., point f). Since the agricultural sector still produces at d some production factors remain unutilized. Unemployment amounts to $L_I L_J$ while the amount of idle capital will be $K_I K_J$. This also means that we produce inside the inner production possibility curve at a point such as F. Consumption takes place at G, which represents a lower welfare level than point E, where all resources are utilized.

If the rate of protection is high enough firms may enjoy 'the best of all monopoly profits': namely, a quiet life. The profit level is satisfactory even though the degree of capacity utilization is low. To some extent firms may influence the rate of protection. Resources are spent on government relations directly or via political parties. Firms prefer a localization close to the centres where the political power is concentrated, and much of the managerial talent and other resources that should have been spent on productive activities are wasted on preventing the wheels of bureaucracy from making too much noise. Often the system encourages corruption. (The

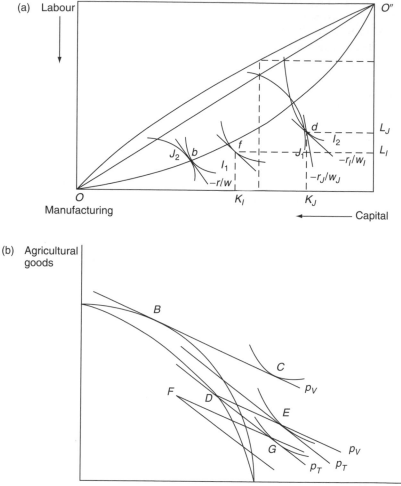

Figure 6.3   Import substitution policy and capacity utilized

phenomenon is known as directly unproductive profit-seeking activities, or
DUP activities. We will deal with these in more detail in a later chapter.)

The protectionist policy has favoured the protected sector – import-
competing manufacturing – at the expense of other sectors. The typical
pattern has been that the import-substitution process has begun within
the consumer goods industry. The latter has been protected while at the
same time imports of intermediate goods and investment goods have been

allowed on favourable conditions. The idea was that the import-substitution process thereafter would gradually be expanded backwards in the production chain.

To extend import substitution to inputs has, however, proved difficult and this has stood out as one of the greatest weaknesses of the policy. The expansion of the consumer goods industry typically built on low tariffs on its inputs. If, however, it is deemed desirable also to protect intermediate production of investment goods an obstacle is immediately put in the way of the consumer goods industry, which now has to be content with more expensive (and often lower-quality) inputs. Thus a conflict of interests arises within the manufacturing sector; this conflict is often solved in a way that favours the established consumer goods producers. If this is the case, the *effective* rate of protection becomes higher on final goods than on intermediate and capital goods.

The effective rate of protection is defined as the relative difference between the value added of the product at tariff-inclusive prices and at world market prices (i.e., without tariffs):

$$ERP = \frac{VA_o - VA_w}{VA_w} \tag{6.1}$$

If we denote the tariff rate for the output, its nominal rate of protection, as t_o and the tariff rate of a (composite) input as t_i, the world market price of the output as P_o and the world market price of the input (per unit of the output) as P_i we may write (6.1) as

$$ERP = \frac{[P_o(1 + t_o) - P_i(1 + t_i)] - (P_o - P_i)}{P_o - P_i} \tag{6.2}$$

or, after simplification:

$$ERP = \frac{P_o t_o - P_i t_i}{P_o - P_i} \tag{6.3}$$

From (6.3) it is easily seen that the effective rate of protection becomes higher the higher the output tariff and the lower the input tariff. For a producer of consumer goods it is advantageous to have a high tariff on the output since this keeps foreign competitors away, while inputs may be imported at a low tariff rate.

Thus the import-substitution policy has strong limitations when it comes to 'propelling' growth in the economy over longer periods. Also in the short run, however, problems easily arise. One such problem is that import substitution decreases the direct need for foreign currency but, since the demand for inputs increases instead, it is far from certain that any net savings of foreign exchange will take place, especially since the export sector is hurt. Often the increases on the input side have been so large that they have more than swamped the savings made on the output side.

Import substitution paradoxically also tends to increase foreign dependence instead of reducing it, as planned. As the import-substitution process runs its course the number of domestically produced commodities increases, and the remaining imports will stand out as strategic for the ability of the economy to function. If many consumer goods are imported it is relatively simple to reduce imports in a crisis. This cannot, however, be done without creating significant problems when the main part of the imports consists of intermediate goods and capital goods. If imports are cut anyway the production of consumer goods must also be reduced. There are no longer any 'non-essential' imports to reduce.

The protectionist policy often favours the rise of luxury goods industries. The planning bureaucracies, naturally enough, often give priority to the exclusion of imports of 'unnecessary' luxuries and hence put high, possibly prohibitive, tariffs on these. In this way, however, strong incentives are created for domestic production of these goods. The distortions in the factor markets have also led to an exaggerated capital intensity within the manufacturing sector. We have already seen how the low degree of capacity utilization has lead to a higher capital–output ratio. The latter is in turn a direct consequence of the favourable conditions in which the manufacturing sector has been able to raise capital. An industry working with techniques that do not correspond to the factor proportions that most often characterize the economies of developing countries – plenty of labour, scarce capital – has been created.

Capital formation has received too much space in the argument in favour of import substitution. A reason often advanced in favour of tariff protection for manufactured goods is that protection would lead to increased savings by stimulating profits in the sector. This is, however, far from certain. In the first place it is not necessarily true that tariff protection leads to higher profits. Rather, there is a risk that the potential tariffs are eaten up by bad cost control and inefficient production. Second, it is not given that increased company profits are the best way of generating capital. If investment must build only on self-financing there are no guarantees that the most profitable projects materialize.

In the end the problem is that of creating efficient financial intermediation. If households are given the opportunity to invest in attractive assets household savings will increase, and if these thereafter, via a functioning bank and finance system, can be channelled to investors the result quite probably is more efficient than when the investors themselves have to generate all savings. It is, of course, purely coincidental if those who have the best potential investment are also the ones that have financial resources to fall back on.

The increase of profits in manufacturing may also be seen in a distributional perspective. The protection policy has turned relative prices in favour of manufacturing. As we know, this is a relatively capital-intensive line of production. At the same time agriculture, and the traditional export sectors, have been punished. Thus capital owners are favoured at the expense of labour. Since capital owners as a rule have higher incomes than workers this tends to increase income differences. Generally speaking, the income level most of the time is lower in agriculture than in manufacturing (this is true of the wage level as well), which means that a policy that favours manufacturing discriminates against low-income groups. In addition the agrarian population is forced to pay more for manufactures as a result of the import substitution policy.

The employment situation is also made worse by import substitution. Agriculture and exports are relatively labour-intensive lines of production, while the artificially high capital intensity in manufacturing holds employment back in that sector. Output tends to expand at a faster rate than the number of jobs available. This, in turn, has contributed to large urban problems. The relatively high wage level in manufacturing pulls people into urban areas, but there it takes time to get a job. In the meantime the number of people who have to make a living in the so-called informal sector (shoe shiners, street vendors, etc.) increases.

Finally, as we have already pointed out, the import-substitution policy has discriminated against agriculture and exports. (Often the two are synonymous.) In next chapter we will come back to a more extensive discussion of agriculture. Here we will simply make a few remarks with respect to exports. These have been hurt in two ways by the import-substitution policy. In the first place relative producer prices have been turned against exports. The production point of the economy has moved towards import-competing products to the corresponding extent. Second, the distorted factor prices have encouraged capital-intensive production when the comparative advantage of the economy would motivate labour-intensive production: that is, a concentration on traditional (agricultural products, textiles) and non-traditional labour-intensive branches (electronics, computers). The import-substitution policy has built up a manufacturing sector with a comparative disadvantage instead of a comparative advantage.

The export-based development model: an alternative

The conclusions that we may draw today from the import-based industrialization strategy do not leave much room for consolation. In a nutshell, the final result has been that industries with comparative disadvantages have developed, that expected linkages have not been created and that the export sector has been discriminated against. In the vast majority of cases the import-substitution policy has run into a dead-end from which it is difficult to back out. The reason is that this requires a huge restructuring of the economy and that strong vested interests have developed behind the import-substitution policy. If these transitional problems are disregarded it is, however, not difficult to formulate an alternative. In this final section that is what we are going to discuss: the export-based model.

The fundamental postulate of the export strategy is that economic growth is driven by production for the world market. The pioneers when it comes to employing this strategy were a number of small and medium-sized countries in east and southeast Asia. More and more countries, especially in the rest of Asia and Latin America, have today followed their examples. The export-based strategy is not problem-free; however, some of the problems have to do with how the strategy has been implemented in practice rather than with the general principles.

The notion of export-based strategy or 'export promotion' has been given somewhat different interpretations in different contexts. The most common one is that the goal for industrial policy is that of the free trade solution. Sometimes, however, the concept is employed in the 'stronger' sense of a distortion in favour of exports. Even in the former case it is often necessary with government intervention of some kind to provide sufficient incentives to firms to export, which is often more risky than selling in the well-known domestic market. These interventions (e.g., in the form of subsidies) impose direct costs on the government, however, which is not the case with protectionist measures. There are hence clear incentives for the government not to provide support any longer than is strictly necessary.

How export promotion works depends entirely on how it is implemented in practice. The simplest case is that of a deregulation of the commodity markets. This in the 'best' case (i.e., when there is perfect competition in both commodity and factor markets) puts the economy back to the free trade point of production and consumption. If, however, the idea is to encourage the manufacturing sector to produce more than under unregulated free trade, we have already seen (in connection with the discussion of Figure 6.1) that this may be achieved in a way which from the welfare point of view is better than tariffs: namely, through the payment of subsidies on the manufactures produced. If we apply Bastable's test (cf. above) it is clear that in this case the welfare losses are more easily balanced by later welfare gains than in the case of tariff protection.

In practice subsidization of production has not been the only or the most common way of promoting exports. Often the incentives have been provided through the factor markets, or via tariff exemptions for imported raw materials when the final product is exported. The latter instrument creates an incentive to sell primarily in the export market. Subsidized credits introduce a distortion in the factor market and, as we have already seen, this has more complicated consequences. We may use Figure 6.2 to see the effect. The factor market distortion (with 'too high' wages and 'too low' capital costs in manufacturing) brings the economy to the production points *d* and *D*, respectively, exactly as before. In this case, however, consumer prices are not distorted. Consumption may hence take place at point F, which from the welfare point of view is preferred to point *E*. In practice – as in Korea – the subsidized interest rates have been combined with extensive regulations in the capital market, rationing credit in favour of the export industry. The result has not been completely positive. The system has tended to lead to overinvestment in branches favoured by the policy, with financial problems, restructuration and bankruptcy as the consequences.

A third form of export promotion has been based on the entry of foreign producers attracted by tax holidays, infrastructure and help in the education of the workforce. The most eloquent example here is Singapore, where the lion's share of manufacturing production takes place in foreign companies. Direct investment makes the production possibility curve shift outwards, as in Figure 6.1. The idea is that the investments, which may be regarded as a 'package' of capital, technology, entrepreneurship, management and marketing expertise, will also indirectly contribute to continued growth and development in the economy through different linkage effects. This has also taken place, although to a differing extent in different countries. For the system to work as envisaged it is important that the investments are on a technological level that makes it possible for domestic employees to absorb the techniques and employ them independently. It is also important, from the point of view of linkages, that the local personnel is engaged in activities other than direct production which is often simple *per se* and mainly consists of assembling components.

The incentives offered in the case of direct investment as a rule do not change the relative prices of either goods or factors. Instead, the costs of establishment are favourably affected, via tax holidays and infrastructure. Thus the risks firms face when investing in a foreign environment are lowered.

The export-based strategy has not escaped criticism, even though this has not been as murderous as in the case of import substitution. A frequent criticism is that it is not certain that a strategy that has been successfully employed by a small number of (relatively similar) countries could work if applied by a large number of countries. The argument, however, is relatively dubious. Countries with large exports will also, at least in the somewhat longer run, import a great deal. The new competitors to the established industrialized countries in the export markets also tend to be increasingly important customers for the same countries. This, however, does not preclude the notion that a strong expansion of export volumes from one country may lead to strained relations in terms of trade policy and to protectionist counter-measures. This, on the other hand, appears to be mainly a short-run problem.

Literature

The ideas behind import substitution are presented in:

Krueger, Anne O. (1993), *Political Economy of Policy Reform in Developing Countries*. MIT Press, Cambridge, MA, and London.

The staples theory of trade and growth is presented in:

Findlay, Ronald and Lundahl, Mats (1994), 'Natural Resources, "Vent-for-Surplus", and the Staples Theory', in Meier, Gerald M. (ed.), *From Classical Economics to Development Economics*. St Martin's Press, New York.

Hirschman, Albert O. (1977), 'A Generalized Linkage Approach to Development with Special Reference to Staples', *Economic Development and Cultural Change*, Vol. 25, Supplement.

Lundahl, Mats (1998), 'Staples Trade and Economic Development', in *Themes in International Economics*. Ashgate, Aldershot.

Balanced and unbalanced development theory is discussed in:

Hirschman, Albert O. (1958), *The Strategy of Economic Development*. Yale University Press, New Haven, CT, and London.

The infant industry argument is presented in:

Gandolfo, Giancarlo (1996), *International Economics I* (2nd rev. edn). Springer-Verlag, Berlin, ch. 5.

The import-substitution policy and its limitations are presented in:

Greenaway, David and Milner, Chris (1993), *Trade and Industrial Policy in Developing Countries*. Macmillan, London, chs 3–4.

Johnson, Harry G. (1965), 'Optimal Trade Intervention in the Presence of Domestic Distortions', in Baldwin, Robert E. *et al.* (eds), *Trade, Growth and the Balance of Payments. Essays in Honor of Gottfried Haberler*. Rand McNally, Chicago, IL.

Krueger, Anne O. (1984), 'Trade Policies in Developing Countries', in Jones, Ronald W. and Kenen, Peter B. (eds), *Handbook of International Economics*, Vol. 1. North-Holland, Amsterdam.

Krueger, Anne O. (1997), 'Trade Policy and Economic Development: How We Learn', *American Economic Review*, Vol. 87.

Lewis, W. Arthur (1980), 'The Slowing Down of the Engine of Growth', *American Economic Review*, Vol. 70.

Little, Ian, Scitovsky, Tibor and Scott, Maurice (1970), *Industry and Trade in Some Developing Countries*. Oxford University Press, London.

The role of financial markets for the efficiency of capital allocation is dealt with in:

McKinnon, Ronald (1973), *Money and Capital in Economic Development*. Brookings Institution, Washington, DC.

The export-based industrialization strategy is discussed in:

Colman, David and Nixson, Frederick (1994), *Economics of Change in Less Developed Countries*. (3rd edn). Harvester Wheatsheaf, Hemel Hempstead, ch. 9.

Greenaway and Milner, *Trade and Industrial Policy in Developing Countries*, ch. 2.

Hong, Wontack (1990), 'Export-Oriented Growth of Korea: A Possible Path to Advanced Economy', *International Economic Journal*, Vol. 4.

Perkins, Dwight H. Radelet, Steven, Snodgrass, Donald R., Gillis, Malcolm and Roemer, Michael (2001), *Economics of Development* (5th edn). W. W. Norton, New York and London, ch. 18.

7
Urban Bias

One of the most original and provocative books about economic develop-ment written during the past 25 years is Michael Lipton's *Why Poor People Stay Poor: Urban Bias in World Development.* This book deals with systematic distortions of the resource allocation of less developed countries. The central idea is that the most important class conflict in the Third World is not the conflict between labour and capital or between domestic and foreign inter-ests; it is the conflict between country and town.

According to Lipton, urban areas are favoured by the politicians at the expense of the countryside. This takes on a variety of forms: the infrastruc-ture is concentrated in the cities, the countryside is taxed more harshly and the price policy turns relative prices in favour of urban pursuits. The import-substitution policy that we looked at in the preceding chapter can partly be seen as an expression of the same phenomenon, just like the priority trad-itionally given by developing countries to manufacturing over agriculture. Too many resources are spent on cities, both from the point of view of efficiency and from the point of view of equality. The fundamental reason why the countryside is discriminated against is political: the countryside is poor because it is politically powerless. The consequence is that the growth of developing countries has been both slower and less equitable than it could otherwise have been.

The origin of the idea of an urban bias is found in a study of India that Lipton carried out in the 1960s. In *Why Poor People Stay Poor* this idea is generalized to what Lipton argues is a theory that bears on the relationship between country and town everywhere in the Third World. His constructive message is that as a rule you have to develop agriculture across a broad range before you start dealing with the remaining sector of the economy. It is only through the development of small-scale agriculture that per capita income can be brought to such a level that the citizens can abstain from as much consumption as is needed to start the industrialization process without inflicting pain and without having to squeeze agriculture. This is not in opposition to industrialization: the latter requires a transfer of resources from agriculture, but this is much more easily accomplished when the agricultural sector is well developed. Lipton's ideas run against much of the conventional current, whether this consists of advocating direct spending on industrialization as the only way of getting away from the poverty related to traditional agriculture or a plea for a balanced growth path where the growth rates of the different sectors are given by the income elasticities of demand for their respective products. Lipton's point of view is controversial, to say the least. How, then, has he arrived at the thesis that resource allocation in the Third World is systematically biased, and how watertight is this thesis? Let us look at these questions in order.

What is 'urban bias'?

Lipton's central thesis is that the poverty found in less developed countries in the main is concentrated in the countryside and that it is a direct result of economic policy. Urban areas, towns and cities with 10,000–20,000 inhabitants or more are consciously favoured at the expense of the countryside. To be able to discuss to what extent urban bias exists we must find define what we mean by a *neutral* policy (a policy that does not favour a certain sector). Lipton himself makes this definition in two dimensions: efficiency and equity.

In Figure 7.1 efficiency is measured on the left vertical axis and equity on the right. On the horizontal axis, from left to right, we measure the share of the resources of the economy that are spent on the countryside. What the

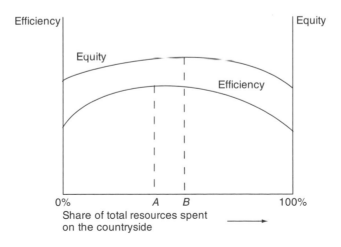

Figure 7.1 Urban bias

figure shows is that both equity and efficiency increase with the share of resources spent on the countryside, but only up to a certain point. Thereafter both of them decrease again. Furthermore the figure shows that the share yielding maximum equity presumably does not coincide with the share yielding maximum efficiency. Which of the 'peaks' lies further to the right is not given. The figure should be interpreted to mean that all resource allocations to the left of *A* favour urban areas, while all those to the right of *B* favour the countryside. Allocations between *A* and *B* are referred to as *ambivalent* by Lipton. In the figure they favour urban areas in terms of equity and rural areas in terms of efficiency. Lipton's hypothesis, however, is that the resource allocation in most countries corresponds to points well to the left of *A*. This means that urban areas are favoured on both counts. How, then, does Lipton define 'efficiency' and 'equity'?

Efficiency

Lipton uses the traditional definition of efficiency in production. A given allocation of resources is efficient only if it is impossible to increase the output of some good without having to decrease the output of at least one other good. This means, as we already know, that the economy is producing on the production possibility curve. We do not know, however, which point on the curve should be chosen unless economic considerations enter the picture. The *economically* efficient point is the one maximizing the value of output at given prices. However, the time aspect also has to come into the picture. A given allocation may generate larger output today but a lower output in the future. Another allocation may have the opposite time profile. In order to compare the allocations future production must be discounted to the present time.

Equity

Defining equity is more complicated. The main problem is that equity is a *normative* concept: that is, it is related to value judgements rather than to facts. In his definition of equity Lipton chooses to use the *marginal utility of money* as his point of departure. This is higher among poor families than among rich. Thus it seems reasonable that from the point of view of equity welfare increases, generally speaking, through a reallocation of money in favour of the poorest. (This, however, assumes that it is possible to make interpersonal utility comparisons, which in turn requires cardinal utility functions, something abhorred by traditional welfare theory. The reallocation also has to face an *intertemporal* problem: if the poor are allowed to consume more today total savings will presumably decrease, and this will lead to lower growth and lower consumption tomorrow.)

On average the countryside is poorer than the cities. An appropriate question, however, is whether increased spending on cities would make the income increases thus generated accrue to poor individuals to a larger extent than would increased spending on the countryside. According to Lipton the answer is no, for two reasons.

In the first place Lipton argues that the fruits of increased spending, both in urban and rural areas, tend either to be distributed according to the actual distribution of income or to favour those who are already well off. In both cases poverty decreases more if the money goes to the countryside. The income distribution is more equal in the countryside and, according to Lipton, the rich in the countryside tend to be politically weaker than the urban rich and will therefore have a harder time obtaining resources. In addition, they tend to consume more goods produced in the countryside. Thus they generate more work and income among the poor, since employment is more evenly distributed between poor and rich in the countryside than in the cities.

Second, most government spending tends to help people who already have a job. In urban areas relatively more capital is spent creating relatively little additional employment. The unemployed, the beggars, the prostitutes, and those who work in the so-called informal sector, on the other hand – the poor – have no part in this. Even if they do, the effect on production as a rule tends to be low, and most often the goal is to increase output. In the countryside most people have some kind of employment, and rural spending hence more easily affects the poor.

The components of urban bias

What does the policy look like which favours the cities and discriminates against the countryside? In Chapter 6 we discussed how the import-substitution policy chosen by many less developed countries favours industry at the expense of agriculture. In the Lipton argument, this policy only constitutes a part of a larger systematic pattern. Urban bias makes itself felt in several different ways. In the first place public investments are concentrated on urban areas; second, the countryside is taxed exceedingly hard in relation to the cities; and third, the relative prices in the economy are manipulated in different ways so as to favour the urban population while the rural population suffers.

Public investment

Public investments, in 'productive' capital, physical infrastructure and social services, are concentrated on the cities. In this context, social services are important. The supply of physicians, nurses, and so on is much worse in the countryside than in the cities and the quality of the rural facilities is usually low. The health care personnel as a rule will have been educated with an eye to the needs of the cities and will prefer to work in urban areas. In the same way the countryside is discriminated against by educational policy. Perhaps it can be argued that agricultural districts get too much education, taking into account that there is not much to use the education on if you stay in rural areas. But, according to Lipton, this is hardly a valid argument. On the one hand the education actually offered in the countryside is worse than the one received in the cities, and on the other hand, it is a matter of increasing the possibilities of using education in the countryside.

In terms of our model the above may be interpreted as an outward shift of the production possibility curve in the manner shown in Figure 7.2. Physical and social infrastructure may be said to act as a 'lubricant' in the areas where it is found. The access to a developed infrastructure makes the existing endowments of capital and labour more efficient than before among the urban sectors (in our model, in the manufacturing sector). The production possibility curve then shifts outwards, from TT to $T'T'$, given the capital stock and the labour force of the economy. Since investment in infrastructure is concentrated in the cities the possibilities of producing manufactures increase proportionally more than the possibilities of producing agricultural goods.

Taxation

According to Lipton agriculture is overtaxed in relation to other sectors in the economies of developing countries. This may show up in different ways. The criteria normally employed to decide to what extent different sectors should be taxed are (1) collection costs, (2) the contribution of taxation to

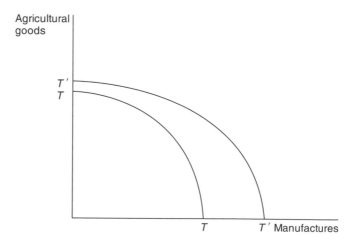

Figure 7.2   Urban bias in public investment

growth and development, and (3) the effects of taxation on the equality of different taxpayers, both horizontally (on the same income level) and vertically (on different levels).

Collection costs are normally higher in the countryside than in urban areas. Households are spread out, communications are poor, peasants are illiterate and average income is lower. If taxes are paid in kind there are in addition valuation, sales, transport and storage costs. This all speaks in favour of taxing cities more harshly than rural areas. There is, however, also a second type of collection cost: the political one. Governments as a rule attempt to avoid political tension. In most developing countries, according to Lipton, this is achieved by taxing the many dispersed and politically weak, and these are found mainly in the countryside.

What, then, is the development effect of a given tax revenue? This depends on the one hand on how much of the tax revenue would have been used for development purposes by those taxed if no taxation had taken place and, on the other hand, on how much of the tax revenue the government decides to spend on development purposes. In addition we have to know the marginal returns to private and public development investment.

Let us begin with the first item on the list. According to the conventional wisdom peasants have difficulties when it comes to saving. They are poor, and recurrent bad years tend to wipe out their economies. According to Lipton, however, this argument is irrelevant. Peasants can be expected to save as much or more of a given income as urbanites. Taxation of agriculture incomes in addition acts as a brake on the will to produce. This may be avoided by using a proportional tax. However, the ability of the peasants to invest and buy inputs will still be reduced.

If negative incentive effects are to be avoided it is easier to tax the urban population. Incomes are on average higher and the distorted prices (in favour of manufacturing) that are found in many developing countries imply that there are plenty of supernormal profits that can be taxed away without negative incentive effects. There is also an excess supply of people looking for employment, which means that wage taxes should not reduce production in urban sectors.

Often the argument in favour of increased agricultural taxation is based on the assumption that this would increase the share which is sold in the market. According to this view taxation constitutes a way of monetizing a subsistence sector, by forcing the sector to pay taxes with cash. The argument, however, is dubious. In the first place hardly any pure subsistence sectors exist any more, even in Africa. A typical farm household tends to receive cash in different ways, among other things by work outside agriculture, through handicrafts and through work outside agriculture and through wage labour on large farms. Thus there is no reason to believe that higher taxes will result in higher sales. The argument that care is required when it comes to taxing farmers should, however, be somewhat modified if it is taken into account that agriculture is not a homogeneous sector. Large farmers often pay relatively little tax, above all because the administrative costs connected with the collection of income taxes in agriculture are high and easy to evade.

When it comes to the returns to rural and urban investments Lipton argues that available empirical data indicate that it would be profitable to increase investment in the countryside in relation to urban investment.

Optimal taxation

The tax problem in developing countries – how the economic burden that is related to financing development is optimally distributed – is complicated, not least because neither agriculture nor manufacturing ('urban areas') are homogeneous sectors. However, under somewhat simplified assumptions it is possible to draw some conclusions. Let us assume that the economy is trading with the rest of the world at international prices and that it is possible for the government to tax foodstuffs differently in the countryside and in the cities. This means that the market price of food may differ between the sectors (this is possible when there is little geographical mobility of goods).

Farmers sell their surplus production to the cities in order to buy manufactured goods. If the sales revenue is taxed the welfare of the farmers is reduced. Normally their supply of food in the market is reduced if the tax rate increases, because the price they receive for their products after tax will decrease and hence lie below the world market price. If the reduction is large enough the tax revenue will fall as well in spite of the increased tax rate. There is thus a limit to how much tax revenue may be extracted from the rural population without producing a result that is non-optimal for all parties.

In the same way, the government may tax the urban population by putting a tax on the sale of food in the cities. This means that the selling price will exceed the world market price. When the tax (and the price) increases the demand is reduced. Here, too, there is a critical limit which means that a tax increase reduces total tax revenue. If this is the case, the tax rate should be lowered.

If the urban price lies below the critical level where a tax increase leads to reduced government revenue, a choice arises: a tax reduction favours the urban population but reduces government revenue and hence the surplus that may be invested to increase the income of future generations. (Strictly speaking, the argument assumes that neither farmers nor workers save.) A similar argument may be constructed for rural areas: the higher the price received by the farmers, the lower will be both the government revenue and the income of future generations.

The balancing of taxation then becomes a question of how the government values private consumption in relation to investment at the margin. It seems reasonable to assume that investment at early stages of development is more valuable at the margin than immediate consumption. If this is the case it may be concluded that both sectors should be taxed, which means that the food prices received by farmers are below world market prices and the prices paid by the urban population are above. This is hardly in accordance with reality in many developing countries where the agricultural sector is taxed but the urban population is subsidized in the trade with foodstuffs.

Taxation and equality

In most developing countries rural areas pay lower taxes per household than urban areas. However, from the equity point of view this gives an incorrect impression, and in any case the difference is small, according to Lipton. The reason for this is that the countryside in general benefits from fewer tax-financed services and that the ability to pay on average is lower in rural areas.

Thus one has to look at what rural and urban areas, respectively, get for their tax money. In most developing countries probably the countryside pays more tax than the cities, in relation to what it gets. Planned public expenditure on agriculture as a rule does not amount to more than 15–20 per cent of the budget even though 70–80 per cent of the population live in the country. In addition the gap between planned and realized expenditure tends to be largest in this sector. This is made worse by the fact that foreign aid as a rule is concentrated on non-agricultural sectors. Lipton mentions a figure of 12 per cent for agriculture. Finally, virtually all infrastructure is concentrated on the cities.

Lipton also argues that taxation is too high in the countryside even if no attention is paid to the fact that the countryside receives less for its tax money than the cities. Rural incomes are less unequally distributed than urban. This means that there are proportionally fewer rural households with a strong ability to pay taxes. The existing capital is smaller than in the cities and its liquidity is lower. It is more difficult to sell assets to get money for taxes. Rural households have more children on average, which also reduces the tax-paying ability. Furthermore, they often have onerous interest to pay on loans. Finally, incomes are seasonal which means that they are forced to pay to be able to consume during the periods when they have no incomes. These savings reduce the ability to pay taxes.

Price policy

Developing countries often pursue a price policy that hurts agriculture and hence the countryside. The price policy may in addition have a redistributive effect within the agricultural sector, to the disadvantage of small farmers. In principle this policy may be designed so as to affect either product prices or input prices. Most commonly, it seems, both methods are used. Interventions on both the product and the factor side change the incentives to produce and hence output volumes. What does this price policy look like?

The inputs used in agriculture are often expensive. A priori this may seem strange, not least because inputs are often subsidized, but the subsidies given often go to large farmers: those who sell for urban consumption or export (and who have a surplus to sell). For them it is easier to approach the bureaucracy than it is for the small farms, since they have cash, wealth and power. They are also the ones who in the first place are compensated for low food prices. Often administrators charge for their services. The credits that often are a necessary condition for using the subsidized inputs are seldom available for the small farmers. These must buy non-subsidized inputs. The existence of input subsidies also makes it easier for consumers to argue in favour of lower prices on agricultural products.

The above distortions are often complemented by direct subsidies to manufacturing on inputs such as electricity, transport, and so on which are sold by public enterprises at artificially low prices. Agriculture does not use these factors to the same extent. There, energy is supplied by animals and humans, not by electricity. Non-agricultural inputs become artificially cheap in relation to agricultural ones also by keeping the price of capital goods down in the farm sector. Often pumps, plans, draught animals and carts are expensive in relation to machine tools, trucks and ball bearings. The latter inputs are favoured by tariff exemptions for imports and an overvalued domestic currency.

The most important price distortion is, however, the one keeping the price of agricultural goods down, but the targets for food prices are multiple and often also contradictory. On the one hand, the government wants to keep prices down to make it possible for the poorest to buy enough food; on the other hand, a secure food supply requires relatively high and stable prices. The need for government revenue means that agriculture is used as a 'milk cow' by those imposing the taxes, while guaranteeing the food supply would require that public funds are used, say, on storage or producer subsidies.

According to Lipton, low food prices are one of the fundamental driving forces behind the urban bias. The urban population has an unequivocal interest in cheap foodstuffs. In this situation a policy is pursued which is detrimental to agriculture. Subsidized food is sold in the cities, especially basic foodstuffs such as cereals. Direct price controls are also common. Often food is imported at low prices, favouring consumers, but hurting producers since these imports compete in terms of price also with domestically pro-duced food items. Frequently the food products consumed mainly by the wealthier part of the population, such as rice, are subsidized, while cheaper foodstuffs consumed by the poor receive no subsidies. Imports of food may also be financed by taxes.

The way agricultural goods are bought from producers also leaves a lot to be desired. Often purchases take place via government marketing boards whose costs are high and who act as monopsonists/monopolists. They work with administratively fixed prices that do not have much to do with demand and supply. With the aid of their pricing these organizations can channel revenue to the public treasury. An investigation by Frank Ellis of marketing boards in Tanzania in the 1970s indicated that this resource transfer corresponded to a 27 per cent tax on the harvest income. Since they are not subjected to the discipline of the market these boards also tend to be inefficient and corrupt, which means that farmers receive lower prices than would otherwise have been the case. When consumer prices have to be kept low, the costs are shifted to the producers in the form of lower prices.

A similar effect is obtained if the state puts an export tax on agricultural goods. Since the world market price as a rule is given, the tax implies that the price received by farmers is lower than the world market price. A more extreme technique is to prohibit exports or use export quotas. These depress the domestic price below the world market level. The idea is either that the price paid by big consumers should be lowered or that forward linkage effects will be created by the supply of cheap inputs to manufacturing.

Consumers are also easily hurt by price regulations. A 'black market' arises almost inevitably. The reason for this is that the regulation creates an excess demand for food at the fixed price. This, in turn, indicates that there are customers willing to pay a higher price to obtain the food. The argument is illustrated in Figure 7.3. (For the sake of simplicity in the diagram we

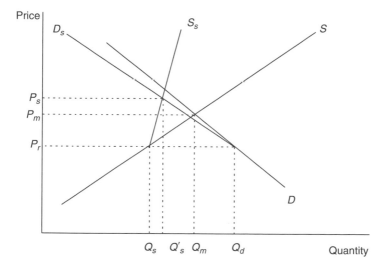

Figure 7.3 The rise of a black market

disregard the idea that producers and consumers may have to trade at different prices as a result of costs in the marketing chain.)

The unregulated price is P_m and the regulated price P_r. At the latter producers are willing to sell Q_s while consumers are willing to buy Q_d. The excess demand then is Q_dQ_s. In this situation it is clear that there are consumers willing to pay more than the regulated price, since the demand curve lies above P_r at quantity Q_s. To be willing to increase their supply above Q_s the producers, however, require higher prices than when the market is unregulated. This is due to the fact that black sales are illegal and subject to punishment. In order to risk this producers demand a higher price for any given quantity supplied. Their supply curve (S_s) becomes steeper to the right of Q_s than without regulations. Analogously, demand becomes more elastic at prices above the official price ceiling (D_s). The price in the black market becomes P_s, which must lie above the regulated price. In the figure it also lies above the unregulated market price. This is, however, not necessarily always the case but depends on the relative slopes of the supply and demand curves in the black market.

In the case of price regulation not only does the resource allocation become non-optimal, but the regulation also has dubious distribution effects. It is far from given that the poor will be given precedence when it comes to accessing to the quantities sold at the regulated, low, price. On the contrary, there is good reason to believe that it is the population groups with most influence (i.e., the best contacts) that primarily benefit from the regulations.

Many developing countries have overvalued currencies. This affects domestic relative prices. In the first place export prices are kept down, in terms of domestic currency, which discriminates against export agriculture. Second, foreign goods, foodstuffs among others, become cheap in terms of domestic currency. This gives rise to food imports, which keep the price level of domestically produced foodstuffs down as well. Agriculture suffers (even though it is not uncommon that the government attempts to counteract the effect by tariffs on agricultural products as well). Third, the manufacturing sector receives tariff protection in order to reduce the imports of cheap industrial products. As a result, the prices of manufactures are pushed up. Industrial products used as inputs in agriculture, or consumed by the farmers, then become comparatively expensive. Finally, raw materials for manufacturing are often imported duty-free. These frequently come from the agricultural sector (such as cotton for the textile industry).

The industrial sector often receives credit at interest rates from below the equilibrium rate in a competitive market. Anti-usury legislation and subsidies may even turn the real rate of interest negative in economies with high inflation. Large parts of agriculture, on the other hand, have no access at all to the organized credit market but are forced to borrow money in the informal credit market, from traders, moneylenders, and so on. In these markets interest rates are considerably higher. The opportunity cost for moneylenders (the return that they would receive from the best alternative employment) may be higher than in the formal sector (especially if the alternatives are illegal). Another factor that pushes up the interest rate is that the lender often takes a high risk. The high rate of interest then reflects a risk premium. Third, transaction costs are often relatively independent of the size of the loan. Hence, the average transaction cost becomes high on informal sector loans, which on average tend to be small. Finally, the moneylender in some cases is a local monopolist.

Marketing and distributional services are also expensive in the countryside. Roads are worse than in urban areas and when something is done it is to improve the roads leading to the cities so that large farmers are favoured, while the roads to nearby village markets where the small peasants sell their produce remain in bad condition. It is also difficult to get information to possible customers or about where such customers may be located. Low literacy rates reduce the value of written information.

The economic consequences of the price policy we have dealt with are negative and often large. Everything works to the detriment of agriculture. In terms of our model they are in principle the same as those illustrated in the preceding chapter. The product market distortions result in a manufacturing output which, from the social point of view, is too large and an agricultural output which is too low. Factor prices are not equalized between the two sectors, which means that the production possibility curve shifts inwards and that the commodity price line will cut this curve.

The situation is illustrated in Figure 7.4. Free trade without interventions in the economy would yield production at point A and consumption at point B, at the world market price, p_v. When the manufacturing sector receives tariff protection or subsidies are used, however both production and consumption will change. In Chapter 6 we dealt with the tariff case. There is hence no reason to repeat this here. We will instead look at the most important distortion according to Lipton: prices of agricultural goods that lie below world market prices to give urban consumers cheaper foodstuffs. Let us therefore introduce a tax on agricultural production and a subsidy on the consumption of agricultural goods that are equal in percentage terms. Thus the price line rotates to p_H. If this is the only distortion the allocation of resources gets worse. Production then takes place at point C. Now consumers cannot make full use of foreign trade but have to consume at the domestic prices at point D.

We must also take into account distortions in the factor markets where, exactly as in Chapter 6, the relative price of capital will be higher in agriculture than in manufacturing. Production will then take place at a point in the box where an agricultural isoquant is cut by a manufacturing isoquant with a flatter slope. The transformation curve shifts inwards, the price line cuts this curve 'from below' and the economy will produce at a point such as E and consume at a point such as F, at the relative domestic price p_H.

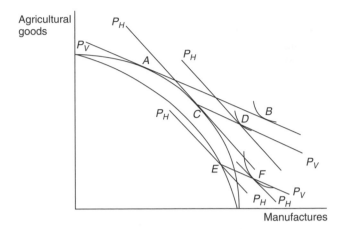

Figure 7.4   Distorted commodity and factor prices

Presumably the situation is also characterized by unemployment of production factors, in the way illustrated in Chapter 6 (i.e., the production point will lie inside *E* and the consumption point on a lower indifference curve than the one going through *F*).

Effects on agricultural incomes

The price policy sketched above reduces farm incomes in three different ways. In the first place farmers receive lower prices on what they sell to other sectors. Second, farm margins are squeezed also by higher prices on inputs. Third, agriculture thus loses production capacity since the poorest peasants are often undernourished and the extent of undernourishment tends to increase when incomes fall, which in turn reduces production and incomes further yet.

The price policy in addition has a number of dubious effects – in the main unintended – on the distribution of income. It is often argued that cheap food favours the poor, but this is a truth with many modifications. First, most of the poor are found in agriculture and are therefore harmed in general by low food prices, especially since prices are kept low not only on the cheap foodstuffs consumed by the poor. Second, the input subsidies employed to compensate farmers for low prices as a rule go to better-off farmers, not to poor ones. Third, lower agricultural prices lead to lower purchasing power in the countryside and hence to negative secondary effects on the production of goods other than agricultural ones. Much of this purchasing power is directed towards cheap craft items, produced by poor artisans. The distributional effects thus become even worse.

Migration and urbanization

If farmers are worse off in the villages than urban dwellers in the cities, it appears probable that farmers would 'vote with their feet' (i.e., tend to leave the villages and be attracted to the cities). If so, the gap between rural and urban incomes should be closed. In the theoretical literature on migration, movements between country and town take place until no new net gains can be made. Thus is the case, for example, in the most well-known model of migration, the so-called Harris–Todaro model. Somewhat simplified, this model may be expressed as:

$$M = M \left(w^u \frac{E^U}{L^U} - w^a \right) \tag{7.1}$$

where M denotes the number of migrants per period, E^U the number of employed in the cities, L^U the size of the urban labour force and w^u and w^a the wage levels in urban and rural areas, respectively. (The ratio E^U/L^U is a measure of the probability of getting an urban job.) Migration is hence determined by the gap between the income the migrants may expect in the city and the (known) income in the countryside.

Lipton, however, argues that not much migration takes place. According to him most of the migration is from village to village or from one urban area to another. Most of the migration from village to town is temporary, or at least does not represent any permanent commitment. Villages close to towns are exposed to migration, and such rural families that have family members in the city also tend to move. These families are often semi-urban even before moving. Some of their members, for example, commute to town to make a living. The very poor, on the other hand seldom migrate; they cannot afford it. If they do, as a rule they do so only temporarily. Those who move rather tend to be those who are best educated or who have the most initiative: that is, those who would otherwise have vitalized and led the villages.

The Harris–Todaro argument assumes that the migrants have information about the alternatives, that they behave 'rationally' and that no obstacles to migration exist. In more developed countries the mechanism provides a rather good explanation of migration. In poor developing countries, on the other hand, it often performs worse. Poor groups (also in richer countries) have problems moving. As a rule it is the literate, those who have better information and who are most dynamic, that move. The poorest, on the other hand, must solve the following problems if they are to migrate.

1 Often they are bound to the village by legislation, tradition or debts that have to be paid or worked off.
2 They are uneducated, often not even literate, and therefore have poor access to information about urban opportunities.

3 If a person is to afford looking for work in urban areas, finance by relatives is needed. Poor families cannot afford this. A decision to send a person to town for the family as a rule implies a lower income now against an (expected) increase in the future. Poor families cannot afford this redistribution of income over time.

4 They are needed in agriculture and their families cannot afford to give them the education that is necessary for moving.

To all this must be added some 'systemic' obstacles. Sometimes there are explicit restrictions on movements to cities. Another obstacle is that transportation is often poor or, if there are better alternatives, too expensive. Finally, linguistic or dialectal obstacles to migration are not unusual.

The big problem with migration, according to Lipton, is that it increases both the gap between town and country and the gap between the classes in the countryside. Migration is selective. Those who leave first are those who would have been in the best position to save the villages from poverty. The villagers have paid for the education they have received and also have to pay for their possible further education in the cities. When the migrants arrive in urban areas they increase the pressure on the politicians to depend on the cities. Those who stay in the countryside are the oldest and the youngest, and those who otherwise have the lowest possibility of getting a job in the urban sector. The young and strong migrants are lacking when they are most needed, during the peak seasons of agriculture. This negative selection hurts the rich in the countryside less since they do not have the same need to move.

How can the systematic relation between talent and propensity to migrate be explained? There are several possible reasons that usually explain some part of what is happening. First, the supply of education in general is lower in the countryside than in the towns. Second, the quality of rural schools is often terrible in comparison with urban schools. Teaching methods are frequently old-fashioned. Textbooks are old or missing altogether. Teachers are few and often not very able, partly because they are underpaid and obtain their main income from other sources. Curricula do not pay any attention to the agricultural calendar, including the fact that children are needed in agriculture at harvest time. This causes many pupils to drop out. Those who, in spite of everything, receive an education seldom stay in agriculture. There is in general too little for educated people to do in the countryside. Higher education is even less directed towards rural needs. Few agronomists and agricultural economists are produced. Many study the humanities, law and medicine. Those who for some reason still choose agronomy stay in the cities.

Not only teachers and agronomists cling to urban areas. This is true also for other categories who can choose where they want to work, such as physicians and nurses. Those who are forced into the countryside return as quickly as possible. The result is that villages lack social services and that villagers do not use urban facilities either to any large extent, according to Lipton.

Does an urban bias exist?

The question that we must tackle next is whether Lipton's urban bias thesis corresponds to reality or, as one of his critics argues, it belongs to the 'pipe-dream' category of neo-populist ideas. Lipton's thesis is in no way uncontroversial or watered down. On the contrary, it has met an often very sharply formulated criticism, concerning the basic design of the analytical scheme, the use of central terminology and the best way of dealing with the empirical materials that Lipton presents in support of his allegations. At the same time it is clear that economic development among other things must mean that the share of agriculture in total production decreases. (Absolutely speaking there is, however, usually a need for *increased* agricultural production.) It must be possible to transfer resources from agriculture to other sectors, which in practice may easily be interpreted as discriminating treatment. It will then be hard to conclude if and when an urban bias exists. Lipton concentrates his analysis on the *end result* of alleged discrimination of the countryside, while the *reasons* are more or less assumed.

The analytical scheme

The first question is what kind of countries Lipton actually analyses. Strictly speaking his description of less developed countries, with 60–80 per cent of the population in rural areas, a large subsistence sector and an industrial share of GDP of the order of 10 per cent, gives a false picture of not only Latin America but also of many countries in southeast Asia. In spite of this, Lipton does not hesitate to present Latin American examples. This, however, hardly implies that it is Latin America that he primarily has in mind. The very origin of the urban bias thesis, as we have already mentioned, is found in an article about India from 1968, and the empirical material presented tends to come mainly from India and other Asian countries.

Second, Lipton employs the very term 'urban bias' in an ambiguous way. On the one hand it denotes an 'explanatory variable' and is then tied to the political alliances and processes that constitute economic policy (Lipton, however, offers no examples of how such alliances have worked in practice); yet on the other hand urban bias is also the dependent variable: the outcome of this policy. A third strong point that has been used against Lipton's fundamental scheme is that the division between town and country is completely artificial. The demarcation line between urban and rural areas is often blurred. In addition, both in the cities and in the countryside there are strong tensions and conflicts of interests between a number of groups that Lipton includes in the same category. If the idea is to bring out actual and potential conflicts it is often more relevant to analyse the interests of large landowners in relation to those of small peasants, tenant farmers and rural workers on the one hand, and those of industrial capitalists in relation to those of urban workers on the other. Why is, for example, the countryside politically powerless when the large landowners clearly are not and could speak for the countryside? The most natural explanation is that they have other interests, which they consider to be more important, to consider.

Lipton is aware of these difficulties, but his way of solving them tends towards escapism. To solve the equation he excludes some urban dwellers from the 'actual' urban group. The slum dwellers, according to this reasoning, are only temporarily in the cities and they may remain only so long as they receive economic support from the countryside. Sooner or later return migration to rural areas and agriculture will be necessary for most people. The credibility of this argument is dubious.

In the same way Lipton tends to blur the distinction that he himself has chosen to make (i.e., the one between town and country) as far as the better-off rural dwellers, above all the landowners, are concerned. These are 'pseudo urbanites' in the sense that they are rich, not least because part of their incomes derive from their urban interests. It is also common that incomes generated by agricultural production by owners of large estates and money-lenders are channelled to the cities instead of being reinvested in agriculture. However, the elite in the countryside also have interests in common with the smaller farms and the rest of the rural population. The low food prices are a common problem as well as, to some extent, the lack of infrastructure and education facilities. In other words, it is uncertain whether the demarcation line is to be drawn between *sectors* or *geographical areas*. To this may be added the fact that the same individual very well may have interests in different sectors. A farmer and his family may, for example, also be making handicrafts or running other small businesses.

Since the borderline is blurred and changes according to what is being investigated at the moment it loses its operationality. What is actually compared, and whether the same entities appear every time, is uncertain. Instead of this Lipton should have tackled the contradictions *within* the urban and rural sectors, respectively, directly, and not least because there are actually important common interests between certain groups which transcend the border traced by Lipton. The landowners have often diversified their investment to include manufacturing as well, and many industrialists simultaneously own land. Contending that these groups oppose each other is not very meaningful.

The above criticism is also related to the expressions of the opposition between town and country in politics. These may, however, extend beyond mere economic division lines. Thus, ethnic controversies often cut right through both cities and rural areas and, if they dominate, may make it difficult to formulate a political strategy for the countryside. Also the alleged weakness of the agricultural sector *vis-à-vis* urban society may be questioned. In some cases technological development (e.g., the 'green revolution') has strengthened the rural sector considerably, and in many countries, such as Bolivia, India and the Congo, the agricultural population has resisted the government low-price food policy more or less violently.

The empirical material

By his critics Lipton has been accused of a careless use of empirical data. First, it is difficult to get an overview of the material. Lipton's apparatus of notes and tables comprises almost a hundred pages and it is difficult to match the references with the contention made in the text. As Lauchlin Currie pointed out: 'After a few efforts to connect statements with their bases, readers are likely to give up and either accept or reject the statements in accordance with their own biases!'

Dudley Seers objects that the size of the welfare gap which Lipton argues exists between town and country is exaggerated by the statistics. The latter cover only incompletely agricultural products. Figures are frequently based on goods sold via officially sanctioned channels, and often these are parastatal buyers. Since the prices paid by these organizations are low, as noted above, an important part of the output tends to reach the customers via alternative distribution channels. Either black markets tend to arise and the peasants prefer to sell their products in these or the goods are smuggled out of the country (especially in border areas). In neither case will the products in question be included in official statistics, which in addition tend to miss goods that are sold legally via channels other than government buyers. In addition, as we have already pointed out, it should be kept in mind that all rural incomes do not derive from agriculture; many come from crafts and trade. These are not always specialized tasks but the peasants often carry them out 'on the side'. Finally, wage labour outside agriculture is not uncommon.

Lipton, does not, however, accept Seers' criticism on this point. Measuring the value of production is only one way of estimating rural incomes. This is complemented by survey materials and direct measurements of what different groups earn, and Lipton uses all three methods in his book. In addition, as Seers himself has pointed out, it should not be forgotten that it may be difficult to find all the income sources in the cities, above all in the informal sector, but also in the formal, organized, one. In the latter case the reason is that tax systems are often designed in a way which makes it easy to make income inaccessible for taxation and consequently, of course, also for measurement.

A much more serious objection that has been made to Lipton's reasoning is that he is selective in his use of source material and facts. He tends to bring out what supports his thesis but material contradicting it is left in silence. Lipton does not dare to expose himself to the risk that 'facts kick', as Gunnar Myrdal used to say.

To decide strictly whether the critics are right when they accuse Lipton of withholding evidence is of course no easy task; for this a large and systematic survey is required. However, a few factors indicate that the critics have a point here. First, Lipton draws his empirical material from a large number of countries. The pattern that is revealed when he assembles his jigsaw puzzle, however, has no direct individual counterpart. The economy that Lipton creates with the aid of data from three continents does not exist in the real world. This would *per se* not be a serious objection to his method, provided that he attempted to weight his observations systematically and treat his material critically and provided that the results are not interpreted too literally. However, the method leads to a plea for case studies of individual economies in order to figure out whether a serious urban bias is present in actually existing economies. If this is not the case, the thesis loses its interest.

Related to the above is the criticism that Lipton's book is actually about India, although he denies this emphatically himself in his answer to Seers' criticism. (He, however, simultaneously defends the use of Indian material by arguing that the country has as many inhabitants as Africa and Latin America together!) Most of the countries from which Lipton gets his material appear sparingly among his references. The majority of the empirical observations come from India and it is difficult to escape from the feeling that it is mainly when no Indian material exists that Lipton is forced to use other, also mainly large, countries and that he puts in such material when he stumbles over it, in an unsystematic way.

India, however, is special in many ways. There is a clear division line between rural and urban areas – densely populated 'semi-urban' areas are exceptions – and cities are spread reasonably evenly across the entire country. In agriculture the cultivation of grain as a food crop predominates, unlike in many other developing countries where export agriculture is at least as important. In the latter case it is not possible, for example, to keep the food price down to dampen the wage demands of industrial workers. It is not possible to ignore the importance of export prices either, not only for the agricultural sector but for the entire economy. To this must be added the fact that Lipton's analytical framework looks 'Indian', in the sense that it relates to an Indian tradition which puts the difference between town and country into focus in discussions of how society is constructed and how it works. The alternative to this approach – a superior alternative since it would acquit Lipton from the accusation of favouring India – would be to work with a number of case studies from other countries to find out the extent to which these countries follow the same pattern as India.

Lipton, however, also points to how urban bias is manifested in a number of concrete instances, and here it is possible to examine the way he presents his evidence in some more detail. As far as taxation is concerned Lipton does not have much concrete data but is content to make reference to 'facts and arguments' in general. Terry Byres, however, has shown that the existing figures for the country most often invoked by Lipton – India – rather tend to contradict Lipton's thesis. According to Byres, during the 1950s and the 1960s Indian agriculture was actually undertaxed; and if India is compared, for example, to China, the result is that the burden of taxation was heavier for the Chinese peasants. Taxes on agriculture to a large extent were used to build up Chinese manufacturing, but it is hardly possible to speak of an urban bias in this context since the existing income differences were smaller than in India and the political power base in China for a long time was well anchored in the countryside.

In spite of this it is not warranted to draw far-reaching conclusions solely from Byres' Indian example. It is difficult to advance any reasonable hypotheses before enough observations are available. It is also possible that it is not meaningful to attempt to generalize the theory too much, especially not when the step is taken from the overall picture to the more detailed interaction between sectors. With this in mind, Robert Bates has suggested that it may be more fruitful to work with relatively homogeneous groups of countries instead of the Third World as a whole.

Terry Byres, however, questions the very fundament of Lipton's study: that the distribution of income in the countryside would be more even than in the cities and that spending on agriculture instead of, for example, on manufacturing would increase the efficiency of the economy. Lipton bases his analysis of the distribution of income on a study by Montek Ahluwalia. This study contains data for ten countries. In these the distribution of income is most even in the countryside in six cases but statistically significant differences are present in only three of these. Lipton thus jumps to conclusions, or at least draws too bold conclusions from his material.

Even if the material had favoured the Lipton thesis in other respects it is not permissible to take for granted, as Lipton does, that a redistribution of resources from town to country will lead to increased income equality. That a certain pattern exists in the static perspective does not guarantee that the same pattern will remain valid when the environment changes. This is perhaps best shown by the 'green revolution', which may represent the most probable form of investment that would take place within agriculture if resources were reallocated from town to country. Those who pocket the fattest profits in the latter are the large landowners, while the small peasants (for different reasons) have been discriminated against by the changes. There is thus a considerable risk that the skewedness of the income distribution increases instead of decreasing if Lipton's recommendations are followed.

Also, when it comes to the relative efficiency of the agrarian and the urban parts of the economy, Lipton's reasoning may be criticized. Lipton bases his conclusion that a reallocation of resources to the countryside would increase GDP on a simple comparison of capital–output ratios in agriculture and manufacturing. The size of these at the margin may, however, differ from their average values. In addition, what such a comparison yields is simply a measure of the once and for all increase of output if an investment is made. In principle, in such comparisons all sectors are treated as if they produced pure consumer goods. In the latter type of sector an investment simply leads to increased consumption. In the producer goods sectors the situation is different. Here, the use of capital–output ratios will produce a bias since the use of producer goods in investment will give rise to additional production in the future (i.e., an adjustment must be made for this if a comparison, say, with food production is to be meaningful).

Conclusions

The idea of an urban bias has been sharply criticized during the entire time it has formed part of the development discussion. Correct or not, at the same time it has contributed to focusing the attention on the relation between town and country in less developed countries. Most development economists favour the idea that there is something behind the Lipton thesis, but also argue that it is incomplete and insufficient in various respects. The identification of urban bias, for example, does not help us when it comes to understanding under which circumstances the problem possibly tends to disappear by itself and when direct intervention can be needed. Above all, however, it may be discussed whether favouring cities and urban trades is a consequence of urban bias in the narrow sense of the term and, in that case, what the propelling mechanisms may be. During the 1980s the theory received a renewed impetus, above all from the contributions by Robert Bates concerning its microeconomic and political economy foundations, and it is today more accepted in this new shape. The generality of the problem is, however, still subject to discussion. Even Lipton himself has conceded that the concept may not be applicable to all countries and that all institutions do not have to fall into the urban bias pattern, even in countries where the concept *per se* appears to be relevant.

Literature

The main source of the urban bias thesis is:
Lipton, Michael (1977), *Why Poor People Stay Poor: Urban Bias in World Development*. Temple Smith, London.

The original idea, however, is found in:

Lipton, Michael (1968), 'Strategies for Agriculture: Urban Bias and Rural Planning', in Streeten, Paul and Lipton, Michael (eds), *The Crisis of Indian Planning: Economic Planning in the 1960s*. Oxford University Press, London.

An earlier contribution to the same type of discussion – however, presumably unknown to Lipton – is:
Malamakis, Markos J. (1969), 'The Theory of Sectoral Clashes', *Latin American Research Review*, Vol. 4.

Haiti as an example of urban bias, especially when it comes to public investments, is dealt with in:
Lundahl, Mats (1979), *Peasants and Poverty. A Study of Haiti*. Croom Helm, London.

A summarizing, critical evaluation of the theory of urban bias is found in:
Varshney, Ashutosh (1993), 'Introduction: Urban Bias in Perspective', *Journal of Development Studies*, Vol. 29.

The entire issue of this journal contains articles that provide a critical evaluation of the urban bias thesis, and so does:
Currie, Lauchlin (1979), 'Is there an Urban Bias? Critique of Michael Lipton's Why Poor People Stay Poor', *Journal of Economic Studies*, Vol. 6.
Harriss, John and Moore, Mick (eds) (1984), Development and the Rural–Urban Divide. Frank Cass, London. (The articles included in this volume were also published as a special issue of *Journal of Development Studies*, Vol. 20, No. 3, April 1984.)

A formal discussion (that constitutes the foundation of the section on optimal taxation in the present chapter) of optimal taxation of farms and urban dwelling, respectively is found in:
Sah, Raaj and Stiglitz, Joseph E. (1992), *Peasants versus City-Dwellers. Taxation and the Burden of Economic Development*. Clarendon Press, Oxford.

A thorough discussion of price policy in agriculture is found in:
Krueger, Anne O. (1992), *The Political Economy of Agricultural Pricing Policy, Volume 5. A Synthesis of the Political Economy in Developing Countries*. World Bank, Johns Hopkins University Press, Baltimore, MD, and London; especially ch. 2.

For a discussion of the structural and the interest rates prevailing in different sectors, see:
Fry, Maxwell (1988), *Money, Interest and Banking in Economic Development*. Johns Hopkins Press, Baltimore, MD, and London.
von Pischke, J. D., Adams, Dale W. and Donald, Gordon (eds) (1983), *Rural Financial Markets in Developing Countries*. Johns Hopkins University Press, Baltimore, MD, and London.

A short overview with emphasis on the effects of government interventions in the credit market is found in:
Poulson, Barry W. (1994), *Economic Development. Private and Public Choice*. West, Minneapolis/St Paul.

The common interest of some groups in the towns and in the countryside is discussed in:
Véliz, Claudio (1963), 'La mesa de tres patas', *Desarrollo Económico*, Vol. 3.

A work that points to the problem of ascribing individuals to a given sector of the economy and hence of evaluating the impact of different interventions is:
Bigsten, Arne (1985), 'What Do Smallholders Do for a Living? Some Evidence from Kenya', in Lundahl, Mats (ed.), *The Primary Sector in Economic Development*. Croom Helm, London and Sydney.

The role of relative prices and marketing boards are discussed in:
Ellis, Frank (1984), 'Relative Agricultural Prices and the Urban Bias Model: A Comparative Analysis of Tanzania and Fiji', in Harriss and Moore, *Development and the Rural–Urban Divide*.

The income distribution study by Ahluwalia that is referred to in the text is:
Ahluwalia, Montek S. (1974), 'Income Inequality: Some Dimensions of the Problem', in Chenery, Hollis, Ahluwalia, Montek S., Bell, C. L. G., Dulay, John H. and Jolly, Richard, *Redistribution with Growth*. Oxford University Press, London.

Lipton has himself taken issue with the criticism of his thesis in:
Lipton, Michael (1984), 'Urban Bias Revisited', in Harriss and Moore, *Development and the Rural–Urban Divide*.

Bates' main contribution to the urban bias theory is found in:
Bates, Robert (1981), *Markets and States in Tropical Africa*. University of California Press, Berkeley, CA.

8
The Apartheid System in South Africa

The best example of ethnically based systematic discrimination can be found in the recent history of South Africa. Discrimination had been applied, in various forms, in the country since the beginning of the European colonization in the mid-seventeenth century until the early 1990s, when the system was officially abolished.

Racial discrimination created a situation that, at times, to a great extent was reminiscent of Arthur Lewis' well-known 'dualistic' growth model, which is based on a division of the economy into a stagnating traditional sector and an expanding modern sector. The growth in the latter sector is explained by unlimited access to labour at a low and stable wage level. This 'unlimited' (infinitely elastic) supply of labour was partly created through denying Africans the property rights to land. Consequently, the Africans had to find work in the European sector. Imports of casual labour from the neighbouring countries contributed, too, increasing competition in the labour market. Over time other types of discrimination emerged as well, particularly in the form of control of geographical mobility and quotas in the labour market, allotting the least qualified jobs to the Africans.

The process can be divided into three stages. The first stage lasted from the beginning of the colonization period until the latter part of the nineteenth century. Both Europeans and Africans practised agriculture using unskilled labour and land. Typical for this stage was immigration from Europe and transfer of land from Africans to Europeans. Traditional African property rights to the land were not honoured and the Africans could not put up effective armed resistance against the intruding immigrants. Gradually the number of immigrants increased and the European sector expanded. Production techniques in European agriculture remained largely unchanged, however. Consequently, more and more land was needed when the number of Europeans increased. The Africans could move between the traditional sector and European agriculture according to the incentives created by, for example, wage differences. Since the Africans were deprived of land the traditional sector slowly declined and income per capita in that sector decreased over time.

Stage two lasted from the great mineral discoveries, of diamonds in 1867 and gold in 1886, until the end of the First World War. A mining and manufacturing sector had now emerged. This sector also needed capital and skilled labour. During this period the transfer of land to the European sector continued. The standard of living in the marginalized traditional sector fell while the European agriculture continued expanding. At this stage land as such was not the most important consideration for the Europeans. The point now was to secure a sufficient supply of African labour. This could be achieved only if the alternatives were few and unattractive.

In the manufacturing sector (including mining) some of the unskilled jobs were reserved for whites. The background to this was the fact that Europeans were now expelled from the agricultural sector, a process which paralleled the increasing urbanization. The reasons for this were an increasingly obsolete agricultural technology, erosion and subdivision of farms into smaller and smaller units as a consequence of inheritance. The result was the so-called civilized labour policy, which was designed to take care of the 'poor whites' (i.e., those who were forced out of the agricultural sector but were unqualified for jobs requiring skills). This group had to compete with the Africans for unqualified jobs in mining and industry. Finally, all jobs requiring skills were reserved for whites. (The fact that little education and only education of low quality was available for blacks had a similar effect. In 1990, when the apartheid system, which had systematically brought about differentiation of education, broke down, 25 per cent of the whites had a tertiary education, while the corresponding figure for the Africans was less than 1 per cent.)

During the third stage the transfer of land from the Africans to the Europeans had come to an end. The Africans were allotted special areas, 'homelands' or bantustans, which they could not leave without permission. European agriculture was gradually mechanized and thus also used capital to an increasing extent. The problem of 'poor whites' was now solved. The whites worked as skilled labour in the manufacturing sector and had priority access to those jobs. Few Africans qualified for skilled jobs, even if they had been allowed to take them, because only low-quality education was available to them as a result of the apartheid system.

In the rest of this chapter we will analyse – with some simplifications – the effects of the discriminatory policies using our model. The three stages of the apartheid policy will be studied separately.

Segregation of the land market

During the first stage the South African economy consisted of two sectors, an African one and a European one. Both produced agricultural goods, including livestock, using land and labour. The production functions of the sectors (linearly homogeneous) are

$$A = A\left(T_A, L_A^A\right) \tag{8.1}$$

$$E = E\left(T_E, L_E^E, L_E^A\right) \tag{8.2}$$

where T denotes land. The African sector uses only African labour while the European sector uses European labour as well.

The total supply of Europeans and Africans is assumed to be given, which implies that

$$L_A^A + L_E^A = \overline{L}^A \tag{8.3}$$

$$L_E^E = \overline{L}^E \tag{8.4}$$

The total endowment of farmland is also given:

$$T_A + T_E = T \tag{8.5}$$

The Europeans are assumed to own the land they till, so their revenue consists of the production value in the European sector minus the proceeds paid as wages to the Africans. African labour is fully mobile between the sectors. The wages, which are determined by the marginal product of labour, will thus be equalized in the two sectors:

$$w = A_L = E_L \tag{8.6}$$

where, for simplicity, we have set the (agricultural) product price equal to unity.

The market for land is partly eliminated. There is segregation in the sense that the Africans cannot buy land from the Europeans even if they want to. On the contrary, during the first stage the discrimination was based on expropriation of African land that was transferred to Europeans. The effects of this can be studied with the aid of Figure 8.1. The figure illustrates the labour market in the European part of the South African economy. On the horizontal axis the use of labour (L) is measured, while the wage rate (w) and the marginal product of labour (MPL) are measured on the vertical axis. The marginal cost of labour is given by the supply curve (S_L).

White employers hire labour as long as the value of its marginal product exceeds its marginal cost. The value of the marginal contribution to production is equal to the marginal cost at point A, with an equilibrium wage rate of w_1 and an employment level of OL_1. We assume OL_1 consists of OL_2 Africans and L_2L_1 Europeans. Knowing this, we can also determine how

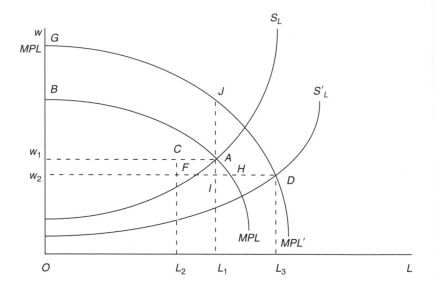

Figure 8.1   The labour market in the 'European' economy

the production value is distributed. OW_1CL_2 will be spent on wages for the Africans, L_2CAL_1 on wages for the Europeans and w_1BA, finally, will accrue to the white landowners.

What would then be the effect on the European sector of transferring land from Africans to Europeans? Since $E_{LT} > 0$ (according to the characteristics of the production function assumed in Chapter 2) the *MPL* curve will shift upwards, to *MPL'*. The S_L curve will shift, too, to (say) S_L'. The reason for this is that the possibilities for the Africans to earn a living outside the European sector have deteriorated since they have lost parts of their land. Consequently, the supply of labour will increase in the European sector. A new equilibrium will emerge, with the wage rate w_2 and employment OL_3. Compared to the original situation, L_1L_3 more Africans have now been employed in the European sector.

As the graph in Figure 8.1 is drawn the white landowners will benefit as a group. The profit consists of the revenue from the new land, *BGDH*, the profit due to lower wages (w_1AIw_2) and the additional surplus generated by the land they already have through lower wages and higher employment (*AHI*). The wages of the white workers decrease with *CAIF* and the wages of the black workers already employed decrease with w_2w_1CF.

Since the European immigrants owned their land it seems natural to assume that they intended to increase the sum of income from land and their own labour, seizing land from the Africans, and, according to the graph, they seem to have been successful. The profit they make as landowners exceeds the loss they make as wage earners. This is not a necessary result, however, but, among other things, depends on the factor intensities in the European and African sector, respectively. Let us assume that the European sector is more land-intensive than the African one: that is, that

$$(T/L)_E > (T/L)_A$$

When land is transferred from the African to the European sector factor prices will be affected and this, in turn, will affect the income of the different groups. Assume, to begin with, that we wish to preserve the original factor proportions in both sectors. When land is then transferred from the African to the European sector African workers are simultaneously released, but in larger numbers in relation to the land transferred than the European sector can absorb if the factor proportions there are not to be changed. For the redundant workers to be absorbed the wage level must fall. Then both sectors will employ new workers. The Africans already employed in the European sector will be worse off and this will be the case for the newly employed workers as well. Their ability to make a living deteriorated when land was transferred from the African sector, and hence they were forced to leave that sector.

The Europeans, in turn, are better off. Their income is given by the value of production minus the wages they have to pay to the Africans. Production increases (at the given price = 1) because the sector receives both land and workers, the Africans already employed get lower wages than before and the newly employed Africans produce a surplus, in excess of their wages, equal to *IJD*, which accrues to the whites. The white group thus gains from seizing land from the Africans. Finally, there are the Africans that remain in the African sector. All Africans there now have less land at their disposal, on average. The sector lost land and labour in the proportion $(T/L)_A$, the original factor intensity in the sector. When the wage level fell, some labour was re-employed, however. Consequently, per capita income in the African sector falls.

'Civilized labour market policy'

When the second stage begins the South African economy has been diversified. A manufacturing and mining sector (here called 'manufacturing') has emerged and both the European agriculture and the industry use capital. We then obtain the following production functions:

$$A = A\big(T_A, L_A^A\big) \tag{8.1}$$

for the African economy (agriculture), as before;

$$J = J\left(T_J, L_J^A, K_J\right) \tag{8.7}$$

for European agriculture, which produces different products from the African sector and where we assume that only Africans work. This assumption is made in order to capture the problem of 'poor whites' who were forced out of the agricultural sector and had to compete with Africans for jobs in manufacturing:

$$I = I\left(L_I^A + \overline{L}_I^E, K_I\right) \tag{8.8}$$

Furthermore, we may assume that the distribution of land between European and African agriculture is given:

$$T_A = \overline{T}_A \tag{8.9}$$

$$T_J = \overline{T}_J \tag{8.10}$$

and that the access of Africans to the European economy is limited:

$$\overline{L}^A = \overline{L}_A^A + L_J^A + L_I^A \tag{8.11}$$

A certain number of Africans had to remain in reserves. Finally, the given capital stock is divided between both European sectors:

$$\overline{K} = K_J + K_I \tag{8.12}$$

We may now limit the analysis to the European part of the economy. (These assumptions have been made since we want to focus on the effect of the 'civilized labour market policy' and tariff protection. A more realistic formulation would take into account the continued segregation of the market for land, the increasing access of Africans to the 'European' parts of the economy when necessary, the use of skilled labour in industry, limitation of the access to education for the Africans and the limited significance of capital in the European agriculture. This would require a mathematical formulation of the model, however, since the box diagram technique in principle is limited to two factors.)

In the box in Figure 8.2 the production would take place at point *a* if there were no distortions, where an agriculture isoquant touches a manufacturing isoquant. Manufacturing cannot choose its labour force freely, however, but has to use Africans and Europeans in given proportions:

$$L_I^E = c\left(L_I^E + L_I^A\right) \tag{8.13}$$

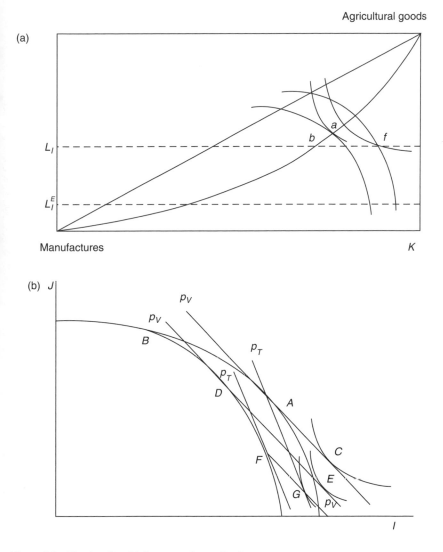

Figure 8.2 The 'civilized labour market policy'

The 'civilized labour market policy' determines the value of *c*: that is, how large a part of the labour input in the sector has to be provided by Europeans. This means that it is no longer possible to increase the use of labour in industry beyond the level L_I. After point *b* the economy is forced off its contract curve, horizontally to the right. Now only capital can be transferred from agriculture to manufacturing (and vice versa). In terms of the production possibility curve this means that to the right of point *B* the curve lies inside the one corresponding to the contract curve in the box. The economy cannot then produce at point *A* or consume at point *C*, at world market prices p_V, under free trade.

If free trade had been allowed when the industrial sector had to apply the 'civilized labour market policy' the welfare loss (for the Europeans) would have been limited to what is given by points *D* (production) and *E* (consumption). In practice this was not the case, however, because the sectors that chose to regulate the proportion of Europeans and Africans were also entitled to tariff protection. Because of this the production point is moved to *F*, at domestic prices, p_T, and the consumption point to *G*, on a lower social indifference curve.

In the box diagram we can express the combination of labour policy and tariff protection as a movement from *a* to *f*. Manufacturing production is higher than it would have been without the interventions in the market mechanism. The relative price of labour is higher in manufacturing than in agriculture. All European labour is employed in manufacturing and, since the number of Africans per European cannot exceed $(1 - c)/c$, the access of African labour to that sector is limited.

Influx control and crowding-out

At the third stage the structure of the South African economy has changed once again. The labour force has now been differentiated into an unskilled and a skilled component, and the forms of discrimination are not the same as before. The Africans have been concentrated in special 'homelands' or bantustans, which they cannot leave without permission. The inflow of Africans into the European economy is regulated. Moreover, the Africans are prohibited from taking qualified jobs. These are reserved for whites, partly through direct legislation, and partly through differentiation of the education system: good education for whites, poor for blacks.

The economy still consists of an African sector (homelands) that uses land and unskilled African labour:

$$A = A\left(\overline{T}_A, L_A^{UA}\right) \tag{8.14}$$

The endowment of land in the homelands is assumed to be given.

In the European sectors only labour, skilled and unskilled, is used. (This assumption is made in order to permit the two-factor approach with the box and production possibility curve to be used.) The production functions are:

$$J = J\left(L_J^{UA}, L_J^{S}\right) \tag{8.15}$$

$$I = I\left(L_I^{UA}, L_I^S\right) \tag{8.16}$$

European agriculture still produces different crops from the African sector. All white workers are assumed to be skilled. The problem of 'poor whites' has ceased to exist. Additionally there is a small number of skilled Africans:

$$L_J^S + L_I^S = \overline{L}^{SE} + L^{SA} \tag{8.17}$$

The unskilled Africans are divided between all three sectors:

$$L_A^{UA} + L_J^{UA} + L_I^{UA} = \overline{L}^{UA} \tag{8.18}$$

If labour is fully mobile in the economy and there are no obstacles against Africans educating themselves and taking qualified jobs, the economy will produce at point a in the box diagram in Figure 8.3, at world market prices, p_V, if no trade barriers exist, or at point b, at home market prices, p_T, if manufacturing is protected by tariffs. (The production isoquant is not shown.) If we assume that manufacturing is the sector that uses skilled labour intensively, the relative price of the latter is higher at b than at a. These points correspond to points A and B on the production possibility curve.

When influx control of unskilled labour is introduced, the box shrinks vertically. Agricultural production now has to be measured from O'' instead of O' and the efficient production points will be on the new contract curve OO''. The production of agricultural goods (which uses unskilled labour intensively) will diminish while manufacturing production will increase at unchanged factor prices. (This follows from the Rybczynski theorem: see Chapter 11.) The economy will produce at point c in the box at unchanged factor intensities. In Figure 8.3b the transformation curve shifts downward from TT to $T'T'$, closer to the vertical axis (agricultural products) and further from the horizontal axis (manufactures); the new production point is C.

The influx control does not lead to any distortions if the discussion is limited to the European part of the economy. South Africa would have been able, in principle, to produce, trade and consume at world market prices. If the homelands are included in the analysis the picture will change, however. As shown by Figure 8.4, the wages in the homelands are forced down, from w_A^u to $w_A^{u'}$, when the supply of labour is increased from L_A^A to $L_A^{A'}$ as a result of the influx control. Earlier the wages of unskilled labour were equalized across all sectors of the economy:

$$w_A^U = w_J^U = w_I^U \tag{8.19}$$

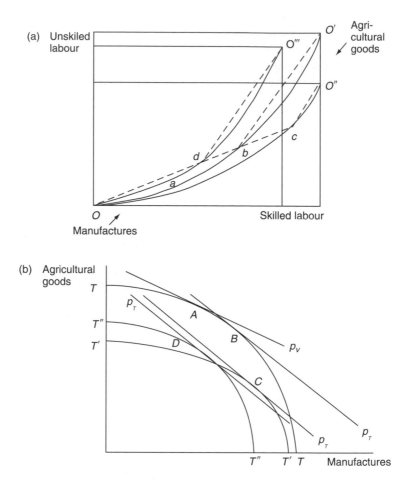

Figure 8.3   Resource allocation with influx control and reservation of skilled jobs for whites

but, when migration is controlled, equality will be established only between the wages in the European agricultural and industrial sectors.

Meanwhile, GDP, measured in terms of domestic prices, has diminished. When the production factors are freely allocated at these prices the value of production is maximized at point *B* on the production possibility curve (and the corresponding point on the transformation surface that corresponds to this curve when all three products are considered). Points such as *C*, in turn, represent a lower production value as they are on a curve (surface) inside the original one.

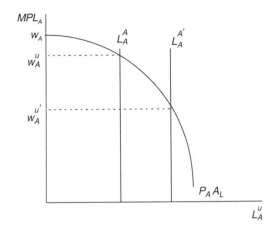

Figure 8.4   The labour market in the homelands

What, then, does influx control imply in terms of welfare? In the South African case, where all population groups except the European one were subject to systematic discrimination, it is no longer meaningful to work with one social welfare function for the whole economy, but a distinction between whites and Africans has to be made. As far as the latter are concerned, those who live in the homelands already and those who are relocated there are worse off. Diminishing returns to unskilled labour cause a fall in both the production value per capita and the wage rate in the homelands. The unskilled Africans that manage to stay on in the European sector will have the same wage as before, however, at given product prices. The latter prices are determined by the world market prices and by the given tariff rates on manufactures and therefore do not change, implying in turn that also factor prices and factor intensities remain unchanged. This also means that the income of the skilled labourers (white and black) remains unchanged.

The income of the whites thus does not increase as a consequence of the influx control. The natural question, then, is why the control is applied at all. This obviously cannot be explained with a starting point in economic rationality, as expressed in our model; other explanations are needed. A possible such explanation of the influx control has to do with the security of the white group. Too many Africans living close to the white areas could be perceived by the whites as a threat to their security. Therefore migration is limited.

The explanation above is not the only possible one, however. The labour contracts that the African migrants had to sign during the apartheid era were temporary and had to be renewed after a certain period of time. This facilitated substituting younger and more productive workers for older ones whose productivity had begun to decrease. In this way the whites could also avoid paying the cost of the physical and social infrastructure needed if Africans had been allowed to migrate freely to the cities with their families.

Considering the economy as a whole, influx control leads to a situation where the wage levels differ between the homelands and the European sectors. As we have seen in earlier chapters, this results in inefficient production. The marginal productivity of labour is higher in the European sectors than in the homeland sector, and thus it would be possible to increase production by moving labour from the latter to the former. Moreover, the relative product prices differ from the slope of the production possibility surface (we now have three products), so that

$$\frac{\partial J}{\partial A_{dI=0}} \neq -\frac{P_A}{P_J}$$

and

$$\frac{\partial I}{\partial A_{dJ=0}} \neq -\frac{P_A}{P_I}$$

This can be shown as in earlier chapters. We may, for example, deduce the expression for $(\partial J/\partial A)|_{dI=0}$ from the production functions (8.14) and (8.15). Differentiating these functions gives

$$\frac{\partial J}{\partial A_{dI=0}} = \frac{J_L dL_J^{UA} + J_S dL_J^S}{A_L dL_A^{UA}} \tag{8.20}$$

The production factors are paid according to the value of their marginal products:

$$P_A A_L = w_A^U \tag{8.21}$$

$$P_J J_L = w_J^U \tag{8.22}$$

$$P_J J_S = w^S \tag{8.23}$$

Solving for the marginal products and substituting into (8.20) gives

$$\frac{\partial J}{\partial A_{dI=0}} = \frac{P_A}{P_J} \frac{w_J^U dL_J^{UA} + w^S dL_J^S}{w_A^U dL_A^{UA}} \tag{8.24}$$

Originally, the wage of unskilled labour is the same in the homelands and European agriculture (and in manufacturing):

$$w_A^U = w_J^U = w_I^U \tag{8.25}$$

$(\partial J/\partial A)|_{dI=0}$ is defined for a constant I. The factor inputs into manufacturing then remain constant when the factor inputs in the homeland sector and European agriculture change. This implies, when we start from (8.18), that

$$dL_A^{UA} = -dL_J^{UA} \tag{8.26}$$

and, starting from,

$$L_J^S + L_I^S = \bar{L}^S \tag{8.27}$$

$$dL_J^S = 0 \tag{8.28}$$

Expression (8.24) can then be simplified:

$$\frac{\partial J}{\partial A_{dI=0}} = -\frac{P_A}{P_J} \tag{8.29}$$

The slope of the production surface coincides with that of the price plane.

When influx control is introduced the wage rate in the homelands falls, so that

$$w_A^U < w_J^U = w_I^U = w_E^U$$

The slope of the production possibility surface then changes to

$$\frac{\partial J}{\partial A_{dI=0}} = -\frac{P_A \, w_E^U}{P_J \, w_A^U} \tag{8.30}$$

where $w_E^U/w_A^U > 1$. The slope of the production possibility surface is steeper than that of the price plane. The two intersect. Similarly, we may show that

$$\frac{\partial I}{\partial A_{dJ=0}} = -\frac{P_A \, w_E^U}{P_I \, w_A^U} \tag{8.31}$$

The other form of discrimination is excluding Africans from qualified jobs. In terms of the box diagram in Figure 8.3 this implies that the width of the box decreases while the height increases, and that the contract curve shifts from O'' to O'''. The Rybczynski theorem can then be applied both 'forwards' and 'backwards'. The production of manufactures decreases because the endowment of the factor used intensively in manufacturing production decreases, and because the endowment of the other factor increases with the same amount. For the same reason agricultural production increases compared to point *c*. If the number of skilled Africans that are forced into unskilled jobs exceeds the number of unskilled Africans that are forced into the homeland sector, agricultural production in the new production point also exceeds production at point *b*. This is hardly likely, however, since more unskilled than skilled Africans are likely to be hit by the apartheid policy. In addition to this the reduction of the number of Africans that are allowed to work in qualified occupations must be taken into account. The net result, hence, is indeterminate in principle, even if it is perhaps most likely in practice that both agricultural and manufacturing production are smaller at the new production point, *d*, than at *b*.

The transformation curve also shifts, to $T''T''$: inwards when close to the manufacturing axis and outwards when close to the agriculture axis. The new production point is *D*. Since the changes do not disturb the relation $DRS = FRT = DRT$ further, but only lead to a change in factor endowments, crowding-out is no distortion in a technical sense, even if it does have production and welfare effects.

The latter effects are negative for the skilled Africans who are crowded out from the more qualified and better jobs and are forced to take unqualified jobs, requiring no education, at a lower wage. The income of other groups is not affected, however, since the product prices remain unchanged. Then the same problem reappears as in the discussion of influx control. What is the reason for discrimination? A possible line of explanation runs in terms of white employment. The whites were afraid to be out-competed in the long run by Africans in the qualified jobs. One of the important tasks for the apartheid system was to guarantee employment for whites.

The breakdown of apartheid

Apartheid was abolished in the early 1990s. An interesting question is why this happened. One possibility is that the international sanctions and isolation that the country was subject to – increasingly so towards the mid-1980s – finally forced the holders of power to give up. Much seems to suggest, however, that international pressure did not topple the system, even if it did cause problems for the regime. Instead, it seems as if the inherent dynamics of the system contained the seeds of its own destruction.

The apartheid system is, to a great extent, a success story, if it is observed from the point of view of the European minority. During nearly a century the system succeeded in generating high rates of growth. The positive development was interrupted in the 1970s, however, and in the 1980s things deteriorated further. Even if the turbulent international economy, as in most other countries, can partly explain the development, apartheid had gradually become a burden for the white minority instead of an asset.

First of all, the system had created severe bottlenecks, particularly in the market for skilled labour. While the economy became more and more sophisticated and the relative share of the industrial sector increased, it was impossible to meet the need for (white) skilled labour fast enough. At the same time the wages of unskilled African labour began to rise as well. The reason for this was that the demand rose at the same time as the supply of labour from neighboring countries dried up when they became independent and started to oppose the apartheid system.

Another problem was the fact that the manufacturing sector had expanded through the strategy of import substitution. The negative consequences of this have already been discussed in some detail in Chapter 6. The attempts made to switch the trade policy regime towards a more export oriented one did not succeed either, partly because South Africans products were boycotted, for political reasons. Finally, the rate of investment fell, partly because of the difficulties just mentioned. The volatile political situation led to capital flight and foreign investors looked on the country with some suspicion, to the extent that sanctions did not preclude investments altogether. Domestic saving had decreased as well, as a consequence of lower growth and increasing insecurity.

In spite of all problems the system might possibly have survived, if this had been in the interest of the dominant Afrikaner minority. During the postwar period this minority had become less homogeneous than before and the interests of different groups began to diverge. The groups gaining from the system were the white farmers and workers, while the industrialists lost out as a consequence of not being able to hire labour at lowest possible cost. This class has long consisted almost exclusively of Anglo-Saxon whites. Gradually, however, an Afrikaner industrial and entrepreneurial class also emerged, for whom apartheid created exactly the same type of problems as for the Anglo-Saxon firms. After some attempts at reform during the 1980s the support for the system finally became too weak and it was abandoned, under strong international pressure.

Literature

Arthur Lewis' dualistic growth model was first presented in:
Lewis, W. Arthur (1954), 'Economic Development with Unlimited Supplies of Labour', *Manchester School of Economic and Social Studies*, Vol. 22.

The growth and development of the South African economy can be studied in:
Horwitz, Ralph (1967), *The Political Economy of South Africa*. Weidenfeld & Nicolson, London.
Nattrass, Jill (1981), *The South African Economy: Its Growth and Change*. Oxford University Press, Cape Town.

The descriptive section on the emergence of the apartheid policy is mainly based on:
Lundahl, Mats and Ndlela, Daniel B. (1992), 'Land Alienation, Dualism, and Economic Discrimination: South Africa and Rhodesia', in Lundahl, Mats, *Apartheid in Theory and Practice. An Economic Analysis*. Westview Press, Boulder, CO.

A survey can also be found in:
Lundahl, Mats and Wadensjö, Eskil (1984), *Unequal Treatment. A Study in the Neo-Classical Theory of Discrimination.* Croom Helm, London and Sydney, ch. 8.

The figures presented on the education level are from:
Lundahl, Mats and Moritz, Lena (1999), 'The South African Economy after Apartheid', in Lundahl, Mats, *Growth or Stagnation? South Africa Heading for the Year 2000.* Ashgate, Aldershot.

An analysis of racial discrimination in South Africa can be found in:
Hutt, W. H. (1964), *The Economics of the Colour Bar.* André Deutsch, London.
Lewis, Stephen R., Jr (1990), *The Economics of Apartheid.* Council of Foreign Relations Press, London and New York.
Lipton, Merle (1985), *Capitalism and Apartheid: South Africa, 1910–84.* Avebury, Aldershot.
Lowenberg, Anton D. and Kaempfer, William H. (1998), *The Origins and Demise of South African Apartheid: A Public Choice Analaysis.* University of Michigan Press, Ann Arbor, MI.
Lundahl, *Apartheid in Theory and Practice.*

The consequences of the apartheid policy can be studied in:
Wilson, Francis and Ramphele, Mamphela (1989), *Uprooting Poverty: The South African Challenge.* Norton, New York and London.

The final analysis of the reasons for abolishing the apartheid system is based on:
Lundahl, Mats, Fredriksson, Per and Moritz, Lena (1992), 'South Africa 1990: Pressure for Change', in Lundahl, *Apartheid in Theory and Practice.*

9

The Socialist Planned Economy: The Price System Eliminated

All earlier chapters have rested on the assumption that prices are formed by the interplay of supply and demand in the world market. The distortions we have scrutinized so far modify the functioning of the market but do not eliminate the price system as such. There is another way of allocating resources in an economy, however: with the aid of administrative processes where *planning* plays a decisive role. The planning system may function in different ways in practice. Here we will concentrate on looking into the effects of the 'purest' variety, the type of planned economy applied in the Soviet Union and a number of Eastern and Central European countries until the early 1990s. In this system there was, in principle, no place for the market at all, even if reality never quite lived up to that ideal. (In several Eastern European countries fragments of a private sector survived. Moreover, illegal, black markets were a reality in all planned economies). Now we know, however, that the system functioned badly and finally it crumbled completely, so that today only North Korea and Cuba remain as orthodox planned economies. From what we know it seems highly unlikely that the planned economy could ever return as an economic system. In this chapter we will show how this type of economy functions and why the experiment of economic planning was unsuccessful.

Principles of a planned economy

The father of socialism, Karl Marx, surprisingly had little to say about the system he propounded. Marx was a determinist. He believed that the inherent contradictions of the capitalist system would inevitably lead to a socialist society, where all means of production are owned by the state (or cooperatives) and the resource allocation, consequently, is completely determined by the state. He was more interested in analysing the development mechanisms of the capitalist system than in trying to predict, with any degree of exactness, what the 'final product' would look like. It was clear, however, that the economy was to be planned and, according to Marx, this

147

was a fairly easy task if only private ownership and the 'anarchy of markets' were abolished first. Marx and his successors were convinced that socialism was a superior system, for purely economic reasons.

According to the so-called labour theory of value the value of a product is determined by its labour content, the so-called socially necessary labour, but is unrelated to the relative scarcity of different products. (Neither does the *exchange* value of the products – i.e., their market price – have to coincide with their labour value.) The labour content is thus, in principle, the correct starting point for pricing under socialism. In practice, this principle seems to have been more liturgy than reality, however, since prices were seldom set according to the labour theory of value. The price was a pure accounting unit. Although a kind of mark-up routine, where the average cost formed the starting point, was used for pricing the costs did not reflect the relative scarcity of goods and factors of production, and thus prices had no signal value. Capital had no price at all, in principle, since interest is banned in the socialist system. The prices were of no significance for the production decisions of the firms, although they were relevant for the choice of consumers. Since a proper price system did not exist the consumers could not influence decisions of what goods were produced and in which quantities. The signal value of prices in a market economy was absent in this case. The quantities to be produced, as well as the allocation of resources to each firm, are determined directly by the planning authorities.

The obvious consequence of all this is that it is unlikely that supply equals demand. The economy is then characterized either by excess demand, leading to rationing, queues and black markets, or an excess supply of products that cannot be sold. Depending on the assignment of resources it is either too easy to reach the production target or impossible to do so. Different investment projects cannot be compared since present values of the projects cannot be calculated without an interest rate and since the prices used to calculate revenues and outlays are distorted. As a consequence scarce capital resources are used inoptimally. In practice, the capital goods industry was favoured compared with the consumer goods sector due to the fact that maximizing economic growth was a paramount aim of the socialist society.

From the latter half of the 1950s pricing, and how pricing procedures could be improved, was the object of much discussion. Three 'schools' can be distinguished in this context: the labour cost approach, implying that prices should be set proportionally to the labour cost; the mark-up school, according to which prices should be determined by the production cost augmented with a profit margin; and the 'planometric' optimization approach, which started out from the idea that the prices of the factors of production should be proportional to their marginal products. In practice the changes were insignificant, however. Particular features of actual pricing procedures were often motivated by some suitable quotations from Marx and his disciples.

The problem of coordination of supply and demand was aggravated by the fact that far from all production goes directly to consumers; many products are intermediate goods that are used in the production of other goods. The quantities required, then, depend on the demand for one or several final products. This network of mutual dependence is very complicated. In practice one plan is not sufficient but several plans, covering different parts of the economy and different time periods, are needed. For this to be feasible the structure of the economy must be very static. The planned economies thus have an inherent tendency towards stagnation.

In principle it is of course possible – as suggested by Oskar Lange and other proponents of so-called *market socialism* – that the prices need not be generated by a market. Instead they might be set by a government planning authority, which keeps changing the prices until a general equilibrium has been achieved. This task is so complex, however, that a functioning market economy with artificially generated prices seems like a pure utopia. Besides, both the quantitatively inclined planning philosophy and market socialism are diffusely related to the ideas of Marx, who came to the conclusion that the state will gradually wither away as unnecessary. A functioning planned economy, on the other hand, would presuppose a strong central power.

Lange's contribution formed part of the so-called socialist controversy (an early discussion on the virtues of the planned economy as compared to the market system). As long ago as 1908 Enrico Barone had shown that, in principle, a centrally controlled socialist system could allocate resources efficiently – that is, Pareto-optimally – provided that the planners had perfect information about consumer preferences, production functions and resource endowments. Also, the planning authority had to be capable of solving the huge system of equations that defines the economy.

The controversy, however, started with Ludvig von Mises' contribution in the early 1920s, when he maintained that no rational price system could be constructed without the aid of a market. Friedrich von Hayek agreed with this view. Hayek above all emphasized the problems of collecting and processing information, and according to him these problems are too severe to be solved. Lange's contribution was actually an attempt to show a way of reducing the complexity of the task and, hence, also to show that a planned economy could function efficiently in practice. The role of central planning in his model was one of setting prices only. The consumers were allowed to choose freely what they preferred to consume at the given prices and the firms would produce the quantity required, equalizing their marginal cost with the unit product price. Since prices were assumed to be adjusted in the case of excess demand or supply production would, furthermore, take place at the lowest possible unit cost. Lange's ideas met with resistance from economists more inclined towards centralism, however. These economists maintained that a centralized system would produce better results in terms of growth and stability. The development of computers would soon render the practical computation problems tractable. Lange was also criticized because his analysis was not based on existing socialist economies.

The problem with the vast amounts of information and the enormous number of computations that the planners had to carry out is a practical one, not one of principle. During the 1950s and later considerable progress was made which could have been expected to facilitate the handling of these difficulties. On the one hand, input-output analysis was developed, which provided the planners with a powerful tool for coping with the complicated interrelations between different industries, characteristic of a modern economy. The development of linear programming, which is based on input-output analysis, had started as early as the 1930s with the Soviet economist, Leonid Kantorovich. This technique can also be used to solve the efficiency problem, (i.e., to construct an *optimal* plan). Also *cybernetics*, the science of self-regulating systems, became part of the tool box of the planners from the late 1950s. This should have solved the problem of deficient feedback during the implementation of plans.

The development of computers that began in the 1950s vastly improved the possibility of utilizing the input-output technique in practice. The planned economies were relatively late starters, however, as far as developing computation techniques was concerned and never managed to catch up with the Western world. Practice also demonstrated that the more sophisticated techniques were not the solution to the problems of a planned economy. The models were still too large despite attempts to split them into different 'levels', which were then linked together. Even the most elementary functions of a market economy required an enormous effort in a planned economy. The models were also unrealistic in the sense that many of them presupposed that the decision-makers had a clear target function. Moreover, many of the problems of the planned economy were such that it was unlikely that improved information and better techniques would be able to solve them. Even in the best of cases the planning bureaucracy used up enormous resources for tasks that the market system could handle at no cost.

Reforms of the price system

Lange's ideas became the theoretical base for several attempts at reforming the socialist planning system. The weaknesses in a system lacking scarcity-based prices gradually became clear and from the late 1950s, especially during the period 1960–67, several attempts at reforming the price system were made. A common trait of the reforms was also the insight that the centralized system had to be changed towards increasing decentralization. Given this, the market entered the picture in three different ways. First, it should be used to verify decisions of the planners and to correct erroneous decisions. Second, the market provides firms with response from the consumers. Third, the market would improve the efficiency of the firms, which was considered the weakest point in the whole planning system. (This is because of incentive problems, which we will return to later in this chapter.) There were great differences in the proposed reforms. Some proponents of reform thought that the system could be improved by changing the incentive system at the micro level. Other, more radical, proposals started from the belief that planning should be limited to the macro level while markets should be utilized at the micro level, where the planning problems had been most obvious. Yugoslavia (which all the time had subscribed to a more decentralized system), Czechoslovakia and Hungary pursued the most far-reaching reforms along these lines. In the other countries the changes remained minimal in practice, although limited reforms were carried out. The most important one was that a price was introduced on the use of capital and that a system with wholesale trade of inputs was introduced. The problem was, however, once again that the reforms of the price system remained half-hearted. With the exception of Yugoslavia, the prices in the East European countries never came to constitute reliable signals of relative scarcity.

The planning routine

The theoretical ideal in a planned economy is that there exists a single body that is both perfectly informed and capable of handling the enormous quantities of information and, based on that information, able to make a nearly infinite number of optimal decisions. In practice this is impossible, however, and some form of delegation and decentralization of the decision processes is necessary. In the Soviet system the planning apparatus formed an enormous pyramid where the executive units, the enterprises, were situated at the base and were supervised by a middle level controlled by different ministries or, in some cases, by local party divisions. Some strategic industries, such as the space and nuclear arms programmes, were controlled directly by the central government.

In the Soviet Union the planning was organized according to three principles, which were partly overlapping: the functional, the sectoral and the territorial. The sectoral principle was the dominant one until 1957. Each ministry then administered a certain industrial sector. Within the ministries the *functional* principle prevailed, however. Different departments organized the allocation of raw materials, labour, energy, and so on. When the economy became more complicated and more and more difficult coordination problems began to emerge, the number of ministries grew. At the same time the tendencies towards 'empire building' increased. Every ministry built its production systems as autonomously as possible, in order to be independent of uncertain deliveries from firms controlled by other ministries. Enormous waste, especially of transport and industrial by-products, was the inevitable consequence. At the same time the regional dimension was neglected.

As part of a reform in 1957 an attempt was made to solve the problems just described. The criterion of decentralization adopted was the *regional* (territorial) principle. A large number of ministries was closed down and, simultaneously, an even larger number of administrative regions was created. The implementation of this system was half-hearted, however, and it worked even worse than the old order. 'Empire building' continued, but was now regionally-based instead of ministry-based. Soon the system reverted to a mainly sector-based structure.

Two main types of plan are often distinguished, known as *perspective plans* and *operative plans*. The former are results of calculations based on given quantitative information and subject to a number of restrictions. The plan is not normative in the sense that it would set targets and provide assignments for different authorities. It is rather a forecast of the likely (and desirable) development of the economy. The time frame for such a plan was usually long, often 15–20 years. The *operative* plans were, in turn, normative. They often expressed concrete targets for sectors, industries and enterprises. Perspective plans were made by special departments within the public service, while the operative plans encompassed the whole planning pyramid, starting from the firms at the base and going all the way up to the central planning authority.

The ideal planning system was supposed to function through feedback to 'higher' organs, so that the macroeconomic aggregates gradually are broken up until the enterprise level is reached. The planning process starts with a statistical compilation of the actual results for the preceding year and the general targets for the current one. This information is used to compile a set of preliminary indicative figures, which are passed on down the pyramid, all the way to the firm level. The firms then have a rough idea of their production targets and can calculate their input needs. This information is passed upwards in the pyramid and undergoes modifications on the way in order to guarantee overall consistency. Finally, all elements are put together into a national plan. Monetary factors, such as prices, wages and credits, are planned separately but they are of secondary importance as compared to the 'real' plan. They are used primarily to calculate the central elements of the national accounts, (i.e., the value of production, income and expenditure).

The incentive problem

A central problem in a planned economy is the question of *incentives*; this problem is built into the system and would remain even if it were possible to eliminate the information problems and cope with the gigantic work necessary to handle the information. Managers have an incentive to meet the planning targets, otherwise they take the risk of being punished or replaced, in which case they lose the material and prestige-related perks that are part of a leading position. For the managers to be able to reach their targets it is important to have good relations with the planning bureaucracy. These relations can be used to influence the targets or to facilitate obtaining accurate quantities of inputs at the appropriate time, which otherwise tends to be a problem. Outright cheating in the reporting of output volumes was not unusual in the socialist planned economy. This rendered the work of the planners more difficult, as the information they based their calculations on was distorted by embellished reporting. A low production target was in the interest of the firm. It also had an interest in exaggerating its need for inputs, in order to be sure to get enough. This made the target easier to reach and provided a safety margin for unexpected disturbances. The planners, on their part, were pressed by the politicians to set high production targets and reduce the supply of inputs. This constellation made it important for the firms to invest in good relations to the authorities (so-called directly unproductive profit-seeking, or DUP, activities; see Chapter 11) and these activities tended to use a good deal of resources. Outright corruption was not unusual. The authorities, in turn, needed control systems to prevent the firms from cheating. Superior authorities therefore tended to interfere in the administration of enterprises. Instead of goods and services demanded by the citizens, the system produced interest-promoting activities, plans and control systems.

The efficiency of the firm is uninteresting, however. It cannot go bankrupt since it is subject to a 'soft' budget restriction. This means that the owner, the state, always provides the funding required for the firm to be able to continue production. The ideological thesis was that the work intensity would increase when the economy was liberated from the capitalist yoke. If the enthusiasm during the first years of the Soviet Union is disregarded, reality was different, however. This was true at all levels in the firms. The managers had nothing to gain personally from efficient production and their power to make necessary decisions was limited in any case. The important thing was to convey a favourable impression to superiors in the decision hierarchy and to reach the production targets. The workers, in turn, had a secure job and, as individuals, had no incentive to work efficiently. It was not worth their while to exceed the production targets either, even if this could increase income in the short run because of bonuses, and even if exceeding the targets was often encouraged by the politicians. The reason was that current production quantities were used as a starting point for deciding the targets for future periods. The best strategy was to be a free rider on the work of other people, if possible, since the targets were set for the collective as a whole, not for single individuals. Moreover, tools and raw materials belonged to the state and thus did not have a 'real' owner. Hence the incentives were strong, both for management and workers, to steal state property and sell it on the black market.

The quality of products also suffers in a centrally planned system because quality standards are difficult to incorporate into the quantitative production targets and because the consumers do not have alternatives. Campaigns for higher quality – which were not unusual – seem to have had little effect. The search for new technology and new products was often more intensive in the state bureaucracy and the state-owned research institutes than in the enterprises. The result was that relevant know-how never reached the firm level. A more fundamental problem, however, was that product development and innovation were not attractive to the firms. Even if they had wanted to achieve high quality standards it was difficult to do so, since they could not necessarily obtain raw material of appropriate quality. Thus they had to choose between not reaching their production target and producing low-quality products. Innovations, in turn, were risky and often caused disturbances to the normal activities of the firm. A failure could prevent a firm reaching its production target. If the innovation was successful it could certainly result in an extra bonus in the short run, but in the longer run it led to an increase in the planning target.

The input problem

The possibilities for firms to function as planned depend on the availability of production resources of the right quantity and quality at the right time. Labour and real capital is not a problem (at least not as far as the quantities are concerned) since these factors are allocated directly to the firms. As already mentioned, inputs are difficult to allocate correctly, however, because in general they can be used in many firms and industries. There may also be difficulties in obtaining the right quality or type of input. This is the case especially as the suppliers have an incentive to tinker with the quality in order to achieve their own production targets easier. For similar reasons the suppliers try to produce as few varieties of their products as possible. Finally it is important to have the inputs delivered at the right time. Even in the most sophisticated planned economy the choice of delivery time has to be left to the single firm to decide. For the receiver it is of great significance, however, whether the delivery is made at the beginning or at the end of the planning period.

The core of the problem is the lack of alternative suppliers. This means that if the supplier of a certain component cannot meet the production target firms further down the value added chain cannot fulfil their quotas either. Problems in one part of the economy thus tend to cause chain reactions.

In order to avoid difficulties with the deliveries of inputs the firms tend to hedge in ways that reduce the efficiency of the economy. One way is to avoid external deliveries and produce as much as possible of the inputs yourself. This usually implies small-scale and inefficient production. Another way is to keep excessive stocks of inputs. This is attractive especially because keeping stock is 'free' (as there is no rate of interest). For society this implies, however, that large resources are tied up in unproductive stocks. Moreover, the products are sometimes destroyed by being stockpiled for too long. This is the case particularly for foodstuffs, but many other products fare badly from being stocked as well. The distorted incentives affect the use of energy too. The manufacturing industry in the planned economies was, on average, twice as energy- and raw-material-intensive as the industry in the West.

Large stocks may lead to a situation where *barter trade* between firms becomes interesting. This trade between firms tends to be awkward and inefficient, however. If you have an excess supply of a certain product you have to find another firm that needs that very product and, at the same time, has something you need to offer in return. In practice, problems of this type lead to the emergence of unofficial, more or less illegal entrepreneurs who specialized in organizing barter deals. The authorities tolerated these activities because they increased the efficiency of the economy. The risk of corruption was obvious, however, since the authorities had to be 'greased' to turn a blind eye.

General scarcity of goods

As we have seen already, prices lack a signal value in the planned economy. Not only the *relative* prices may be distorted, however. The *absolute* price level was also too low compared to the purchasing power of the consumers. (In the Soviet Union the absence of inflation was often emphasized, even if this was a truth with modifications.) The wages were allowed to rise while the product prices were kept unchanged. The inevitable consequence was scarcity of goods, queues and rationing. It was usual for a household to have to spend several hours a day queuing and looking for the product it wanted in several shops. Furthermore, the buying pattern was affected, since the consumers bought the products that were available, as a precaution, even if they had really planned to buy something else; this phenomenon has been named *forced substitution*. Often there was no alternative other than postponing the purchase. The savings rate was high as a consequence, but it was hard to find meaningful savings objects. The better the authorities managed to keep inflation in check the higher was the savings rate. This did not mean that there was not excessive production of some other product in spite of the fact that consumers were buying more of it than they had planned because of the lack of alternatives.

Scarcity of goods almost inevitably leads to black markets (cf., Chapter 7) and other abuse. Goods disappear from the shelves (the shop assistants buy them or steal them) and are sold at a higher price, with the thieves pocketing the profit. The service in shops tends to be slow and indifferent. There is a shift of power from the consumer to the seller. Moreover, the scarcity of goods reduces the work incentives for employees, since a higher wage does not lead to a higher level of welfare. The workers reduce their efforts both quantitatively and qualitatively. A vicious circle emerges: the scarcity of goods diminishes the work incentives, which adds to the scarcity, and so on.

Overemphasizing the production of goods

According to Marx and his successors only production of goods counted as a productive activity; services did not create any value according to this view. The service sector remained very underdeveloped in all centrally planned economies and its share of total production was much lower than in market economies at the corresponding level of income. At the end of the 1970s the relative share of the service sector in the Soviet Union was only 20 per cent while the 'expected' value (calculated with the aid of a cross-section regression) for an economy at that income level was 56 per cent. Since no scarcity prices existed there were no incentive for investing more in service production. Services such as transport and communication, repairs, banking and insurance are crucial, however, for producing goods efficiently.

Heavy industry, like the base metal industry and the chemical industry as well as energy production, was particularly emphasized. Another priority was the arms industry. A reason for emphasizing heavy industry was that the relatively large industrial sector created a great demand for inputs, not least because the inputs were used inefficiently. This was the case for investments, too, which did not have to pass any profitability test. When the production of inputs was increased to overcome the scarcity, industrial production increased even more, which again increased the demand for capital goods and intermediate goods. A vicious circle thus emerged. The heavy and extractive industries were also those most suitable for a planned economy since the products are homogeneous and relatively simple and production is usually subject to large economies of scale.

The thesis of the superiority of the socialist system also put strong pressure on the decision-makers to achieve results. This implied that the production of investment and intermediate goods was given priority. The arms industry, in turn, reflected the reverse side of the alleged superiority, the feeling of being threatened by international capitalism. The emphasis on heavy industry laid the foundations for a high growth rate in the early phase of the industrialization process but neglected the needs of the consumers, ignored the environmental consequences almost completely and resulted in a lack of efficiency in the economy at large.

The large share of industry can also be explained without the ideological point of view, however. An important reason is probably the import-substitution policy pursued in the Soviet Union, which led to an overexpansion of the production of, above all, intermediate products. This prevented specialization according to comparative advantage, which was a problem especially in the smaller planned economies. Another reason was the so-called do-it-yourself syndrome at the micro level. Firms preferred to make themselves independent of uncertain deliveries of inputs by producing as much as possible of these products themselves.

The production units in the planned economies were rather large on average, but the firms were very diversified and the production series for single products were short. One reason for the large average size was that a few big firms facilitate the planning process. Another reason is the one we mentioned before: the perceived need to produce as much as possible instead of subcontracting from other firms. Moreover, distorted prices and 'soft' budget constraints give unclear and erroneous signals about the optimal production capacity. Most products could be sold and capital equipment was free, at least before the reforms of the 1960s. In case of serious difficulties the firms could always rely on being rescued by the soft budget constraint. The system worked reasonably well as long as the issue was that of producing large quantities of a few standardized products. However, even then it can be expected that the unit cost will start to rise after a certain limit, but it is hard to tell where exactly this limit is, however, since the optimal size varies across different industries and different points of time.

Foreign trade

As we have already mentioned, socialist ideology took for granted – not entirely without reason – that socialism is surrounded by enemies trying to destroy it. Therefore the socialist planned economies strove to be as self-sufficient as possible, within the realm of their organization for economic cooperation, known as the Council for Mutual Economic Assistance (CMEA) or COMECON. Trade with the market economies could not be completely avoided, however (even if the volumes were rather small). Foreign trade was a strict state monopoly, handled through special export and import companies. Hence contacts between the foreign customers and the producing firms were indirect. The situation on the import side was similar, too. It was mainly the need for imports (such as foodstuffs, luxury goods and technically advanced products) which determined export volumes as imports, by and large, had to be paid for in convertible currency. The firms did not have any incentives to attempt to export more than the plan called for. Such behaviour would have increased the planning target for the next period and the quantities that could be exported were much more difficult to predict than domestic sales.

There were other circumstances, too, which made exploitation of potential profits from foreign trade difficult. One problem, already touched upon, was that the quality of the goods produced in the planned economies was low, which made them hard to sell in the West. It was certainly possible to obtain an acceptable quality, but only at higher cost than for the standard product. Often imported intermediate goods were needed to reach this goal.

In practice, the exports to the West were heavily dominated by raw materials. For the firms that might have been able to sell to the West the incentives to do so were limited, however, since the firms could not retain any foreign currency they earned. The proceeds were instead channelled directly to the authorities, which compensated the firms with domestic currency at a rate of exchange that did not encourage exports before sales to the domestic market. Thus the firm was not compensated for being compelled to improve quality and there was no import competition, which would have forced them to do so. Hence there were, by and large, no real economic incentives for exporting. (Foreign trade may still have been attractive for other reasons, however, such as the chances for overseas trips it may have given.)

A more fundamental problem is that the logical basis for foreign trade, comparative advantage, may not be reflected in the trading pattern of the planned economies. Since the prices do not reflect the opportunity cost of different products it is perfectly possible that goods for which the country has a comparative advantage are imported, and vice versa. Foreign trade then causes a social welfare loss instead of a gain. As we have seen already, the East European planned economies had problems with their exports of manufactured goods despite the fact that the share of manufacturing in GDP was much larger than in the market economies. Since exports of these products still took place it has often been suspected that there was a systematic bias in favour of capital-intensive goods, because the capital costs were ignored or underestimated in the planned economies. The products then seem cheaper than they are in reality. Some recent research seems to suggest, however, that the lack of prices with a signal value tended to result in a wide spread of factor intensities of export goods. This was the case particularly in the smaller economies, which were less resource-abundant than the Soviet Union.

The trade between the planned economies, most of which was organized by the CMEA, was intended to take advantage of potential specialization possibilities between the member countries. A consistent application of the basic idea of a planned economy would have implied that an additional, supranational, level should have been imposed on top of the national planning hierarchies. This idea was never fully implemented, however, due to its implications for the sovereignty of the member countries. The thought of an international division of labour between the countries remained a paper construction.

The trade within the CMEA did not work very satisfactorily although the member countries had the same economic system and in spite of the fact that the trade volumes were relatively large as compared to those with the capitalist countries. One reason was that the countries, by and large, had the same range of products to offer, and they all suffered from the quality problems we discussed earlier. Another reason was that the system presupposed that the trade for each pair of countries would balance. An export deficit in the trade with one country thus could not be compensated by a surplus in the trade with another one. The reason for this was that the currencies of the planned economies were not convertible. The only way to handle this situation was to decrease imports in the former case and exports in the latter case. The total volume of trade decreased due to the required bilateral balance of the foreign trade. In order to escape the problem of bilateral balance the so-called transferable rouble, a calculation unit, was introduced as a clearing instrument. This system did not work as planned either, however, since the prices in the internal trade within CMEA differed from the world market prices.

A model analysis

We will now interpret the world of the planned economy in terms of our model. The simple model cannot capture all problems related to planning. The complicated input-output problems are rather incompletely illuminated but the model still gives a good idea of some of the typical problems. As before, the model can be formulated in terms of two graphs as shown in Figure 9.1.

At world market prices, p_V, the economy would, as before, produce at point A and consume at point C. These points will not be reached in a planned economy, however. For one thing, the planning process itself uses resources that cannot simultaneously be used for producing goods. The planning also implies that resources are wasted, which shifts the production possibility curve inwards even more. The economy thus produces inside the efficient production possibility curve, at a point such as B. Moreover, it is unlikely that the relative prices, determined by the planners, will coincide with the world market prices. Since there is, in principle, no rate of interest the relative price of the capital-intensive manufactures will be lower than the world market price. Since manufacturing is the favoured sector the allocation of capital to that sector takes place at more favourable terms than the allocation of capital to agriculture. The domestic price line, p_H, cuts the new production possibility curve (not shown), and its slope is less steep than that of the curve at B. The nominal income is allowed to rise above the nominal value of production. Hence the consumers would like to consume at point D. This is not possible, however, given domestic production. Instead, we end up with an excess demand of KI for agricultural goods and LH for manufactures at prevailing prices.

In a market economy the difference between desired consumption and desired production would be imported (and the economy would draw on its foreign exchange reserves or incur a foreign debt), but this would not happen automatically in a planned economy. How extensive foreign trade is allowed to be is also centrally determined. The rest of the world is, however, likely to insist on applying world market prices in international trade, while domestic consumption takes place at p_H. The planned economy

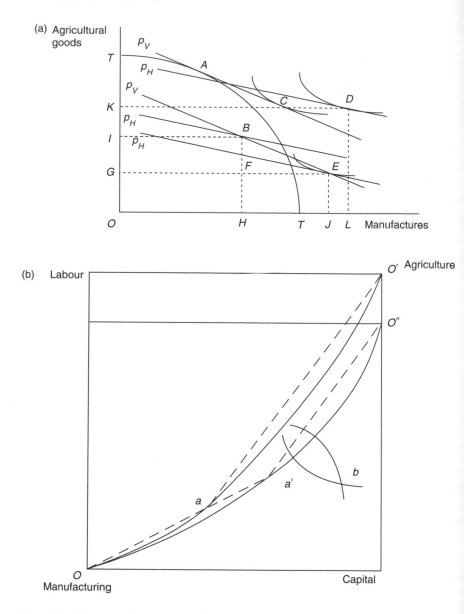

Figure 9.1 Resource allocation in a planned economy

can then exchange, say, $IG = BF$ agricultural products for $FE = HJ$ manufactures. The scarcity of manufactures then decreases to LJ while the scarcity of agricultural goods increases to KG. The world market price line passing through B is closer to the origin than the one passing through A and represents an unambiguously lower real income. E must be on a lower indifference curve than C and is thus inferior from a welfare point of view.

In a market economy with perfect competition the factors of production would be allocated between agricultural and industrial production at a point such as a in the box diagram, Figure 9.1b. We have already seen, however, that the same production volume as in a market economy is not possible in a planned economy, since the planning process itself uses up part of the available resources. We assume here that planning demands and wastes only labour, while all capital can be divided between the agricultural and industrial production. The availability of labour then decreases with $O'O''$ and the box shrinks vertically. According to Rybczynski's theorem the (labour-intensive) agricultural production would decrease and the (capital-intensive) industrial production would increase. We would end up at point a' in the box diagram (the corresponding point in the graph with the production possibility curve is not shown) where the factor intensities of the two sectors would be the same as at point a. In a planned economy it is, of course, unlikely that point a' can be found. This is because the problem here is to allocate labour and capital directly, without the help of the market mechanism. The most likely outcome is therefore that we end up at a point such as b (corresponding to point B in Figure 9.1a) which is located off the contract curve in the new box, where two production isoquants intersect, because the use of capital is more subsidized in manufacturing than in agriculture. This is only one example, however. An infinite number of other possibilities exist as well, but the fact that production is inefficient is common to all.

Conclusions

Against the backdrop outlined above it is clear why the planned economy fell apart as an economic system. We may distinguish between three types of reasons. First, performing the functions of markets requires substantial resources while the market system performs them at almost no cost. Second, the need for information and information processing technology are so great that they tend to be unattainable. Third, the incentives of firms and individuals alike are distorted, not least because risk taking and innovation tend to be unattractive. The system has performed best in simple, undeveloped economies with hard ideological control.

The problems of the planned economies tended to become more and more difficult over time. The more sophisticated the economy, the more difficult the information problems became and the greater were the effects of the distorted incentives. The constant scarcity of goods put pressure on increasing the production of goods while the service sector withered away. The reserves available (for instance, low-productive farmers who could be recruited by the manufacturing sector) gradually dried up. After some half-hearted attempts at reform the East European planned economies crumbled about 1990.

Literature

A concise survey on the economic history of the Soviet Union is given in:
Nove, Alec (1989), *An Economic History of the USSR*, (2nd edn). Penguin Books, Harmondsworth.

The discussion on Marx and the socialist controversy is based on, among others:
Fine, Ben (1975), *Marx's Capital*. Macmillan, London.
Kornai, János (1992), *The Socialist System. The Political Economy of Communism*. Clarendon Press, Oxford, ch. 21.
Nove, Alec (1983), *The Economics of Feasible Socialism*. George Allen & Unwin, London.

Oskar Lange's ideas on market socialism can be found in:
Lange, Oskar and Taylor, Fred M. (1964), *On the Economic Theory of Socialism*. McGraw-Hill, New York.

The ideological foundations of the superiority of socialism are described in:
Kornai, *The Socialist System*, ch. 4.

The discussion on different pricing systems and the section on pricing reforms and planning routines in the Soviet Union are based on:
Turner, R. Kerry and Collis, Clive (1977), *The Economics of Planning*. Macmillan, London.

The principles of the planning system are also described in:
Kornai, *The Socialist System*, ch. 7.

A survey of Kantorovich's contribution to developing the planning techniques is given by:
Johansen, Leif (1976), 'L. V. Kantorovich's Contribution to Economics', *Scandinavian Journal of Economics*, Vol. 78.

The incentive problem and the problem with inputs, as well as the scarcity of goods and the overemphasis on goods production have been treated as a starting point in:
Kornai, *The Socialist System*.
Winiecki, Jan (1991), *The Distorted World of Soviet-Type Economies*. Routledge, London, especially chs 3 and 4. (Winiecki discusses the various forms of inflation in a planned economy in ch. 2.)

In this context we have also used:
Kornai, János (1982), *Growth, Shortage and Efficiency*. Basil Blackwell, Oxford.
Kornai, *The Socialist System*, esp. chs 11 and 12.

The role of foreign trade in a planned economy has been described with the aid of:

van Brabant, Jozef M. (1989), *Economic Integration in Eastern Europe*. Harvester Wheat-sheaf, New York.

Kornai, *The Socialist System*, ch. 14.

Winiecki, Jan (1991), *The Distorted World of Soviet-Type Economies*. Routledge, London, ch. 5.

10
Interest Groups and Collective Action

This book has so far (with the aid of a simple model) shown, on the one hand, what an optimal situation looks like from a welfare point of view and, on the other hand, why common economic policy interventions – not least in foreign trade – often tend to reduce potential welfare. (We have also looked into situations where interventions can *increase* welfare.) Moreover, we have given examples of policy-generated distortions. In the rest of the book we will try to explain why it is so common for the state to pursue 'wrong' economic policies. When we do this we will use economic theory, not only to show in what way the policies are 'wrong' but also *why* they go wrong.

So far, we have treated the state as something of a 'black box', as an institution which intervenes in the economy for reasons that we have not really specified, except by referring to more or less non-economic arguments. As an example of this, historical factors may be mentioned, such as the effect of the Depression and the Second World War on the import-substitution policy. From a more general perspective this way of reasoning is unsatisfactory, however. Specific historical events offer only part of the explanation of why a given government at a given moment chooses to formulate one particular policy instead of another.

If we want to reach a higher level of generalization other types of explanations are called for. The remaining chapters will concentrate on methods for achieving such a generalization. A central feature of the argument is the view of the state as a representative of the special interest of various groups or as a moderator between different groups. In opposition to traditional theory, the behaviour of the state and the interest organizations is endogenously determined by the model.

In several of the preceding chapters it became clear that the activities of the public sector are not necessarily determined by a concern for the welfare of the general public, but can be influenced by various special interests which try to make the state act in a way that is favourable to them. In extreme cases the state (or, rather, the groups that act in the name of the state) is a special interest group itself, (an issue we will return to in Chapter 12). The influence of pressure groups is channelled through various organizations and institutions including the state, whose behaviour can be seen both as a consequence of the activities of these groups and as a reason for them. In this chapter we will look into some theoretical approaches to the behaviour of interest groups. The leading name in this field is Mancur Olson.

Olson's ideas are closely related to the so-called *public choice* school or the *new political economy*, which studies the principles of public decision making, and *institutional economics*, which analyses economic development and how it is related to the development of social *institutions* (i.e., 'the rules of the game' of society). In Olson's work a theory is deduced for the behaviour of interest groups trying to bring about production of a public good useful for the group, and the implications of this behaviour are followed up in different cases. A common characteristic of these research programmes is that they analyse the behaviour of organizations and politicians with the neoclassical principle of utility maximization as their starting point.

To begin with, however, we will see how a pressure group (i.e., a 'lobby' that already exists) determines its optimal behaviour. After that we will consider the preconditions for forming a successful lobby in the first place and, if this is the case, how the lobby manages to look after its interests through interaction with the state.

The behaviour of lobbies

Olson's starting point is that individuals often act through different types of organizations in order to promote their interests. People with a common interest join in different organizations: trade unions, industrial associations, cartels, companies, and so on. Trade unions press for higher wages and better conditions of work for their members, branch organizations try to make legislation favourable for themselves and cartels endeavour to increase the prices that can be charged for the products of its members. All this is well known. The interesting thing here is the consequences for the behaviour of the state and the economic consequences that result. Let us consider tariff protection as an example of this general problem.

It is fairly easy to say something in general about which groups in society are for tariff protection and which groups are against. The import-competing industries are often protectionist and so are the trade unions active in these industries. Consequently the industry and the trade unions tend to cooperate in order to secure tariffs or other trade barriers. They both usually have a great deal to gain from protection, and the gains are immediate and easy to measure. Trade barriers can, furthermore, be defended because they 'save jobs'. The efficiency loss incurred by the economy is much more difficult to concretize; it is often small in per capita terms and is likely to go unnoticed by most citizens.

The exporting industries are losers, as far as tariffs are concerned, and thus tend to be opposed to them. First, they may be hit by retaliation from other countries, which may increase their own protective barriers. Second, imported inputs become more expensive while the prices of the final products cannot be increased. Third, resources are competed away from the export industries to the import-competing industry.

Consumers usually stand to lose from trade barriers as well. They seldom resist them, however, perhaps because most consumers are also employees and thus may have conflicting interests. As we will see later, they also have difficulties organizing a pressure group. Finally, the benefits from free trade are hard to identify.

The behaviour of lobby groups may be discussed in terms of a 'political market'. Take, for instance, the case of tariff protection. On the demand side we then have interest groups benefiting from protection, and on the supply side the political parties, single politicians and government bureaucrats. The lobby invests real resources – money and time – to persuade the politicians to provide the desired protection. (Since these activities do not create any new resources but, on the contrary, use resources they have been called 'directly unproductive'. We will return to this issue in next chapter.) The politicians, in turn, use the campaign contributions from the lobbies for their efforts to win elections. The question for them is then how much tariff protection it would be worthwhile to promise considering the fact that some voters are opposed to protection. Below, we are going to see how a lobby can decide on the optimal level of its campaign contributions and how a political party chooses what level of protection it wants to go for.

The demand for tariff protection

Assume that the political parties strive to maximize the number of votes in their favour. Assume also, for simplicity, that the only issue of the election is the level of the import tariff. The party that is for protectionism receives contributions for its election campaign from a lobby gaining from tariffs. How the lobby can decide how much it would be worth paying is shown in Figure 10.1.

We assume that the only cost for the lobby is the monetary contribution to the protectionist party. (This can be done since the cost of organizing the lobby can be regarded as fixed and thus does not affect the behaviour of the lobby.) The cost function then is linear and forms a 45-degree angle with both axes. The curve, B, the expected utility of lobbying, has been drawn for a given tariff level, the one that the party has promised to introduce if it assumes power after the election. According to the figure, lobbying has diminishing marginal utility. The curve still has a positive slope because larger contributions to the protectionist party increase the probability that the party will win the elections and introduce the tariff corresponding to B.

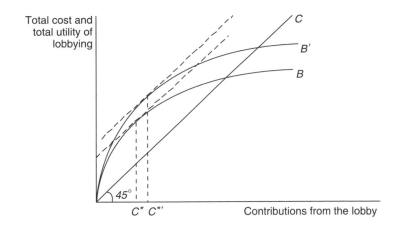

Figure 10.1   Optimal lobbying

It is now easy to see that the optimal contribution is C^*, since this level maximizes the difference between benefits and costs. If the protectionist party decides on a higher tariff rate the curve shifts upwards, say, to B'. The sum that it is worth paying as a campaign contribution rises as well, to $C^{*'}$.

The figure also demonstrates that lobbying for tariff protection is not always worthwhile. If the prospective level of protection is too low (i.e., if the slope of the utility curve never exceeds 45 degrees) lobbying will be meaningless.

The supply of tariff protection

Tariff protection is supplied by politicians and government bureaucrats. The former wish to be re-elected and thus try to make themselves popular. One way to do this is by trying to satisfy the often vocal demands for trade barriers, especially since those who lose as a result of protectionism tend to be unaware of this, or at least relatively uncommitted compared to the tariff lobby.

The civil servants, in turn, easily tend to identify with the sectoral matters they are in charge of. This gives them prestige and influence in their 'own' industry. The bureaucrats may thus function as an extension of the lobby within the civil service and are in a position to behave in a way that furthers the interests of the lobby, even if they cannot decide on legislation directly. (Imports may be obstructed through bureaucratic procedures, 'safety standards' for products, and so on.)

How then, can, a political unit (such as a political party or a government) determine how much protection it would be worthwhile to offer? Let us take a look at the behaviour of the protectionist party. The contributions of the lobby have two different effects. On the one hand, the party gains votes

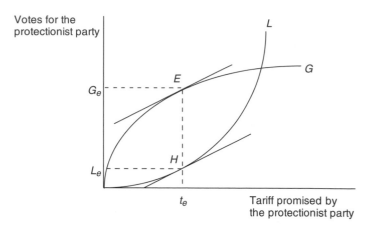

Figure 10.2   The optimal tariff from the point of view of the protectionist party

because the contributions add to the effectiveness of the election campaign (the 'contribution effect'). On the other hand, it loses votes because some voters realize that the party is going to favour the lobby by increasing tariffs (the 'distortion effect'). If we assume that the aim of the party is to maximize the number of votes in its favour, the argument can be illustrated by Figure 10.2.

The L curve shows the loss of votes at each tariff level: higher tariffs lead to larger distortions and fewer votes. The G curve, in turn, shows the votes gained at each tariff level. The curve has a positive but decreasing slope since successively higher tariff barriers attract fewer and fewer additional votes. The campaign contributions display diminishing returns. The optimal tariff level is t_e, where the number of votes is maximized. At this level the marginal contribution effect is equal to the marginal distortion effect.

We now know a lobby's logic of reasoning and how governments and parties react to the activities of pressure groups. We can then demonstrate how the tariff level can be determined endogenously in an economic system where the citizens can influence the behaviour of the government.

Endogenous tariffs

We will shortly return to the costs incurred by the activities of the interest groups but before that we will give an example of endogenous tariffs in a trade policy context. The preceding discussion showed how a lobby can determine its optimal input of resources to obtain, for instance, tariff protection. This setting was oversimplified in the sense that it did not take into account the countervailing actions of a possible anti-tariff lobby. We will discuss how the effort by the two competing lobbies can be determined. As an analytical device we use Figure 10.3.

Assume that there is a farmer lobby wanting import tariffs on agricultural goods in order to increase the income of the farmers, and a manufacturing lobby which wants to keep the tariffs down because tariffs increase the prices of agricultural goods. This leads to intensified competition for labour and, consequently, to increasing wages in manufacturing. Assume, furthermore, that the final tariff level is determined by the amount of resources used by the two lobbies:

$$T = T(R_J, R_I) \quad T_{R_J} > 0, T_{R_I} < 0 \tag{10.1}$$

The broken lines in the diagram show what combinations of resource inputs by the two pressure groups produce the same level of protection. If we choose an arbitrary point on one of the broken lines and let the efforts of the farmer lobby increase, the manufacturing lobby has to increase its lobbying effort as well just to keep the level of protection unchanged. At a given level of farmer lobbying, the level of protection will be lower the more pressure there is from the manufacturing lobby. The tariff level thus decreases as we move upwards in the diagram. Similarly, it can be shown that the tariff level increases when we move to the right.

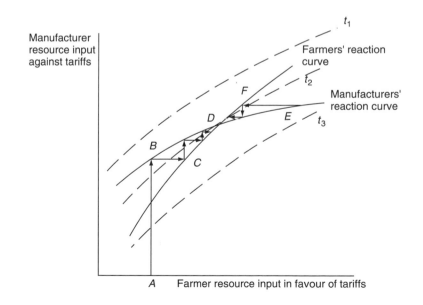

Figure 10.3 The tariff-seeking process

Hence we have:

$$t_3 > t_2 > t_1$$

The two bold lines in the diagram are the *reaction curves* of agriculture and manufacturing, respectively. The former shows how the farmers react to different given resource inputs on the part of the manufacturing lobby while, correspondingly, the other shows how the manufacturing lobbying effort varies for different values of R_f. Both curves have a positive slope, implying that both parties increase their effort when their opponent does so.

Moreover, the farmers' line has a steeper slope than the tariff lines. This means that when manufacturing increases its lobbying efforts the farmers follow suit, but not to the extent that the original tariff level can be preserved. The slope of the manufacturing curve, on the other hand, is less steep than the tariff line. In other words, we assume that when farmer lobbying increases, the efforts of the manufacturing lobby will increase as well, but not enough to take us back to the original tariff level.

The equilibrium level is given by the intersection of the two reaction curves. Let us start at an arbitrary point, say A, with a given resource input by the farmers. Manufacturing will react to this with an input corresponding to B, but then the farmers, in their turn, react with an increase of their resource input, leading to C, and so on, until equilibrium is reached at point D. This is a stable equilibrium since no party wants to change its resource input at that point. We could also start at point E, on the reaction curve of manufacturing, and proceed to the equilibrium point from the northeast.

For the process to converge to D the reaction curve of the tariff proponents (farmers) must be steeper than the one of the opponents (industrialists). A given increase of farmer efforts to increase tariffs is met with weaker and weaker resistance, at the margin, on the part of the manufacturers, while a given increase of the efforts of manufacturers leads to successively stronger pressure, at the margin, from the farmers. The latter sector is thus more interested in increasing protection than the former sector is in reducing it.

When can lobbies be formed?

In this chapter we have so far assumed that the interest groups are homogeneous and that they have a given objective they try to achieve, using some kind of optimizing behaviour. The is an oversimplification, however. The interest groups are often heterogeneous (i.e., there may be conflicts of interest between the members). If these conflicts grow strong enough it is not possible to form an interest group. Even if that can be done the groups may differ in strength and, hence, have different leverage with regard to promoting the interest of their members.

In Mancur Olson's basic theory of interest groups, two fundamental questions are posed:

1 What determines whether a certain group can organize a lobby or not?
2 If organized, is the lobby able to promote its interests to an extent that is optimal for the group?

Every group consists of individuals, and in order to satisfy the interest of the group the *individuals* must act. The interests relevant here are public goods for the group. The members may, for example, operate firms in the same industry and stand to benefit if the state subsidizes the industry. Thus they have a common interest in subsidies.

The activities of interest organizations may run into difficulties, however, especially in large organizations with many members. The question is therefore whether the entrepreneurs are ready to use their time and money to achieve their goal: the subsidy. This is far from certain. Since the subsidy is a public good there is a 'free-rider' problem. All members share the benefits but it is often difficult to force everybody to share in the cost. Consequently, everyone tends to expect 'the others' to do the job.

Olson takes two illuminating examples. The first one focuses on firms in a perfectly competitive industry (i.e., an industry where the number of firms is large, by definition). In such an industry the incentives for the individual firm are very small when it comes to putting pressure on the government in order to secure support. This is because the firm would have to bear all the costs alone, while the benefits are reaped by all members of the industry. The incentives to form a lobby are therefore weak and, consequently, the industry has problems getting its message through to the government.

The other example presented by Olson is the largest of all organizations: the state. No state would be able to survive on voluntary contributions from its citizens, despite the fact that the state provides many services that they want to take advantage of. The citizens must be forced to pay (i.e., they have to be taxed).

In both cases the problem is that the services or 'products' provided are of the public good type: that is, the fact that one group member uses the service does not preclude others from using it as well. Moreover, it is usually impossible to charge people for using the service, so 'free riders' cannot be excluded. In order to do this there must be some sanctions or incentives which make it possible to identify the individual members of a group. It is often difficult (e.g., in the case of trade barriers) to see how this could be done if the favoured groups are large.

It is not only large groups that face this problem, however, even if the issue is more clear-cut in that case. As soon as a group has a common interest in the production of a public good the problem is how the production could be organized. Are there any incentives for such production?

Small groups and collective goods

Assume that an individual considers using time for making a certain public good available for 'his' group (take, for example, an entrepreneur in an industry that wants tariff protection to secure a higher price for its products). The total cost of the individual for doing this, C, depends on the 'level', T, of the public good aimed at (i.e., how high the tariff barrier should be):

$$C = C(T) \tag{10.2}$$

What value, V_g, does the utility represent for the group as a whole? If the 'size' of the group is S_g, we have

$$V_g = S_g T \tag{10.3}$$

Note that the 'size' of the group does not necessarily refer to the number of individuals; it also depends on the value of the public good for each individual, measured by their sales volume, for example. (S_g could then be the total number of product units sold by the industry.)

The value of the public good for the *individual* is thus

$$V_i = F_i V_g \tag{10.4}$$

where $F_i < 1$ is the share of the individual in the value of the utility for the group. We can then write

$$V_i = F_i S_g T \tag{10.5}$$

The net utility of the individual, A_i, is given by

$$A_i = V_i - C \tag{10.6}$$

that is, the value of the utility minus costs incurred to produce it. The net utility is maximized when

$$\frac{dV_i}{dT} = \frac{dC}{dT} \tag{10.7}$$

that is, when the value and cost of the utility are equal at the margin.

Assume now that F_i and S_g, the individual's share of the utility and the size of the group, are given and constant (this is denoted with barred symbols below). Using (10.4), we obtain

$$\frac{dV_i}{dT} = \bar{F}_i \frac{dV_g}{dT} \tag{10.8}$$

so that

$$\bar{F}_i \frac{dV_g}{dT} = \frac{dC}{dT} \qquad (10.9)$$

Equation (10.9) thus expresses the optimum as the point where the increase in value for the individual (equal to the increase in value for the group multiplied by the share of the individual) is equal to the marginal cost for producing the utility. This is illustrated graphically by Figure 10.4.

In the figure, the cost curve is increasing. This is based on the plausible, and traditional, assumption that the marginal cost for producing the good rises when the volume increases. The curve denoting the value of the good for the individual, V_i, is a straight line. (This follows directly from (10.5) and the assumption that F_i and S_g are constant.) The optimal level of production, from the individual's point of view, is the point where the marginal cost and value for the individual are equal: that is, where the slopes of the two curves are equal.

We now know the optimal level of the public good for the individual. The question then is whether it pays for the individual to make any effort at all for the good to be provided. For this to be the case, not only the marginal value and marginal cost for the individual have to be equal, but the *total* value of the utility must exceed the *total* cost incurred:

$$V_i = \bar{F}_i \bar{S}_g T > C \qquad (10.10)$$

This means that the C *curve cannot lie above the* V_i *curve throughout*. This implies, in turn, that groups with many members may have problems bringing about provision of public goods. The larger the number of members is the

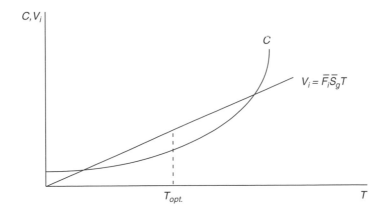

Figure 10.4   The optimal level of a collective good

more individuals have to share the total utility, V_g. The average, F_i, is then small, the V_i curve in Figure 10.4 is relatively flat and the individuals have weak incentives, on average, to be involved in working for the good to be produced.

The same model can be used to show that public goods usually are supplied in suboptimal (i.e., too small) quantities for the group, taken as a whole. Consider the situation depicted in Figure 10.5.

The value for the group is given by $V_g = \bar{S}_g T$ where $\bar{S}_g$ is a constant, while the value for the individual is given by $V_i = \bar{F}_i \bar{S}_g T$ where $\bar{F}_i < 1$. The slope of the V_g curve exceeds the slope of the V_i curve. The optimum for the group can thus be found to the right of the optimum for the individual. The smaller the share of the total value that accrues to the individual, the more the two optimum positions differ. This implies that large groups have more difficulties than small groups in securing the 'correct' production level of the public good.

There is also an obvious tendency for individuals with a smaller share of the total value (lower F_i) to 'exploit' those who have a higher share. This can be done since the latter have a stronger incentive to engage themselves in trying to bring about production of the good. Their optimum T is higher. If this T is achieved, the individuals with smaller F_i values obtain more than they would have been willing to secure themselves, without incurring any cost. The group members with a high F_i thus tend to bear a disproportionally large share of the cost.

Applications of the theory

According to Olson, his theory of groups and public goods has great applicability. In his book, *The Rise and Decline of Nations*, he uses the theory to

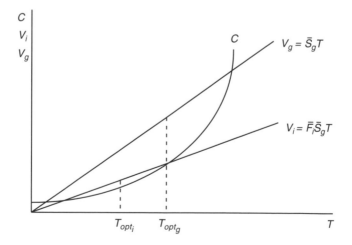

Figure 10.5 Suboptimal production of collective goods

explain why the economies of some nations grow rapidly while others tend to stagnate. He takes as his starting point the fact that during the postwar period the West German and Japanese economies grew rapidly, and the growth rate of the French economy was relatively high as well. The British economy performed poorly, however.

What could be the reason for the differences in growth rates? Olson begins by looking into a 'folkloristic' discussion as an example of the shortcomings of ad hoc explanations. According to popular belief the 'explanation' is often found in the alleged industriousness of Germans and Japanese (i.e., some kind of 'national character'), while the British – according to this line of reasoning – would value their leisure more. (In the early days of development economics similar explanations of differences in economic level were often invoked: that is, people in developing countries were allegedly uninterested in economic progress and therefore less industrious.) Other frequent explanations of the low British growth rate include the militancy and stubbornness of the trade unions, the lack of entrepreneurial spirit of the firms and the rigidity of the British social class system.

There need not be anything 'wrong' with this type of explanation: there is often a grain of truth in popular wisdom. The problem is rather that the explanations were formulated ad hoc, in such a way that they cannot be systematically tested using a large number of observations which display enough variation to make it possible to see whether they possess general validity or not. Moreover, they are often formulated in terms of concepts that are hard or impossible to operationalize.

A consequence of this problem is that ad hoc explanations are usually limited in time and space. They seldom hold in a wider perspective. An explanation of the low British growth rate in terms of strong preferences for leisure, for instance, seems to be almost impossible to maintain in a historical perspective. The British, of course, were the ones that 'invented' economic growth. The Industrial Revolution started in Britain and, from the mid-eighteenth century to the mid-nineteenth century, the growth rate in Britain was the highest (or one of the highest) in the world. Those who want to explain the sluggish postwar growth using 'national characteristics' or institutional features must then also be able to explain why these characteristics have changed over time.

We can find a similar case in the attempts to explain the high growth rates in East Asia during the last few decades with the aid of the old Chinese state philosophy, Confucianism, which emphasizes industry, thrift, respect for authority and education. The argument appears quite convincing. The only problem is that some years ago Confucianism used to be invoked as a reason for the earlier economic *stagnation* in the region. Hence, a more systematic approach is called for. The theories constructed for modelling institutions, the behaviour of organizations and the political decision process with the aid of the economic toolbox seem to have a considerable explanatory value.

Olson finds an approach in his theory of groups and public goods. Several implications follow from this theory. The most important one is the observation that efficiency will not prevail in a society with many interest groups. First of all, bargaining power is not distributed proportionally (according to group size). This follows directly from Olson's theory that 'large' groups, such as 'consumers', 'the unemployed', 'tax payers', and so on, have difficulties organizing themselves in such a way that their pressure would bring about the optimal production of the public good. The difference between the optimal level of the individual and the group is too large. The individuals have no incentive to act on their own since their share of the result is small. 'Small' groups can often do that at the expense of the social groups, which are unable to organize themselves and which therefore cannot prevent interventions that reduce their welfare. This leads Olson to formulating the following hypothesis:

1   There will be no countries that attain symmetrical organization of all groups with a common interest and thereby attain optimal outcomes through comprehensive bargaining.

Even groups which, in principle, are capable of organizing themselves for the common good need time. To induce the individuals to act it is usually not enough to give them a share in the public good. Selective incentives, 'group benefits' or coercion, which favour those who act, are needed as well. (Trade union members may, for example, obtain larger unemployment benefits than non-members, non-members may be harassed, etc.) This characteristic is stronger the larger the group is. The organization is then complicated and time consuming to create. Sometimes this can be achieved only under very favourable circumstances. In Sweden, for instance, it took several decades to create trade unions of any real significance, despite the fact that their potential benefits for members are obvious. In the case of farmers' organizations the situation was similar.

If society is stable, however, without any great disruptions or wars taking place, the possibilities of organizing increase. It can then be expected that the number of interest groups tends to increase over time, particularly as an organization, once created, tends to survive even if the public good it was once created to produce may no longer be relevant. In Japan, Germany and partly also in France the political structures were destroyed during and after the Second World War and this was also, to some extent, true for economic structures, while the UK was not at all affected by the same kind of disruptions. Organization structures and institutions developed there more gradually and continuously, without periods of strong turbulence. Olson's second thesis is therefore that:

2 Stable societies with unchanged boundaries tend to accumulate more collusions and organizations for collective action over time.

Small groups can organize themselves quickly because the benefit per capita is greater, the selective incentive needed is smaller and the members can control each other more easily. This, in turn, has implications:

3 Members of 'small' groups have disproportionate organizational power for collective action, and this disproportion diminishes but does not disappear over time in stable societies.

What implications does the existence of interest groups have for efficiency and growth? A lobby can, in principle, further the interest of its members in two different ways. Either it works to increase the efficiency of the economy and, thus, to increase total production, or it concentrates on *redistributing* the already existing production to its members.

Under certain circumstances interest groups *may* contribute to increasing efficiency of the society, but this is not usually the case. The reason lies in the very core of the rationality of collective action. When individuals act, they incur a cost but they receive only a small part of the benefit. An organization, which represents 1 per cent of the citizens, cannot count on receiving more than 1 per cent of the incremental production. This means that it pays for the organization to act only if it can bring about an output increase at least one hundred times as large as the cost of acting. It is usually only in a situation when an interest group is hit directly and selectively (e.g., by a tariff), that there is an incentive for the group to increase efficiency by trying to abolish the tariff. In such a case, of course, the group captures most of the gain for itself. An example of this could be an industry that is hit by a tariff on some key component and, consequently, has difficulties competing in international markets, or a well-defined group of consumers who are dependent on a certain imported product (e.g., a medicine) whose price increases because of the tariff.

Alternatively, the interest groups reduce efficiency in the economy. By spending resources on redistributing goods to themselves they restrain the production of the economy with potentially large losses as a consequence. A group with command over 1 per cent of the GDP has an incentive to redistribute income as long as the resulting decrease of the GDP (which affects the group as well) is less than one hundred times the benefit captured by the group through redistribution. This implies that there are hardly any restrictions for small groups on the costs they are prepared to inflict on society through their redistribution efforts. Chapter 5, which can be interpreted as an illustration of how the farmers' interest organizations have been able to bring about regulations favourable for the members but at the expense of considerable welfare losses, is a case in point. We may then draw the following conclusion:

4 On balance, special-interest organizations and collusions reduce efficiency and aggregate income in the societies in which they operate and make political life more divisive.

The incentive picture is different for large groups. The larger the GDP share that one commands the weaker are the incentives to redistribute in a way that reduces the GDP, and the greater are the incentives to promote efficiency and growth. The strongly centralized Swedish trade union movement is a case in point. Industrial associations that comprise a large part of the industrial production capacity are another example. The consequence, then, is that:

5 Encompassing organizations have some incentive to make the society in which they operate more prosperous, and an incentive to redistribute income to their members with as little excess burden as possible, and to cease such redistribution unless the amount redistributed is substantial in relation to the social cost of the redistribution.

Interest groups tend to be slow decision-makers because they have to resort to methods that are based either on consensus or on 'constitutional' procedures. The reason for having to use such procedures is that there is a latent conflict about how the costs for upholding the organization are to be shared among the members. This type of decision-making takes time, especially in large organizations. The output quantities of the organization must often be decided for each member, as in cartels, where the precondition for higher profits for the members is that the total production of the cartel is kept down. There is a tendency for free riding in this case, however: a firm that cheats and produces more than its quota will gain at the expense of the others.

It is usually easier to fix prices than quantities – in principle, only one decision is then necessary – provided that there is an acceptable way of sharing the costs between the members. For this purpose, some rule of thumb (or even an external 'arbitrator') may be used. Even if this does not necessarily result in an optimal outcome for everybody involved, it is usually preferable to losing all benefits inherent in collective action. For a trade union, for instance, the price for higher wages is a lower level of employment for present and potential members. This cost is usually borne only by those who lose their jobs, and thus a mechanism is needed for determining who these people are. Usually seniority rules are used, or the decision may be left for the employer to make.

As a result of the complicated decision-making process the agendas of interest organizations tend to be very extensive. The conclusion is that:

6 Distributional coalitions make decisions more slowly than the individuals and firms of which they are comprised, tend to have crowded agendas and bargaining tables, and more often fix prices than quantities.

If the interest groups function in a slowly changing environment their sluggish decision-making does not matter too much. The environment often changes quickly and suddenly, however. Slow decision-making precludes the economy from keeping up with the development through growth-inducing innovations. Interest organizations, such as trade unions, also tend to discourage structural changes in order to 'protect jobs', when changes would be necessary, say, because of innovations or the emergence of 'newly industrializing countries' which take over industrial production, starting from the 'easy' end. Even if they may be prepared to adapt, in principle, the complicated negotiation and decision-making procedures may lead to delays. After the Second World War the Japanese and German industrial sectors were rebuilt from scratch and were therefore fully up-to-date. The British, whose industrial capacity was intact after the war, had no chance to catch up with the development embodied in the new industrial capacity. This acted as a brake on growth in Britain. The consequence of this is that:

7 Distributional coalitions slow down a society's capacity to adopt new technologies and to reallocate resources in response to changing conditions, and thereby reduce the rate of economic growth.

When interest groups have existed for some time they tend to become exclusive. If the number of members increases there is a risk that the price of the 'product' of the group decreases. Increasing the number of members increases the complexity of the decision process and, consequently, the costs as well, but contributes less and less to the utility of the group. Examples are doctors' and lawyers' associations, which often try to limit the access to education for these occupations. To be successful, the lobby has to reach a certain minimum size but, having done that, the result for the members is usually better if the size of the group is kept down. A telling, but extreme, example is a ruling clique which creates a dynasty, excluding new members and applying endogamous rules of marriage (marriage is to take place between members of the group) which contributes to keeping the number of members down. These groups can be held together easier if the differences in incomes and values are not too great. Newcomers are let into the group only if they can contribute to preserving the position of the clique. The need for common values, equal income and other qualities that tend to distinguish the group from the rest of the population lead to social interaction and selective social incentives:

8 Distributional coalitions, once big enough to succeed, are exclusive, and seek to limit the diversity of incomes and values of their membership.

Interest groups use lobbying to promote their interests and cooperate in the markets. They are frequently allied to certain political parties (trade unions cooperate with left-wing parties, farmers' associations with parties in the political centre, etc.). This tends to increase the complexity of society and provides stronger incentives for regulations and contributes towards more complicated negotiated solutions. The more complexity increases the more there is a need for specialists in charge of lobbying and regulations. These experts may, in turn, develop into a special interest resisting deregulation, and the bureaucracy needed for administrating the regulations tends to increase the need for personnel in the public sector. A dynamic process results whereby regulations give rise to attempts to circumvent them, which in turn leads to new regulations. As a consequence, the social costs for having a regulation apparatus tend to increase over time. Bureaucracy increases. In the market, complexity increases as well, in a similar vein, since firms cooperate in a time-consuming decision process. The complicated decision-making processes also contribute to a reluctance to change agreements that have already been concluded, which leads to more and more inertia in the social adaptation mechanisms. Finally, a consequence of an increasing number of interest groups and coalitions along with regulating activities and increasing complexity of the economy is a tendency not to concentrate on productive activities but on redistribution:

9 The accumulation of distributional coalitions increases the complexity of regulation, the role of government, and the complexity of understandings, and changes the direction of social evolution.

To conclude, we may note that all of Olson's theses tend to support the hypothesis that stable societies with slow social changes have a tendency to become more and more tied up in a network of interest-promoting activities and redistribution activities. Less and less energy is invested in achieving economic growth and more and more on redistributing the existing income.

An example: urban bias

The phenomenon of urban bias, which we discussed in Chapter 7, is a good example of how group interests influence the economic policy. How is it possible that the rural population accepts being discriminated against? In Lipton's work we do find some discussions on the political forces behind discrimination, but it is, above all, Robert Bates who has developed this aspect (mostly using Africa as his object of research), starting from the theories of collective action.

Bates's argument contains three steps. First, food prices are set at such a low level that the interest of the countryside is impaired, in order to channel resources to urban industries and the public sector. Second, the state divides the rural sector into two groups: the relatively resource-rich one, which can take advantage of subsidized inputs, and the relatively resource-poor one, the poor peasants whose interests are opposed by the policy. In this way it can pursue a 'divide-and-rule' policy which pre-empts the formation of a united front against the policy. Third, collective action is difficult for the peasants since their number is very large and they are widely spread geographically.

Even in China, which often – rightly or wrongly – is regarded as a country where the rural population is the political power base, the peasants have complained about the absence of channels for airing their grievances. The free rider problem (the fact that peasants who do not participate in putting pressure on the state also benefit from the actions), among other things, prevents the peasants from taking action. The urban industries, especially manufacturing, are often concentrated, however, which makes it easy for them to organize themselves. The government bureaucrats, finally, are mostly inclined to be urban oriented, which tends to be reflected in their work.

Finally, urban bias may be a mistake in the sense that when there is a large number of policy measures, all of them having allocative effects, it is hard to see who the winners and losers are. The government often tries to convey the impression that all groups benefit from subsidies. This is, however, logically impossible.

The possibilities for the rural population to make itself heard depends, to a great extent, on specific institutional conditions. A system where several political parties compete (e.g., Costa Rica) tends to give a better chance for different social groups to get attention. The number of persons to be elected from each constituency plays a role, too. Even in one-party states the peasants may have their say provided that there are several competing candidates. It seems clear, however, that the behaviour of the state is of paramount significance for the presence or absence of urban bias. This behaviour depends on the interplay of different special interests, however. The idea of a neutral, benevolent state that intervenes mainly to correct various distortions in the economy does not stand up to a closer scrutiny.

Conclusions

The theory of collective action explains many traits of the modern organization society which traditionally have been out of reach for economic theory, such as how do interest organizations decide how to act? Why do political parties and single politicians advocate distorting regulations in spite of the fact that it is relatively easy to show that they are non-optimal? How is it possible that public goods which are demanded are not produced unless the state takes on the producer role? Why does nobody seem to protect the interest of large majorities, while small key groups are able to promote their interests effectively regardless of the social costs incurred? Why is there a tendency for stable societies to become entangled over time in increasingly stifling networks of special interests? In Olson's theory, analyses of these and other similar questions are used for drawing conclusions about the macroeconomic dynamics in different countries. A stable environment, according to him, gives the special interests time to develop their instruments of leverage causing gradual petrification of the society.

Olson's theory is controversial, however. On the one hand, it is easy to find examples that seem to support it; but on the other hand, the institutional structure at the beginning of the stable period cannot be without significance. If this structure is dominated by elites whose main interest is redistributing of the production in their favour, the results differ from the outcome when the political system is independent of the special interests and able to keep their advances under control. In Chapter 11 we will formalize the effects of interest group activities with the aid of our two-good model.

Literature

Olson's ideas are documented in the following works:

Olson, Mancur (1965), *The Logic of Collective Action: Public Goods and the Theory of Groups*. Harvard University Press, Cambridge, MA, ch. 1.

Olson, Mancur (1982), *The Rise and Decline of Nations. Economic Growth, Stagflation, and Social Rigidities*. Yale University Press, New Haven, CT, ch. 3.

Olson, Mancur (1983), 'The Political Economy of Comparative Growth Rates', in Mueller, Dennis C. (ed.), *The Political Economy of Growth*. Yale University Press, New Haven, CT, and London.

James Buchanan and Gordon Tullock are the leading names of the Public Choice school. The classic work in this field is:

Buchanan, James M. and Tullock, Gordon (1962), *The Calculus of Consent*. University of Michigan Press, Ann Arbor, MI.

The greatest name in institutional economics is Douglass North; see:

North, Douglass C. (1981), *Structure and Change in Economic History*. Norton, New York and London.

North, Douglass C. (1990), *Institutions, Institutional Change and Economic Performance*. Cambridge University Press, Cambridge.

North, Douglass C. and Thomas, Robert Paul (1973), *The Rise of the Western World. A New Economic History*. Cambridge University Press, Cambridge.

A short overview of many of the ideas discussed in this and next chapter is given in:

Poulson, Barry W. (1994), *Economic Development. Private and Public Choice*. West, St Paul, MN.

The discussion of the behaviour of lobby groups is based mainly on:
Frey, Bruno S. (1984), *International Political Economics*. Basil Blackwell, Oxford.
Magee, Stephen P., Brock, William A. and Young, Leslie (1989), *Black Hole Tariffs and Endogenous Policy Theory. Political Economy in General Equilibrium*. Cambridge University Press, Cambridge, ch. 2.

See also:
Mayer, Wolfgang (1984). 'Endogenous Tariff Formation', *American Economic Review*, Vol. 74.

Whether political stability is an obstacle to economic development in developing countries is discussed in:
Goldsmith, Arthur (1987), 'Does Political Stability Hinder Economic Development? Mancur Olson's Theory and the Third World', *Contemporary Politics*, Vol. 19.

Robert Bates's ideas on the political economy of urban bias are presented in:
Bates, Robert (1981), *Market and States in Tropical Africa*. University of California Press, Berkeley, CA.

11
Directly Unproductive Profit-Seeking Activities

In the preceding chapter we outlined a theory for how individuals (or firms) organize themselves into interest groups when there are public goods for the group which may be produced as a result of putting pressure on the government and the legislators. We will now take one more step in our analysis and see what the economic consequences of this behaviour may be. The activities of the interest groups towards securing favours for the members are known as *rent seeking* or *directly unproductive profit-seeking (DUP) activities*.

A characteristic of these activities is that interest groups invest resources in securing the public good they want, inflicting costs both on the groups themselves and on society at large. Gordon Tullock has characterized these activities as a 'negative-sum game'. In the description of Olson's analysis in the preceding chapter we saw that the public goods would not be produced unless their value for the *individuals* who try to promote them exceeds the cost incurred by the same individuals. Only privately profitable lobbying is pursued.

For society as a whole, the situation is different. The interest groups invest resources. It is possible that different groups compete and some of them come out as winners with a positive net value for the group. From society's point of view no new goods or services that would be part of the welfare function of the citizens have been created, however. Instead, resources have been used for redistributing a 'pie' that already exists. The point is that the size of that pie has shrunk in the redistribution process as a direct consequence of the activities of the interest groups. The gain for the winning group is more than made up for by what society as a whole loses. 'Political' competition of this type usually results in a loss for society.

Directly unproductive profit-seeking activities and their costs

The costs for this type of activity can be seen in different ways. We start with a partial approach. Moreover, let us consider the clearest possible example of this phenomenon: theft. The situation is illustrated in Figure 11.1.

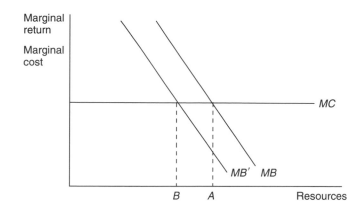

Figure 11.1 The costs of theft

In the figure, *MB* denotes the potential marginal returns on investing a given quantity of resources (i.e., time and equipment) on criminal activities. *MC* is the marginal opportunity cost representing the return on the same resources in the best alternative use. We assume that this opportunity cost is constant. The *MB* curve has a negative slope as the easiest objects for theft are assumed to be exploited first. The distance of the curve from the horizontal axis depends on how much other members of the society (including the public sector) invest in preventive measures. The more policemen society appoints, for example, the closer to the axis the curve would be.

In traditional partial analysis, where a dollar is a dollar no matter who earns it, where redistribution from one group to another does not count but only 'dead-weight losses' that do not benefit anybody, theft is a pure transfer from the victim to the thief. There are no welfare effects.

The preceding reasoning seems rather dubious, however, not only from a judicial but also from an economic point of view. The reason for the latter is that theft, and the risk of theft, uses up resources in the society. This may be illustrated in several ways with the aid of Figure 11.1. Let us begin by looking at the thief's situation. The marginal return on his criminal activity is given by the curve *MB* (i.e., the curve denoting the marginal product of theft). This benefit has to be compared to his marginal cost (working time, crowbar, mask, hood, sack). The thief's optimal resource input can be found in the usual way by locating the point where the marginal benefit and the marginal cost coincide (point *A*). (An additional effort, on the part of society, towards preventing crime would shift the curve to *MB'* and the optimal resource input for the thief to point *B*.) The value of the transfer granted by the thief to himself is given by the area below the *MB* curve from the origin to *A*, but from this area we have to deduct his costs, shown by the area below the *MC* curve between the origin and *A*.

The thief is not the only one to incur costs, however. It is reasonable to assume that the potential victims of criminal activities protect themselves (using locks, alarms, batons or tear gas). The more resources put into preventive measures the more the potential victim gains in terms of loss reduction, but the more it costs him. The marginal utility can be assumed to be decreasing because the greatest risks – such as unlocked doors – are taken care of first. (More crime prevention by society shifts the *MB* curve of the crime victim *upwards*.) The victim's decision problem is similar to the one demonstrated in Figure 11.1. It pays to invest in incremental preventive measures up to the point where the marginal benefit and the marginal cost are equal.

The conclusion of our discussion is that transfers of the directly unproductive, profit-seeking type are not costless for the parties involved, even if they would be for a society that turns a blind eye towards the distributional effects. In our example, both the thief and the victims use resources for achieving and preventing redistribution, respectively. The case of tariff seeking and tariff prevention, discussed in the preceding chapter, is a direct parallel.

If we take the step from a partial analysis to a general equilibrium framework the direct cost for directly unproductive activities is expressed by an inward shift of the production possibility curve. Since the existence of theft implies that resources are used both on carrying out and preventing this activity, the production possibility frontier of the economy shifts inwards in the way shown in Figure 11.2. The resources that have to be used for theft and its prevention cannot be used for producing agricultural goods and manufactures which are the products demanded by the public.

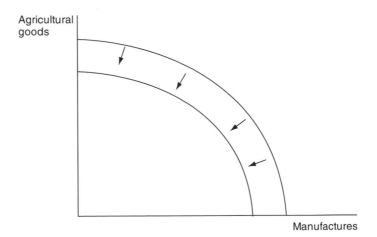

Figure 11.2   Production capacity and directly unproductive profit-seeking activities

A classification

Unproductive activities have different welfare effects depending on whether they are distorting or not. An unproductive activity may, paradoxically, increase the welfare of the economy. Jagdish Bhagwati distinguishes between four categories of unproductive activities.

1 The original and final states are both distorted. (DD)
2 The original state is distorted but, as a consequence of the unproductive activity, the final state is free from distortions. (DF)
3 The original state is free from distortions but there are distortions in the final state. (FD)
4 The original and final states are both free from distortions. (FF)

The most important distinction is the one between categories 1 and 2 (with distortions in the original state), on the one hand, and categories 3 and 4 (no distortions in the original state), on the other hand. In the former case the unproductive activities *may* be welfare enhancing – even if that is not necessarily the case – while this is impossible in the latter case. The former case is a typical example of a so-called second-best situation: if we already have a market imperfection somewhere in the economy, the optimal policy may not be elimination of all other imperfections. Optimality may rather depend on introducing some other distortion (cf. Chapter 1). Figure 11.3 gives some examples of unproductive activities that belong to the different categories. A distinction between legal and illegal activities is also made in the figure.

1.DD		1.DF	
Legal	Illegal	Legal	Illegal
1. Revenue seeking 2. Premium seeking	Evasion of tariffs, smuggling	Lobbying eleminating tariffs	Lobbying, eliminating tariffs by bribing politicians
3. FD		4. FF	
Legal	Illegal	Legal	Illegal
Tariff seeking	Evasion of tariffs in a situation with optimal tariffs at the outset	Lobbying for tariffs without result	Theft

Figure 11.3   Different categories of unproductive activities

Case 1 (DD)

In the first case there are distortions both in the original and the final state. Legal activities of this type include revenue seeking, where pressure groups try to obtain tariff-generated revenues, and premium seeking, where importers try to secure import licences in the case where the imports are limited by quantitative restrictions (and the price is bid up). Examples of illegal activities in this category are smuggling and attempts by importers to evade tariffs. (The importers who manage to evade the tariff can, of course, sell at the same price as those who pay the tariffs.)

Revenue seeking

Let us look into the case of revenue seeking and then, specifically, into what happens when interest groups try to capture the revenues created by a tariff. This situation is depicted in Figure 11.4, for a small economy with given product prices. In the free trade situation the economy produces at B and consumes at C. If a tariff on agricultural goods is introduced the domestic relative price relation becomes p_T. Production takes place at D and consumption at E, on a lower indifference curve (not drawn) than the one passing through C. The tariff revenue generated can be measured as the distance DF (in terms of manufactures). At international prices, GD manufactures are exchanged for GE agricultural goods. If we introduce a tariff, the

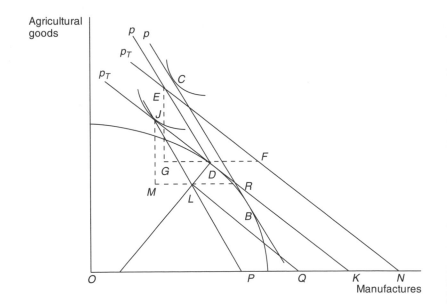

Figure 11.4   Revenue seeking

price relation changes to GF/GE, where the tariff rate is DF/GD. This can be shown as follows: the relative prices without and with the tariff, respectively, are:

$$\frac{P_J}{P_I} \equiv p \text{ and } \frac{P_J(1+t)}{P_I} \equiv p_T$$

The relation between p_T and p is then $1 + t$, where t is the tariff rate. The same price relation may also be expressed in terms of the figure, however, as:

$$\frac{p_T}{p} = \frac{GF}{GE}\frac{GE}{GD} = \frac{GF}{GD} \tag{11.1}$$

We can then write

$$1 + t = \frac{GF}{GD} \tag{11.2}$$

which gives

$$t = \frac{GF - GD}{GD} = \frac{DF}{GD} \tag{11.3}$$

Since export and imports have to be equal in the model, the real tariff revenue is obtained as the product of the tariff rate, t, and the export quantity, GD (i.e., $tGD = DF$).

The tariff revenue, in this case, is assumed to be returned to the consumers as lump-sum transfers (which do not affect behaviour) when there is no revenue seeking. Assume now that revenue-seeking activities take place and that the 'production' of these requires inputs of both capital and labour. If the revenue seeking takes place under competition the K/L quota is chosen so that the costs are minimized for a given wage rate (w) and a given capital cost (r). If the production functions are linearly homogeneous, the relevant r/w ratio (and thus the optimal K/L ratio) for the revenue seekers is determined, as we know already (Chapter 2), by the relative commodity price, p_T.

When revenue seeking takes place under competition, the value of the factors used up for this activity is equal to the available tariff revenue because revenue seeking continues as long as there is any revenue left to capture. This value corresponds to DF in the figure.

Revenue seeking affects the production side as well. Resources corresponding to DF are taken out of the production of the two goods. The economy then has to produce at a point inside the production possibility curve. Capital and labour are taken out of commodity production in the proportion $(K/L)_{DUP}$ which is determined by the production function of revenue seeking. The straight line DL connects all production points that are chosen when the factor input into commodity production successively shrinks in the proportion $(K/L)_{DUP}$. The argument is based on the Rybczynski theorem. According to this, in a model where the production functions are linearly homogeneous, with constant commodity prices, the production of the good using the shrinking factor intensively decreases, while the production of the other good increases. If the supply of both factors decreases, the production of the good using intensively the factor that shrinks relatively more decreases more, proportionally speaking. (The production of the other good may, but need not, increase.)

This is easy to see. If the total factor input in the economy is K/L when there is no revenue seeking, we have:

$$\frac{K}{L} = \frac{K_I + K_J}{L} = k_I \frac{L_I}{L} + k_J \frac{L_J}{L}; \quad k_I \equiv \frac{K_I}{L_I} \text{ and } k_J \equiv \frac{K_J}{L_J} \tag{11.4}$$

When K shrinks, the value of the left-hand side of the equation decreases. But, as shown in Chapter 2, factor prices and factor intensities are also given if commodity prices are given. Therefore k_I and k_J remain unchanged. Assume now, as before, that manufactures are relatively capital-intensive (i.e., $k_I > k_J$). For the value of the left-hand side of the equation to decrease, L_I/L must decrease compared to L_J/L. L_J must increase and L_I decrease, but unless k_I and k_J change, K_I must decrease and K_J increase. This implies that the production of manufactures must decrease and the production of agricultural goods must increase.

Assume, instead, that both K and L shrink and that L shrinks relatively more than K (as in Figure 11.4). The effect is most easily seen when it is divided into two steps. The first one entails the full decrease of K and an equiproportional decrease of L. This also reduces the production of both goods in the same proportion. (The scale of the economy shrinks, a movement along a straight line (not shown) between D and O. The structure of the economy does not change, however, since neither the shape of the production possibility curve nor the relative prices have changed.) The second step consists of an additional decrease of L, which decreases the production of agricultural goods and increases the production of manufactures. It is, however, not certain that the increase is large enough to result in a net increase in the production of manufactures. (In Figure 11.4 we depict a situation where the labour force shrinks more than the capital stock but where the difference is not large enough to result in a net increase of industrial production.)

We can now return to Figure 11.4. The decrease of agricultural and industrial production takes place along the line DL, until resources corresponding to $QK = KN$ have been used up (i.e., the entire tariff revenue). The consumption point is J, which must be at the intersection of a world market price line and a domestic price line (the domestic price line through D and K, since

LR = the tariff revenue in the final situation and $LR = QK$). Trade takes place at world market prices, p, and the new production point (after revenue seeking) is L. LM manufactures are exchanged for MJ agricultural goods. The welfare level has fallen compared with both the free trade situation and the situation with tariff protection but without revenue seeking.

Revenue-seeking activities do not necessarily lead to a reduction in welfare, however. The preceding argument was based on the assumption that the entire tariff revenue was absorbed by the interest group. We will now consider a case where only part of the tariff revenue is sought. (The state does not allow the entire revenue to be channelled to the interest group but distributes part of it as a lump sum transfer.) This case is illustrated by Figure 11.5.

Assume that capital and labour are taken out of production – and used for lobbying – in such proportions that the production point moves along the line DL. The tariff revenue at the outset is DH. Revenue seeking is for a smaller amount, however, such as $DK = MN$, and real income decreases by $MN = PN$. We find the new production point at L and the consumption point at G, which implies a higher welfare level than originally. LQ of the tariff revenue accrues to the interest group and $QU = NT$ to the consumers as a lump-sum transfer. After introducing the tariff the economy produces at D and consumes at E. A necessary (but not sufficient) condition for achieving a higher welfare level is that the revenue seeking moves the production point to the right of the world market price line through D. This is possible if the revenue seeking is so labour-intensive that the new production point entails an increase of industrial production and a decrease of agricultural production.

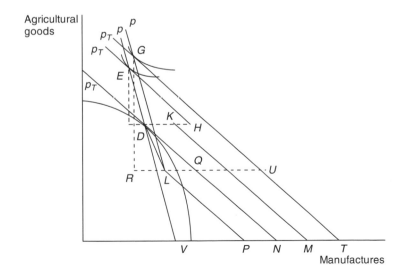

Figure 11.5 Revenue seeking when the entire revenue is not sought

Premium seeking

Revenue seeking is an example of a price-related unproductive activity. (The profit that may be the object for rent seeking is created by a direct price change.) Such activities may also be quantity-related, however. An example of the latter is premium seeking. That type of unproductive profit-seeking activity becomes interesting, for instance, when the state chooses to regulate imports with a quantitative restriction instead of using a tariff. This results in an import premium through the restricted supply of the imported product, created by the quota. The value of the premium is determined by the value of the imports allowed in terms of domestic and international prices, respectively. The import premium accrues to those who are allowed to import the restricted product (in our case, agricultural goods). Those who want import licences are therefore prepared to spend resources to secure them.

Unlike the situation with price-related unproductive activities, quantity-related unproductive activities do not entail the possibility of increasing welfare, provided that the unproductive activity is the only distortion in the economy (except the quota itself). This is shown in Figure 11.6.

Assume that the economy produces at point D at the domestic prices given by the quota (EF) of agricultural goods, p_K. This results in exports of manufactures of DE at world market prices, p, and consumption at point F, at domestic prices.

The quota (premium) that is subject to rent seeking is EF. We know already that an increase in welfare implies that the premium seeking would have to use such a combination of capital and labour that the new production point

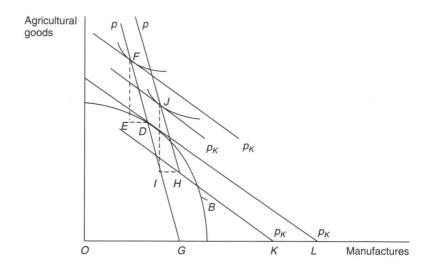

Figure 11.6   Premium seeking

is to the right of the line *DG*, otherwise it is impossible to end up on an indifference curve higher than the one passing through point *F*. Agricultural production then has to decrease and manufacturing production has to increase. Hence, proportionally more labour than capital should be taken out of goods production, to such an extent that industrial production increases, absolutely speaking.

Assume that the new production point is at *H*. The import quota is unchanged; that is, $IJ = EF$. Trade takes place at international prices, *p*, and consumption takes place at point *J*, at domestic prices, p_K. The resources used on premium seeking correspond to *KL* in terms of manufactures, measured at domestic prices (i.e., the difference between the production value without (*OL*) and with (*OK*) premium seeking, respectively).

As such, the move from *D* to *H* implies a reduction of the distortion of the production structure. The economy moves towards the free trade point, *B* (the relevant price line is not shown). This improvement on the production side is not sufficient to increase the welfare level, however. To do this, foreign trade would have to grow to the extent that the economy could consume at a point on the *p* line, above the indifference curve passing through *F*. This is prevented, however, by the fact that the import quota is given as $EF = IJ$. Premium seeking thus unambiguously leads to a welfare loss, and the reason for this is that a quantitative restriction is imposed on the volume of foreign trade.

In the preceding case the premium was not fully spent on the profit-seeking activity. Since it is likely that the premium created by the quota becomes an object for competition by several profit seekers, it is more probable that the profit seeking proceeds until the whole value of the premium has been spent (i.e., resources are used to an extent corresponding to the whole premium). This is shown in Figure 11.7.

Resources are used on premium seeking in such proportions that the production point moves along the line *DH*. The import quota, *EF*, corresponds to *EI* in terms of manufactures. (*FE* agricultural goods can be exchanged for *EI* manufactures.) *DI* is the tariff equivalent of the quota. The value of the production given by *D* is *OK*, in terms of manufactures. The production value achieved when resources equivalent to *DI* are spent on premium seeking is $OL = OK - LK$, where $LK = DI$. To find the new production point, we move to the northwest from *L*, along a line parallel with *KD* until this line cuts the *DH* line at *H*. At the latter point, resources equal to $HM = LK$, in terms of manufactures, have been used for premium seeking. The economy imports the permitted quota, $FE = NJ$, at world market prices. From a welfare point of view this case is inferior to the one presented in Figure 11.6 because more resources are used on premium seeking.

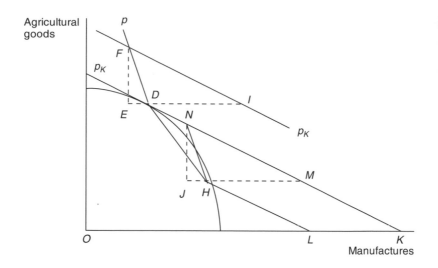

Figure 11.7   Premium seeking when the entire premium is competed away

Case 2 (DF)

In case 2 the original state is distorted but the unproductive activity removes the distortion. An example of this is lobbying that aims at abolishing tariffs. (This may possibly take place in an illegal fashion: the lobby may bribe politicians.)

Also in this case welfare-enhancing paradoxes are possible. The effect of an unproductive activity can be divided into: (1) the effect of the activity with a given distortion (this is identical with case 1), whether positive or negative, and (2) the effect of eliminating the distortion, which must be positive. Hence, the net result is not clear. A case where lobbying results in a tariff being abolished and the welfare increases as a result, is presented in Figure 11.8.

Let us start from a situation with tariff protection. The economy produces at D and consumes at E. Now, resources are employed in lobbying which results in an inward shift of the production possibility curve. If the tariff had not been affected, production would have taken place at F and consumption at G. This implies an increase of welfare. If the lobby, furthermore, succeeds in abolishing the tariff, production will take place at H, with consumption at I, at world market prices. The positive effect will be strengthened. A closer look at the figure shows, however, that this is not a necessary result. If capital and labour had been used by the lobby in such proportions that point F had been on a p line to the left of the one passing through D, a negative net outcome may have resulted. (The positive effect following from

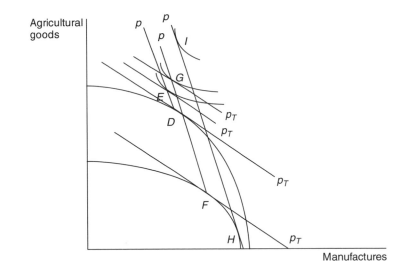

Figure 11.8 Lobbying that eliminates a tariff and increases welfare

the abolition of tariff is insufficient to outweigh the negative effect of the employment of resources in lobbying.)

Case 3 (FD)

In case 3 the initial situation is free from distortions but, as a result of the unproductive activities, such distortions are introduced. A legal example of this type of activity is a branch organization using resources to obtain tariff protection for the industry. An illegal example is when there is an optimal tariff (cf. Chapter 4) and this is evaded by importers. In the final situation the tariff then is not optimal since, on average, less than the optimal tariff revenue is collected. In this case, two negative effects contribute to the end result: (1) the inward shift of the production possibility curve resulting from the unproductive activities, and (2) the effects of the distortions when the production possibility curve has already shifted.

Let us look closer into the case of *tariff seeking*. Here the original state is free from distortions but not the final state. This is illustrated by Figure 11.9.

In the initial state there is free trade, with production at *B* and consumption at *C*. Next, we introduce a farmer lobby which uses resources in order to obtain a tariff on agricultural goods. The production possibility curve then shifts inwards. The direct welfare loss from this – as long as the tariff has not been introduced – is given by the movement of the consumption point from *C* to *E*, at constant prices. When tariff protection has been introduced, the

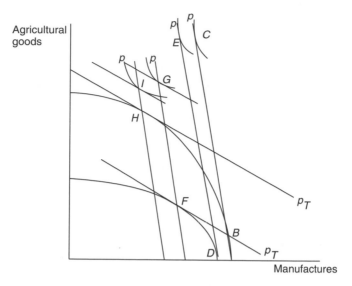

Figure 11.9 Tariff seeking

relative price of agricultural goods increases to p_T, however. The new production point is *F* and the consumption point moves from *E* to *G*. In addition to the loss that follows from the shift of the production possibility curve, the economy makes the usual loss from the introduction of a tariff.

The losses due to lobbying and tariff protection, taken together, may be smaller than the loss resulting from a tariff being imposed 'exogenously' (i.e., without lobbying). Assume, as before, that we start at points *B* and *C* and that a tariff is imposed which moves the production point to *H* and the consumption point to *I*. *I* is on a lower indifference curve than *G* and is therefore inferior from the welfare point of view. The explanation for this is that lobbying in this case leads to a smaller deterioration of the resource allocation: that is, the proportions of agricultural and industrial production, respectively, change less than when the tariff is imposed without lobbying. Consequently, the starting point for exchanging manufactures for agricultural goods on the world market is better.

The latter result does not necessarily hold, however. The outcome depends on the factor proportions employed in lobbying. In our case, lobbying was a relatively labour-intensive activity. This implies that the production of agricultural goods, which are labour intensive too, decreases more than that of manufactures. A higher capital intensity of lobbying may change the shape of the production possibility curve and result in a reduction of welfare in the case of lobbying as compared to the case without lobbying.

Case 4 (FF)

In the last case both the starting point and the final situation are free from distortions. A legal example of this is when two lobbies spend resources for and against tariff protection, respectively, and no protection is introduced. Theft is an illegal example. For the case of tariffs the situation is illustrated in Figure 11.10.

Since the lobbying uses resources, the capacity to produce agricultural goods and manufactures decreases. The production possibility curve shifts inwards. The price relation remains unchanged, however, since the pro-tariff lobby fails to achieve its goal. Consequently, welfare is reduced.

Conclusions

The theory of unproductive profit-seeking activities provides an apparatus for analysing the economic consequences of the behaviour of interest groups and organizations. The selfish actions of such groups have in common the fact that they use resources that otherwise could have been spent on producing goods and services demanded by the public. We have shown, however, that the consequences of the unproductive activities are unambiguously negative only if the initial state is free from distortions. In a 'second-best' situation, where we have distortions to begin with, it is possible that they have positive welfare effects, provided that they contribute to alleviating the original distortions.

In the next chapter we will look into some examples of directly unproductive profit-seeking activities. These examples illuminate what happens

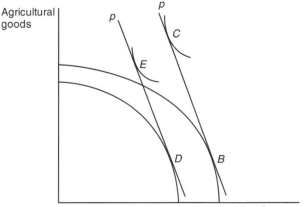

Figure 11.10 Tariff seeking that yields no result

when politicians and government officials establish themselves as an interest group aiming at satisfying their own interests rather than the needs of the state they have been authorized to manage.

Literature

Systematic research on rent seeking was begun by:
Krueger, Anne O. (1974). 'The Political Economy of Rent-Seeking', *American Economic Review*, Vol. 64.

The ideas on unproductive profit-seeking activities as a negative-sum game are discussed in detail in:
Tullock, Gordon (1980), 'Rent Seeking as a Negative-Sum Game', in Buchanan, James M., Tollison, Robert D. and Tullock, Gordon (eds), *Towards a Theory of the Rent-Seeking Society*. A&M University Press, College Station, TX.

The social costs of transfers are illuminated in:
Tullock, Gordon (1967) 'The Welfare Costs of Tariffs, Monopolies, and Theft', *Western Economic Journal*, Vol. 5.

The classification of DUP activities presented in Figure 11.3 is based on:
Bhagwati, Jagdish (1983), *The Theory of Commercial Policy. Essays in International Economic Theory*. Vol. 1. MIT Press, Cambridge, MA, ch. 17.

The analysis of the different cases of unproductive profit-seeking activities is based mainly on:
Bhagwati, Jagdish N., Panagaryia, Arvind and Srinivasan, T. N. (1998), *Lectures on International Trade* (2nd edn). MIT Press, Cambridge, MA and London, ch. 34.

The Rybczynski theorem is proved in any textbook on international economics, such as:
Södersten, Bo and Reed, Geoffrey (1994), *International Economics* (3rd edn). Macmillan, London, ch. 7.

12
The State as an Interest Group: The Economic Logic of Wielding Power

As we have seen in the preceding chapters, government interventions in the market tend to create distortions and excess profits, which special interests try to capture. There are also incentives for various groups in the economy to join forces and try to secure favours by persuading the state to introduce distorting policy measures.

In traditional public finance theory the state is perceived mainly as a force opposing the special interests or as a benevolent arbitrator who, taking into consideration the interest of the public, balances different special interests against each other. In the light of more recent theories on public decision-making this view seems rather naive, however. In a world of lobbies there are also cases when the state itself is the leading interest group. This happens either if an interest group 'hijacks' the state and uses it for its own benefit, or if an 'autonomous' state, spurred by the economic incentives of those in power, begins to act as a special interest. Furthermore, in less extreme cases it is easy to detect selfish traits in the exercise of power. The results of an analysis of the role of the state depend, however, on how exactly we define the 'state' concept. In a broad sense, the state is constituted by the citizens as an organization for taking care of common affairs. In the present context, however, the 'state' stands for the political power elite, including the central government bureaucracy: that is, the decision-makers acting in the name of the state.

A central thesis of the modern political economy literature is that the 'state' consists of individuals who, like all other economic agents, aim at maximizing their own utility instead of the utility of the public at large. Such a state redistributes resources primarily in order to secure its own existence and also to maximize the economic benefits of the power holders. The more concentrated the power, the more it can normally be abused.

Still, it is rather difficult to find an unambiguous relation between the type of state and economic development. Government power can indeed be abused to a certain extent. Much depends on what it is most profitable for the power elite to do. State interventions, ultimately introduced to benefit

199

the power holders, *may* enhance economic efficiency but need not do so. If a measure makes it difficult for the government to stay in power or to use the system for its own benefit, it will not be taken. Efficiency and economic development are not necessarily the most important goals for an 'egotistic' state; they are only two among several possible ways of achieving maximum utility for the power holders. This reasoning emphasizes the importance of the *incentives* encountered by decision-makers. These incentives, in turn, depend on the 'rules of the game' in the economy (i.e., its institutions).

This interpretation is far from the traditional one, which considers the state as a benevolent – albeit sometimes badly informed – exogenous force in the economy. The interplay between altruism and egotism in the public sector is complicated, and which of these two forms dominates depends on the circumstances. Even if it would probably be too extreme to deny the relevance of idealism and unselfish work for the public good, it is a fact that corruption, self-serving redistribution and egotistic behaviour on the part of politicians, officials and political parties exist, to a varying extent, in all countries. It is a long way, however, from this 'minor' abuse to a situation when rent seeking is endemic and systematic in the state bureaucracy and the political system. In the extreme case, the main task of the state apparatus is to maximize the income of the ruling clique, while the state gives next to nothing in return to the public. This is a pure *predatory state* (kleptocracy), which has severely distorting effects on the economy.

The view of the role of the state in the economy

At least during the past century, economists have had a divided view of the significance of the state for the functioning of the economy. Most agree that a state can be justified by the need for defining and enforcing property rights in the society and for producing public goods such as defence or law and order. How the state functions, how it should function optimally, and why it functions as it does in different situations have been relatively little discussed. Much work has been carried out on the clarification of targets and instruments for economic policy and on the effects of this policy. The behaviour of the state has seldom been explained *endogenously*, however. Ineffective measures have usually been regarded as unintended consequences of imperfect information or incompetence, while successful measures have not received any particular attention but have been considered 'normal'.

The 'pre-classic' David Hume stressed, more than two hundred years ago, the need for including checks and balances in every constitution, because individuals can be assumed to act in their own interest. The view of the classic economists of the behaviour of the state and the role of institutions in the economy was rather broad and nuanced as well. John Stuart Mill, for instance, notes that a constitutional type of government a priori presupposes that political power would be abused, not because this is always the case but because it is the natural tendency. The later, neoclassical, view of the role of the state is much narrower. It is confined partly to the role of the state as a supervisor of law and order, partly to the need for interventions implied by, say, imperfect markets and external effects. A *minimalist* state appears to be the ideal. The neoclassicists also perceive the state as a monolith: an 'outsider' that consistently strives to maximize the welfare of society.

Even in the Keynesian world, where the state and state interventions are of crucial significance, the state played the role of a benevolent 'Santa Claus', regarded as an exogenous agent in the system. The case of development economics is similar, too, even if schools influenced by Marxism tend to be more nuanced in this respect. (The state is regarded by the Marxists as the passive tool and the extended arm of the ruling class, facilitating the exploitation of the rest of the population.) In the planned economies of Eastern Europe the state was a tool for the 'dictatorship of the proletariat', but in a society without class conflicts – the communist society – the state would be redundant.

Within the realm of development economics the discussion has mostly concerned the justification of various interventions, and much less why some states perform better than others. During the first quarter century after the Second World War, the interventionist policy was successful (or at least this was the general picture), and the positive role of the state in the economy was seldom called into question. A decisive change of the analysis of the behaviour of the state took place only later, with the emergence of the *public choice* approach in the 1960s and the so-called new political economy, a school that really began to develop only in the 1980s.

Opinions on how and how much the state should intervene in the economy have varied strongly over time. During the early postwar period the desirability of interventions was considered self-evident. The reason for this can be found both in Keynesian economics, which stresses the role of the state for the stability of the economy, and in the new welfare economics, which identifies cases where the market system functions poorly or not at all, and where interventions are needed to solve the problems. Moreover, the fact that the Soviet Union and other planned economies displayed high growth rates, during their first few decades, seemed to speak for a high degree of state intervention in the economy.

Especially regarding developing countries the common view was that ill-functioning markets and 'vicious circles' were obstacles to industrialization and other development. The market was the problem, not the solution. The consequence of this view was a strong emphasis on the role of the state. Development could be achieved only through a strong and organized contribution by the state, which called for both a strong public sector and extensive interventions in the private sector. The doctrine of import-substituting industrialization emerged, since the industry of the developing countries could allegedly not compete with established firms from developed countries unless they received protection. Closely related to this was the use of planning models, combined with regulation of prices, wages, investments and foreign trade. In socialist economies markets were substituted for planning models wherever possible.

Import substitution and the strong emphasis on planned development eventually resulted in a strong counter-reaction. Even if there had always been single critical voices against the planning philosophy, the criticism grew stronger and more serious only in the 1970s. One reason for this was the theoretical developments about, for example, the logic of the behaviour of interest groups, put forth mainly by Mancur Olson, the *public choice* school, the rational expectations school and the so-called neoclassical counter-revolution in development economics. Another, perhaps more important, reason was the fact that it became more and more obvious, from an empirical point of view, that import substitution led to a dead end. Also the planning approach appeared as more and more untenable. The problems were reflected in the (largely unsuccessful) attempts at reforms carried out, especially in Hungary and Czechoslovakia. The pure planned economies lagged behind more and more until finally they broke down completely.

The consequence of these obvious examples of unsuccessful state-led development was that the attention was turned from market failures to problems emerging as a consequence of overambitious state interventions, or *government failures*. It seemed that economic success could be related to the absence of state interventions rather than to the use of such measures.

Lately, the pendulum has begun to swing again, away from the view that the extremely minimalist state would be the ideal if the aim is rapid economic development. To some extent, newer research on institutional economics has played a role. A central result of this research was the insight that a functioning market system needs an infrastructure of social institutions. The main reason for the reappraisal of the minimalist state as the ideal was, once again, however, mainly empirical. On the one hand, the most successful economies during the last 30 years, the East and Southeast Asian countries, are hardly good examples of minimalist states. It is also questionable whether these states have been particularly benevolent. Many of them have intervened strongly and purposefully in the economy and some have been quite repressive. On the other hand, the state has been weak and passive in most of the economies of the former Soviet Union and Eastern Europe. Other social institutions, 'rules of the game', have not yet emerged either. The market economy is thus uncontrolled. The economy of these countries has not developed nearly as well as expected; in fact, it is often difficult to see any positive development at all.

Market failures and government failures are two sides of the same coin, however. The former, combined with the goal of influencing the distribution of income, provide the rationale for government intervention. At the same time, these interventions often tend to cause government failures. The original goals may be undermined by rent-seeking special interests, and self-serving politicians and bureaucrats may take the interventions further than would be optimal from an economic point of view. Furthermore, vote-maximizing politicians may produce 'political business cycles', where, for instance, government expenditures tend to rise before elections in order to win votes for the ruling parties, regardless of their long-run effects (which may well be negative). Government failures may finally be due to incompetence and a tendency to overstretch the available resources. The outcome of an evaluation of the relative importance of market and government failures, respectively, is the main reason for different ideas as to what the role of the state should be.

To summarize, it is hard to see a clear relation between the *degree* of state intervention and more or less successful economic development, given the experience we have today. Douglass North once noted that the existence of a state, on the one hand, is a precondition for economic growth; on the other hand, the state is the reason for the cases of economic decline that can be related to human factors. Therefore it is not enough to regard the state as an exogenous agent. This does not imply that evaluations of exogenously formulated policy alternatives are meaningless as such, but in order to understand the role of the state for economic development we have to endogenize it, which means that the incentives guiding the group of individuals that 'personalize' the state have to be scrutinized.

The central concept when the state is endogenized is directly unproductive profit-seeking (DUP) activities, exactly as when the behaviour of other interest groups is concerned. As an economic agent the state is unique, however, in the sense that it does not only react to incentives; it also creates incentives for the rest of the economy insofar as it determines the 'rules of the game'. It is also unique as an organization because of its legal monopoly of using violence, if necessary. The important things in this context are, on the one hand, what consequences the interventions have for efficiency – which can be studied with the aid of traditional theory – and, on the other hand, why different types of state appear and why the state behaves differently in different situations.

The older literature on the problem of *public choice* tends to emphasize the negative aspects of the wielding of power by the state. There seem to be cases where the experiences of state interventions have been good, however. In the case of East Asia, agreement is stronger about what policy variables promote growth than about what the optimal political environment looks like. Is, for instance, an authoritarian state a necessary (but not sufficient) condition for development? The interplay between economics and politics is complicated and the causal relations often go both ways. All market transactions and government interventions take place in an institutional environment which – perhaps over an extensive period of time – creates a certain incentive structure, which depends, for example, on the legal system defining and upholding property rights, the political structures and constitutional arrangements, the existence of private organizations, special interests, cartels, and so on. These are, in turn, affected by the direction economic development takes, according to the principle of 'trial and error'.

Different types of state

A precondition for successful interventions is that the state is genuinely willing to develop the economy and enhance economic efficiency. It must also be possible to implement decisions on interventions without the costs of information becoming too high and too many administrative complications. Otherwise the state remains inefficient despite good intentions. Even a benevolent state may take erroneous decisions, from an efficiency point of view, because the consequences of a decision may not be clear. Moreover, the ambitions of the state may be too high given its competence. It is not unusual that economic advisers have different views on how to reach a certain goal. Even if the decision is the 'right' one, the measures taken may have unexpected consequences because of transaction costs not included in the calculations.

Civil servants seldom have an incentive to be efficient (as opposed to firms, government offices do not have a profitability restriction), and they may also have private goals that differ from the official ones. Moreover, the tasks assigned to the government bureaucracy may be too complicated, considering what would be required in terms of competence, coordination between various authorities, and so on. The result is that the policy actually pursued may differ considerably from the official intentions. Worse still, the interventions themselves may be the result of lobbying, where rents are channelled to a certain interest group at the cost of efficiency losses for the economy at large. Finally, the image of the state as a benevolent guardian of the public interest cannot be taken for granted. It may have objectives that differ from the promoting of economic efficiency and development, such as the maximization of the welfare of the power elite. The interventions then reflect this. If the interest of the elite depends on economic development, the state tends to be developmental, but not otherwise.

A basic tenet of the new political economy is that the type of state is important for the results of an active policy of interventions. According to Deepak Lal and Hla Myint the state may be of two types, factional and autonomous. The factional state may either be democratic or authoritarian, while the autonomous state is always authoritarian, geared towards either development or predation. In each case it may be tempting for the power holders to line their pockets at the expense of the citizens. The crucial question is then why all states do not develop into downright predatory ones.

Douglass North distinguishes between the *contract based* and the *exploitation based* views on the state. For economic development to be possible, there must, according to the former view, be social 'contracts' – explicit or implicit – which define existing property rights. The state plays the role of third party in every contract, being the 'arbitrator' who guarantees and, as the last resort, enforces it. According to this view, the state is a 'battlefield', where the 'battle' concerns the rights to define the property rights in the most favourable way possible for one's own group. The exploitation based view, in turn, concentrates on how the groups controlling the state can manipulate property rights to their own advantage, so that the most lucrative activities are monopolized for the ruling clique. A variety of this type of reasoning is the 'clientelist' view, which perceives interest groups as networks of individuals who try to secure personal favours through the groups.

The two approaches are not necessarily alternatives, however, but complement each other. According to North the difference is that the potential for violence is relatively evenly distributed in the former case but unevenly distributed in the latter. In other words, it is possible that all states, in fact, are potential predators, but that predation in some cases is easier and more lucrative than in others: 'If the highest rate of return in an economy comes from piracy, we can expect that the organizations will invest in skills and knowledge that will make them better pirates.' There is no reason to believe that the state a priori would be different from other organizations in this respect.

A common trait of all types of state is that the government wants to remain in power, and tries to do so either using violence, 'buying' support from powerful special interests or trying to win elections, using different methods. A favourable economic development is one way of securing power, while power is a necessary precondition for pursuing a consistent, long-term policy-promoting development.

The factional state is often weak and 'soft' in the sense that it is forced to find a balance between the demands of special interests. Here the potential for violence is relatively evenly distributed but some group may temporarily have the upper hand. Even if the group in power at the moment may count on willing supporters, their loyalty is weak. They bet on winners and change camps as soon as they think it is favourable. Pranab Bardhan analyses a society dominated by strong special interests in terms of game theory. The result, according to him, is often what has been called 'the prisoner's dilemma' in game theory, where each group chooses an alternative that is non-optimal for society as a whole but which protects the group against the worst outcomes. Bardhan applies this framework to the economic development of India, where inefficient use of resources, extensive regulation and slow growth, at least until recently, have been salient features.

For a favourable economic development it is important that the state is strong enough, and independent of special interests, to be able to uphold fundamental property rights, say, and see to it that laws and regulations are obeyed. There must also be countervailing forces, however, preventing the state itself from abusing its power. In the *democratic* state a limit to predation is set – even if it can hardly be prevented completely – by the fact that the power holders have to submit themselves to general elections at regular intervals. The redistribution of income made by a democratic state is usually aimed at improving the chances of the ruling parties to win the next election. This entails economic favours as well, however, especially for the party elites. The political parties also have to court the special interests which easily creates client relations. A democratic state is more open and information is more available than in authoritarian states, however, due to (among other things) the fact that mass media have greater freedom and that the legal system is separate from the polity. Those who abuse their position must therefore accept a high risk of being held responsible. There is a 'grey area', however, which allows power holders to enrich themselves without losing their legitimacy. Abuse may be endemic but still not systematic. North points to the inherent tensions between the social responsibility of the state and its own rational behaviour, considering the incentives it faces. Olson, in turn, emphasizes the tendency of government decision-makers to ally themselves with special interests. The efforts of the state to please the electorate has been regarded as a reason for the tendency of the public sector to expand in democratic states.

In the rest of this chapter we will concentrate on authoritarian regimes. This is done mainly for the sake of the argument, however. Many of the means used by the authoritarian state to channel resources into the pockets of the ruling clique can be used – to a greater or lesser extent – by any state.

The state as a predator

The authoritarian factional state lacks most of the mechanisms mentioned above that could prevent abuse of power. Political and economic power are confused and the special interests may directly influence – often through their economic clout – both legislative and executive decisions. Since there are several competing power centres in this case (these are actually organized special interests in the sense of Olson, dealt with in Chapter 10) the ruling clique is often too weak to stay in power long enough to organize systematic predation. Sooner or later a *coup d'état* takes place and the clique is replaced by another one. The policy seldom changes and large resources are used both by the power holders, in order to stay in office, and by their competitors, in order to take over.

If the authoritarian state manages to suppress all competing power centres it turns into an autonomous state. (The very possibility of keeping the special interests in check is an argument frequently presented as an advantage in the context of economic development. The 'autonomy' concept is a relative one, however; 'autonomous' states have often developed close relations with, say, big business.) This type of state may also appear in different shapes. On the one hand, it may develop into a pure predatory state, concentrating on maximizing the income of the ruling clique without giving anything in return; on the other hand, the result may be a developmental state.

The extreme type of predatory state evolves around one single individual, who 'is' the state, and functions with the ultimate aim of maximizing his income (e.g., François Duvalier in Haiti, Jean-Bedel Bokassa in the Central African Republic, Mobutu Sese Seko in Zaire and Ferdinand Marcos in the Philippines). Another variety originates in an interest group, such as an ethnic group or a political party, and strives to maximize the utility of the group members. This can be arranged by giving group members well-paid public offices, via monopoly rights or government procurement. Those who are already 'insiders' in the system work towards including relatives or fellow tribesmen. Systems resembling this can be found in Zimbabwe or Brunei, even if neither of them is extremely predatory. Over time privileges may be concentrated in the ruling group through education, which is then reserved for members of the group.

A less extreme variety of the latter type of state can be found in states with a strong bureaucracy working to enhance their own welfare. In that case the bureaucrats have to justify their actions to the politicians. This can be done, for example, by referring to 'national interest', 'cultural identity' or 'social improvement'. The objective is expanding the public sector, which tends to lead to higher salaries, better career openings and higher status for bureaucrats even when they are not corrupt.

It is important to see that the extreme predatory state is an exception, even if not a very unusual one. Practice indicates that we rather have a whole range of authoritarian states. Starting from downright predation the range encompasses totalitarian regimes with strong predatory traits but who still contribute considerably to the economy through public goods and so on (cf. Indonesia under Suharto), and paternalistic but fairly benevolent regimes striving to maximize the welfare of society at large, provided that the regime cannot be questioned and that the establishment takes direct advantage of the system in the form of high income (such as Korea and Taiwan, until recently).

Judging a regime as more or less 'benevolent' may be misleading, however. Few commentators would have regarded the Kuomintang regime of Taiwan, with its background as an extreme predatory state, as developmental in the early 1950s. *Ex post*, however, most evaluators would be prepared to make such a judgement. It is entirely possible that a regime which only aims at enriching itself pursues a developmental policy out of pure self-interest. The opposite case is just as conceivable. The interesting question is, then, why some autonomous authoritarian regimes develop into predatory states while others become more or less developmental. One, albeit not exhaustive, answer to this question may be obtained by considering the economic incentives of the power holders. Another possible answer is that the system is sensitive to the personal competence of the rulers. Let us take a closer look at the significance of economic incentives in this context.

As noted before, the state is an organization with a 'comparative advantage in violence'; the state can always take what it wants from the citizens by resorting to violence. The coercive apparatus is also needed to secure the other paramount goal of a predatory state: to stay in power. The problem is that the use of force is expensive because the police, military and prisons are costly to uphold and the expenditure on them reduces the net income of the regime. Additionally, there is a risk for the regime of being toppled if it becomes too onerous for the citizens. In reality genuine revolutions are rather rare, however. A greater risk for the regime is being either toppled by a competing clique or a faction of the ruling one. The end result in both cases is usually a regime that continues preying, in its turn, until it is ousted.

The ruling clique thus strives to maximize its income under the restriction that it has to stay in power. Economic development has two advantages from this point of view. On the one hand, it results in more income to redistribute also to the state; on the other hand, the chances of being able to stay in power increase. Economic prosperity is of interest also for a predatory state. Methods which are too rough may result in high revenues in the short run but have a negative effect in the longer run because the income base is destroyed. In practice, the time perspective of the predatory state is often too short for it to consider investing in economic development, especially if it has to start from a low level. The quality of the tax system (and hence the bureaucracy) plays an important role. If taxation is difficult and the state still wants to maximize its income, it is easier and cheaper to try to extract what is possible with cruder methods.

Paradoxically, a weak, factional state may be more detrimental for the economy than an autonomous state, since the latter has better control of the system and can more easily take into account the total effect of its interventions.

One of the basic tasks of a state is to define property rights and uphold the right of making and enforcing contracts between economic agents. These rights are public goods that a private producer will not produce because it is impossible to make the users pay. The state can guarantee respect for such rights because it always has the option of using force, if necessary. If property rights are protected, individuals cannot be deprived of what they have produced. There are no guarantees, however, that the property rights protected by the state are such that they encourage efficiency. On the contrary, the regulations may be used systematically to produce revenue for the state, often with considerable efficiency losses as a consequence. The judicial system then becomes a passive tool for the state and the difference between making and applying laws becomes blurred.

Arbitrary and high taxes on firms may, for instance, cause the latter to go underground and operate with the aid of informal networks and at high transaction costs. The predatory state may, of course, also use more 'traditional' distortions, such as trade barriers, with part of the income going directly into the pockets of the power holders, but also render favours to domestic firms. The latter then have to pay part of the proceeds to the state as taxes or bribes, and also incur costs for lobbying.

A dictator or a governing elite cannot take for granted that the administrative machinery of the state is loyal. The bureaucracy, in turn, may consist of one or several rival interest groups. The power elite must then be able to control its organization, the state apparatus, while the public is exploited. To make this possible the government officials have to benefit from part of the spoils. This is a so-called principal-agent problem which implies that the rulers have to set up rules and systems for monitoring the officials. The latter have their own preferences, however, and can be expected to act in their own interest if they can. The methods vary from direct extortion – police officers pocketing the fines for made-up crimes, for example – to bribes. Hence there is reason to believe that decisions taken at the central level are 'diluted' on their way to implementation, and that part of the income generated by the state apparatus through interventions end up in the pockets of government officials, at different levels.

In order to maximize its income and still stay in office, the predatory state has to optimize the size of the clique taking advantage of predation. (We will analyse the optimization problem in detail in Chapter 13.) This is problematic, since the optimal size regarding income maximization may differ from the optimal size regarding the security of those in power. The larger the clique, the more revenue can be squeezed out but probably at a decreasing rate, while the costs of collecting the revenue are likely to accelerate (because the 'easiest' sources of income are tapped first and because the number of victims of predation decreases as the number of predators increases). This implies that the net income begins to fall after a certain size of the state apparatus has been reached. When the size of the clique increases, its chance of staying in power increases as well. Also in this case there is likely to be an optimum, however. When the size of the administration increases, the risks for emergence of internal conflicts and factions tends to increase as well, which may lead to the downfall of the government for internal reasons. If there is some kind of solidarity between the members of the clique, such as kinship (as in Saddam Hussein's Iraq) or ethnic group (which is common in Africa), the likelihood of a *coup d'état* decreases at a given size of the clique, however.

If the optimal size of the ruling clique coincides with regard to both income and security of the incumbent government it is not a problem, in principle, to choose the correct size of the administration. There is no reason to believe that the two maximum points would coincide, however. On the contrary, it is unlikely. Figure 12.1 illustrates a situation where maximizing revenue calls for an administrative apparatus large enough for security to suffer. In Africa examples of such a situation can be found. In the typical case, the army has been relatively large in relation to the revenue that can be extorted in countries with poor communications and a dispersed population. Coups within the military have therefore been common. The Philippines under Marcos is another possible example. In that case the number of 'insiders' eventually grew very large and the government finally crumbled because it was not supported by a sufficient number of influential members of the clique.

The opposite situation may also occur, however, whereby incomes are maximized at such a small size of the clique that it would have difficulty clinging to power. This situation seems to be illustrated by several cases in nineteenth-century Latin America, where income maximization called for a small clique which thus remained weak and was relatively easy to topple for its rivals. This is also what actually happened, with the consequence that many countries in the region displayed a rapid turnover of dictatorial, usually military, regimes with little control of the country they were supposed to rule. In Thailand the situation was similar for a long period of time – even though the country is hardly a very good example of a kleptocracy – in that power was usually held by different, often quite small, army factions which could easily be exchanged without notable policy changes.

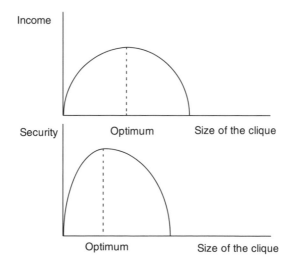

Figure 12.1   Optimal clique size regarding income and security

Techniques of predation

The possibilities for the state apparatus to line its pockets at the expense of the public depend ultimately on what resources those in power can use in their hunt for revenue. These resources are of three kinds: coercion (which we touched on already), and political and economic resources. By definition the state is in charge of the police and military. It can always, as a last resort, use violence in order to have its way. This is expensive, however, since the coercive apparatus has to be in place and must be maintained in order to be useful. If this is the only or main means of enforcing the decrees of the government, it has to be relatively big. Not least for this reason, other means are of interest as well. There is no lack of such means in a predatory state, however.

In all societies where governments exist there is also rent seeking. In predatory states the situation is extreme in that the unproductive activities tend to dominate behaviour both in the public and the private sector. For the latter, it pays to use the prospects for excess profits created by various distortions, such as trade barriers, and to work towards introducing new distortions. It is worth paying something for these possibilities. As long as the value of a privilege exceeds its costs, it is worthwhile. The public sector obtains income through distortions either directly (tariffs, licence fees) or indirectly, through 'selling' privileges to private agents. Who exactly collects the profit depends on how the decision-making power is delegated. Licences, for instance, are often granted at a rather low administrative level. The bribes would then be paid at that level, but may partly be channelled upwards in the hierarchy. Direct embezzlement of public funds is not unusual either.

Taxation is the most important tool for the predatory state. The interesting thing for the state, in this case, is not the allocation or stabilization effects of taxation, which traditionally are the focus of the analysis. The point here is rather the redistributive effects. Income is redistributed to the ruling clique. It is also important that the costs of collecting taxes and controlling the objects of taxation are as small as possible. The essential thing is maximizing the *net* income. This means that tariffs and export duties are the most important taxes, since income taxes, for example, are rather expensive to administer and require a large (and reasonably honest) civil service. Agriculture can, for example, be taxed through 'marketing boards', which have a purchasing monopsony, keep the prices paid to the farmers as low as possible and resell the products at a high price. The difference accrues to the state, if it is not absorbed by costs generated by a corrupt and inefficient system.

To the extent that there are income taxes these are often administered by 'farming out' the taxation privilege. Local chiefs or administrators are made responsible for collecting the taxes. As a reward they may keep part of the proceeds. Direct confiscation – for instance, when members of the ruling clique buy real estate at artificially low prices – has been prevalent in many predatory states.

Tariffs also facilitate another way of making money: smuggling. A tariff entails high domestic prices. The smuggler thus can pocket the difference between the world market price and the domestic price. If the product is not allowed to be imported at all, the profit is particularly big, of course.

Trade barriers favour the groups of society that take advantage of import-substituting industrialization while the government can force them to pay for their privileges. Since it is easy to find objections to import substitution – a populist one would be that big business is favoured – it is likely that the state prefers to conceal its real objectives through different diversions. The argument that import substitution 'promotes employment' is one such diversion. Quantitative, or so-called non-tariff, trade barriers are less transparent than tariffs and can thus be used if the government wants to divert the attention of the public from what it is actually doing.

Budget deficits may also be financed by printing money. The ensuing inflation can be regarded as a tax since real resources are bought with money whose value deteriorates rapidly. Foreign debt is a possibility that has been frequently used by predatory governments in spite of the fact that the loan conditions are often unfavourable. The point is that the borrowers do not intend to pay back the loans back and, in fact, they are often channelled into foreign bank accounts through some detour. The loans are left to be paid back by future governments. Development assistance is an even better alternative, but can seldom be directly confiscated by the government since the donor usually monitors the use of the proceeds. It is often easy to abuse aid funds, however (e.g., through paying too much for deliveries and charging 'administrative fees' to be paid by the recipients). Moreover, aid releases domestic government funds which are easier to abuse.

Another way of increasing the state revenue is by granting monopoly rights to entrepreneurs with close links to the rulers. Part of the monopoly rent is kept by the monopolists themselves and part goes to the state as 'licence fees', for example. A notorious example of this was the administration of Ferdinand Marcos in the Philippines, where the state systematically granted monopolies to family members, friends and relatives. Government procurement is another method for supporting 'loyal' firms, and usually takes place against payment under the table.

Government appointments can be used in various ways for rent seeking. In an authoritarian state based on one party or one ethnic group, lucrative government appointments are the natural way of exploiting the revenues generated by the state apparatus. In other cases public offices have been 'sold' to the highest bidder. In practice, the usual way to do this is bribing the official in charge of a certain appointment. The consequence is incompetence in the administration combined with negative incentives for those officials who, in spite of everything, are competent.

The costs of predation for the economy are very high. The income and wealth distribution tends to become very distorted. The resource allocation becomes inefficient and the effects on technical development and long-run growth are negative. Prices are distorted by subsidies and arbitrary sales taxes and by (say) trade barriers and overvalued exchange rates, while the real rates of interest are often negative, and so on. Additionally, there is the risk of so-called X-inefficiency (i.e., a lack of cost efficiency for a given activity).

An economy with strong traits of corruption and DUP activities (see Chapter 11), where resources are used extensively for securing privileges of special interests, runs the risk of getting stuck in a state of poverty and stagnation. If predation becomes endemic, the expected return on product-ive activities tends to be low, which affects the will to save and invest negatively. Investments tend to be small in a predatory state because there is a considerable risk that investors will lose their capital. Innovation activ-ities are particularly unattractive, since the risks are high even under normal circumstances. Furthermore, the allocation of investments is disturbed by the fact that profitable investments are unattractive, being the most inter-esting ones for the state to confiscate.

Firms are forced to devote much of their resources and time to creating good relations to the government through DUP activities and therefore neglect their proper tasks: producing goods and services and making cost-reducing innovations or new products. It also pays to coopt politicians and senior civil servants as 'partners' in the firms. These 'partners' function as promoters of the interest of the firms in the public administration, for which they obtain a share of the profit. The public investments in infrastructure and so on tend to be small, since they do not yield a direct return (but generate positive external effects). It is attractive to invest in security forces, the police and the army, however, since these organizations directly create the preconditions for predation.

The investments in education tend to be small. The children of the ruling clique are often educated abroad. As far as the rest of the population is concerned, education is rather a problem for the rulers, due to the fact that an ignorant population is easier to control than a well educated one. The demand for education is often low as well, since the return on education is low. It is more important to be well connected than to have a degree. Those who do have an education often emigrate.

Distortions of the economy favour certain interest groups, but the overall result in terms of welfare is usually a disaster. The problem then is to keep an unhappy population in check. One method for the regime is to try to conceal what it is really up to, through tinkering with the government budget or even avoiding channelling some revenues and expenditures through the official budget. Systematic attempts at misleading the population (and foreign donors) with respect to the real objectives of the rulers are a standard technique of the predatory state. (See Chapter 13 for details.) Ideology, often relating to nationalist or religious sentiment, is also a cheaper way to secure the cooperation of the population than using police and military force. Ideology has frequently been used in order to obtain development assistance as well. It cannot be considered an independent factor affecting the state's choice of policy but rather a way of rationalizing self-interest. It makes people behave in a way that deviates from their immediate interests. Compared to arms, ideology has a weakness, however: its ability to convince tends to diminish over time, especially as ideological constructions often contain attractive visions of the future. When these are not realized it becomes difficult to uphold the enthusiasm. The legitimacy of the system comes under scrutiny and it becomes more and more expensive for the ruler to uphold it, through, say, the education system or pure coercion. Also in minor issues marketing has an important role in the arsenal of the predatory state. The measures utilized have to be 'sold' to the public: introducing trade barriers 'saves jobs', but the fact that they create excess profits that can be expropriated by special interests is not mentioned.

Factors that limit predation

As we have already noted, some writers claim that all states basically are predators. According to this reasoning it is only the ability to extract revenues that differs, since the constraints on what the state can do are different. Democracy is one important constraint because it tends to limit the arsenal available to the decision-makers. Authoritarian states are subject to various constraints, too, however. An important such constraint is that the larger the share of the economy that the predatory state controls the weaker are its incentives to create distortions. (We have already applied the same logic, in Chapter 10.)

Assume that the ruling clique controls 1 per cent of the national income. In order to gain, for instance, 1 million from redistribution, it is willing to allow the national income to decrease by 100 million, since the likely loss of the clique would also be about 1 million. Alternatively, the clique would gain 1 million from stimulating the economy to grow by 100 million. This is usually more difficult, however, as it calls for increasing efficiency and more investment. If the ruling clique controls 50 per cent of the economy, an increase of its revenues by 1 million can only be allowed to lead to a decrease of the national income by 2 million. The incentives to distort the economy are much less in this case. In the extreme case, the state controls 100 per cent of the economy and then the incentive to distort the economy disappears altogether. This implies that predators who manage to stay in power for a long time tend to become more 'developmental' because, with the passing of time, intervening negatively the economy will be less and less in their interest.

Another factor that limits the scope for predation is the ability of the rulers to protect their interests against domestic or foreign rivals. To be able to stay in power, the ruler needs sufficient resources. The greater the potential for violence and the more economic and political resources the power holders command, compared to their rivals, the more possibilities they have for distorting the economy in their own favour. The government thus needs support from powerful groups in society. This may, on the one hand, lead to inefficient property rights (e.g., monopoly rights that favour certain groups), since a small number of monopolies is easier to control for the government than a more decentralized economic structure. There are cases, however, when a strong economy is a necessary condition for the government to stay in office. Sometimes the issue may even be the very existence of the state and the nation. National security and economic progress are then two sides of the same coin. In this case the state cannot afford to impair the efficiency of the economy. Taiwan and South Korea – states that have been subject to a permanent external threat – are two of the best examples of developmental states that can be found.

Redistribution of resources that belong to the citizens, finally, entails *transaction costs* for the rulers. This contributes to setting limits to predation because the interesting thing is *net income*. In order to redistribute, the government has to enter into explicit or implicit contracts with the citizens, specifying which the relevant resources are, how they should be measured and at what stage part of them are to be transferred to the state. An administrative apparatus has to be built up to handle this and to monitor the adherence to the 'contract'. This causes costs, not least because the administration itself is corrupt. In that case, a sizeable part of the revenue 'disappears' on its way to the treasury. Considering the efficiency of the economy it is best if the citizens can be made to comply voluntarily, since it is not in the interest even of a predatory state to have an inefficient economy if this can be avoided. Often it is most efficient to enter into (explicit or implicit) contracts with interest groups instead of individuals. The special interests are then given favours in return for payment. They are turned into a political resource for the government.

The productive predatory state

The predatory state reduces the efficiency of the economy only when this is the most profitable alternative. To a regime whose major interest is to enrich itself it may very well be advantageous to reduce the transaction costs in the economy by strengthening its fundamental institutions. Overall, it pays for a single organization – the state – to specialize in providing these institutions. Trade may be furthered by making laws that define economic rights and obligations, for example. This is apparent from trade and company legislation. Law and order is another central, collective good that the state may offer in order to receive incomes. It is not always in the interest of the government to make rules that paralyse the economy. Even a state that is mainly predatory may find it profitable to be economically productive. This increases the revenue that the state can confiscate. In addition, it increases the probability that the rulers may stay in power. The result may, however, not be optimal from an overall perspective, since the main interest of the decision-makers is government revenue.

The idea of the productive predatory state may be illustrated with the aid of a model constructed by Ronald Findlay and John Wilson. In this model, national income is produced by a private sector. The government taxes this sector and employs at least part of the tax proceeds (possibly all) to produce collective goods (law and order, infrastructure) that increase the productivity of the private sector. The tax is levied as a given percentage of the national income and the wage rate in both sectors is determined by the marginal product of labour in the private sector.

Formally, the national income is given by

$$Y = A(L_g)F(L_p, \overline{K}_p) \tag{12.1}$$

where L_p and $\overline{K}_p$ denote labour and capital in the private sector. If no private sector exists, $L_g = 0$ and $A = 1$. By allocating labour (L_g) to the production of law, order and infrastructure (and so on) the government may, however, increase the productivity of the private sector, but only at a decreasing rate: that is

$$A_L > 0 \text{ and } A_{LL} < 0$$

The total labour supply is given:

$$L_g + L_p = \overline{L} \tag{12.2}$$

When $L_g > 0$, $A(L_g) > 1$. At the same time, the use of labour in the private sector will decrease. The optimal allocation of labour is obtained by maximizing the national income (12.1) subject to the restriction imposed by the supply of labour:

$$dY = FA_L dL_g + AF_L dL_p = 0 \tag{12.3}$$

where

$$dL_g = -dL_p \tag{12.4}$$

or

$$FA_L = AF_L \tag{12.5}$$

The marginal product of labour in the public sector has to be equal to that of the private sector. This determines the optimum size of the public sector: $L_g{}^*$.

Since no market exists for the services produced by the public sector, this sector must be financed by taxation. In optimum the tax revenue will suffice to finance the wage bill in this sector. The tax is proportional to the national income:

$$R = tY \tag{12.6}$$

In the labour market there is competition, so that the wage rate equals the marginal product. The workers also pay taxes at the rate given by t. The net wage paid by the state in the public sector hence becomes $(1 - t)AF_L$ and the total wage bill of the sector amounts to

$$(1 - t^*)AF_L L_g^* = t^* Y^* \tag{12.7}$$

financed by taxation, where the asterisks denote the size of the public sector and the tax rate that maximizes the national income.

The problem of finding the optimal size of the state (the public sector) is illustrated in Figure 12.2. The national income that would arise if no state exists, and hence no collective goods are produced, is Y_0. If the public sector grows, with a given tax rate, production within the private sector will increase as long as the addition to output produced by the use of collective goods exceeds the output loss resulting from workers leaving the private sector to take up public employment (i.e., up to point L_g^* in Figure 12.2. A ruler who wants to maximize national income should choose the tax rate, t^*, that just suffices to finance L_g^*, no more and no less. The Y and R curves drawn in Figure 12.2 have been drawn for precisely this tax rate. Since R is a given share of Y, R reaches its maximum at the same level of public employment as Y. The cost curve, C (the wage bill in the public sector) increases, becoming steeper and steeper, with L_g since the public sector can expand only if it bids up the wage rate. It cuts the revenue curve in the maximum of the latter (i.e., the entire government revenue is used to finance the public wage bill).

Kleptocratic rulers have no incentives to deviate from this behaviour, provided that they are in a position to confiscate a suitable share of the output value, such as $Y^* - Y_0$. This is the maximum that they can take without risking an uprising. In certain cases, however, kleptocratic rulers are also bound by a 'contract' with the citizens, which implies that they cannot extract more than a given share of national income as taxes (and cannot confiscate anything). In that case, the public sector will be

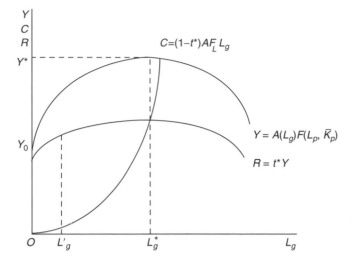

Figure 12.2   Optimal size of the public sector

too small, even though the tax rate might happen to be the optimal one. The only parameter that can be manipulated will then be the level of public employment. This will be chosen in such a fashion as to maximize the surplus of revenue over costs, $R - C$, in L'_g, where only part of the tax revenue is used for wages and the rest will end up in the pockets of the ruler.

There is, however, also a kind of predatory state that attempts to maximize public revenue. The best example is the *nomenklatura* of the previous communist regimes of Eastern Europe that had an incentive to increase employment in the public sector until the wage bill absorbed the entire tax revenue. This type of kleptocratic state can be 'tamed' in the case where it cannot decide the tax rate itself, by fixing the latter at t^*, the level that maximizes national income. This will automatically lead to the optimum size of the public sector.

If the bureaucrats themselves are allowed to decide the tax rate, the result will be a state apparatus which is 'too large'. Assuming that the public sector is allowed to expand until it absorbs the entire tax revenue, at any tax rate, the national income becomes a function of the tax rate. This is illustrated in Figure 12.3. The national income reaches its maximum when a further increase of the tax rate no longer increases it. Tax revenue, however, continues to increase also thereafter, until reaching the point where the increase resulting from a higher tax rate is balanced by the loss of tax revenue as a result of the lower national income.

Formally, we take the derivative of the tax revenue, $tY(t)$, with respect to t, which yields

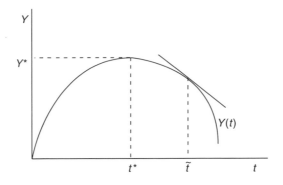

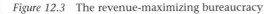

Figure 12.3 The revenue-maximizing bureaucracy

$$Y = -tY_t \tag{12.8}$$

or

$$Y_t(t/Y) = -1 \tag{12.9}$$

that is, the maximum is on the part of the national income curve (as a function of t) that has a negative slope, hence to the right of Y^*, at the tax rate t, where the elasticity of income with respect to the tax rate is equal to -1.

Not only the public bureaucracy but all workers, regardless of whether they work in the private or the public sector, have an interest in the expansion of the public sector. The workforce is given. Its income will increase with the after-tax wage rate $(1 - t)AF_L$. This wage increases when the public sector swells at a given tax rate:

$$\frac{dw}{dL_g} = (1 - t)\left(A_L F_L + A F_{LL} \frac{dL_p}{dL_g}\right) = (1 - t)\,(A_L F_L - A F_{LL}) > 0 \tag{12.10}$$

The capital owners, on the other hand, have clear incentives to limit the growth of the public sector after a certain point. Also the given capital stock is remunerated with its marginal product, so that

$$r = (1 - t)AF_K \tag{12.11}$$

and

$$\frac{dr}{dL_g} = (1 - t)(A_L F_K - A F_{KL}) \tag{12.12}$$

r reaches its maximum when

$$A_L F_K = A F_{KL} \tag{12.13}$$

that is, when the increase generated by an increased use of labour in the public sector is balanced by the reduction resulting from the fact that the workers in the public sector are taken from the private sector. In contrast to the workers, the capital owners will not be prepared to increase public employment beyond this point.

It is significant that the state bureaucracy in many predatory states is larger than in the industrial countries. In several African countries the number of employees in the public sector increased rapidly during the first years after independence. (The model's prediction of an increasing wage level in the public sector is, however, not very relevant for Africa.)

The developmental state

The preceding discussion suggests that the inclination of the state towards development to a great extent is an economic question, not an ideological one. If it pays better to be developmental for those in power this is a superior strategy, at least as long as it does not jeopardize their position. Successful state-led industrialization depends, on the one hand, on a strong autonomous state, which is able to discipline the private sector and does not have to bow to special interests. A strong state also presupposes a strong and competent bureaucracy.

On the other hand, the state itself has to be disciplined. In order to become developmental the state itself must be dependent on the performance of the economy. The prospects for and probability of successful development represent one factor in this context. If a country is too poor and undeveloped for favourable economic development to be likely within a reasonable period of time, the predatory alternative is probably more attractive from the rulers' point of view. What is 'reasonable' here tends to vary with the discount factor of the government, which in turn depends on how long it can reckon on staying in office.

This argument appears plausible. There are cases, however, that suggest that things may be more complicated. The East Asian newly industrialized economies (NIEs) are good examples. None of them was regarded as having good prospects for development in the late 1950s. Instead, the Asian favourites of development economists were Burma, the Philippines and South Vietnam! *Ex post* we now know that the former group of countries is among the best examples of successful development that can be found, while the favourites stagnated, at least until very recently. Hence a good expected growth potential is not enough. It is possible that the decision-makers must encounter a crisis, economic or political, that they have to resolve quickly in order to stay in office. A regime must also be able to fend off threats that do not originate from domestic challengers. Sometimes the threat against the very existence of the state (and perhaps even the nation) can be obvious. If foreign states threaten to take over – that is, there is a threat against the national existence – the state may be forced to be developmental. The economy must then be strong in order to ward off the threat. As mentioned already, the Asian NIEs are good examples of this, as they all began to develop under strong external pressure. Indeed Japan, nearly one hundred years earlier, is a similar example. Without the external threat all preconditions for a development towards a kleptocracy would have been met, especially in Taiwan and Korea. Ultimately, it was a question of preventing 'foreigners' from taking over the property rights of the economy. The external threat was not always enough, however. In China the state virtually collapsed due to the external pressure about the same time as the progress of Japan had become evident.

Conclusions

It is difficult to pinpoint exactly what the role of the state is in the economic development process. In any case, it is clear that regarding the state as a purely positive or negative agent in the economy is untenable. The degree of interventionism – or the size of the public sector – does not seem to play a decisive role. The government's degree of 'benevolence' is not necessarily crucial either. A state apparatus built with the good intentions of developing the economy can become an effective instrument of predation. An example of this is the regime of Kwame Nkrumah in Ghana, where Nkrumah was known for idealism and incorruptibility, but where the system itself developed into a typical predatory state. An example to the contrary is found in Taiwan. The Kuomintang regime was one of the most developmental in the world, but Chiang Kai-shek was not known for being 'benevolent', especially not during his time in Mainland China. Instead of the personal benevolence of the elite, it seems as if the economic incentives encountered by the state are decisive for what type of regime will emerge. Successful development is apparently explained neither by *laissez-faire* nor by an interventionist state. The state and the market need one another and positive synergy in the interaction between state and market appears to lie behind the examples of successful development.

Literature
The idea that those in power tend to maximize their own utility can be found in:
Brennan, Geoffrey and Buchanan, James M. (1983), 'Predictive Power and the Choice of Regimes', *Economic Journal*, Vol. 107.

John Stuart Mill's observation on abuse of political power was republished in:
Mill, John Stuart (1986), *On Liberty.* Longman Green, London.

Hume's ideas are referred to by:
Doshi, Tilak (1996), 'Chaining the Leviathan', in Tan, Kevin and Lam Peng Er (eds),
    Managing Political Change in Singapore. The Elected Presidency. Routledge, London and
    New York.

For ideas on the shortcomings of the market economy and the need for government
planning, see:
Srinivasan, T. N. (1985), 'Neoclassical Political Economy, the State and Economic
    Development', *Asian Development Review,* Vol. 3.
Cf. also:
Myrdal, Gunnar (1957), *Economic Theory and Under-Developed Regions.* Gerald Duck-
    worth, London.

Problems of a planned economy are analysed in:
Kornai, János (1992), *The Socialist System. The Political Economy of Communism.* Clar-
    endon Press, Oxford.

For a discussion on market failure and government failure, respectively, see:
Lal, Deepak (2000), *The Poverty of Development Economics* (2nd revised and expanded
    US edn). MIT Press, Cambridge, MA and London.

North's view of the state as both a source and an impediment of growth can be found in:
North, Douglass C. (1979), 'A Framework for Analyzing the State in Economic His-
    tory', *Explorations in Economic History,* Vol. 16.

The classification of states in different types originates in:
Lal, Deepak and Hla Myint (1996), *The Political Economy of Poverty, Equity and Growth.*
    Clarendon Press, Oxford.

The distinction between the contract based and the exploitation based state is made in:
North, Douglass C. (1981), *Structure and Change in Economic History.* W.W. Norton, New
    York and London.

The idea that all states are fundamentally predatory is presented in:
Levi, Margaret (1988), *Of Rule and Revenue.* University of California Press, Berkeley, CA.

The quotation on piracy is from:
North, Douglass C. (1997), *The Process of Economic Change.* UNU/WIDER, Working
    Papers, No. 128.

Bardhan's analysis of special interests in game theoretical terms can be found in:
Bardhan, Pranab (1984), *The Political Economy of Development in India.* Basil Blackwell,
    Oxford.

The quality of the taxation system and its significance for how developmental the regime is, is emphasized by:
Aoki, Masahiko, Murdock, Kevin and Okuno-Fujiwara, Masahiro (1997), 'Beyond the East Asian Miracle: Introducing the Market-Enhancing View', in Aoki, Masahiko, Kim, Hyung-Ki and Okuno-Fujiwara, Masahiro (eds), *The Role of Government in East Asian Development.* Oxford University Press, Oxford.

The reasoning on the optimal size of the ruling clique is based on:
Lundahl, Mats (1985), 'Government and Inefficiency in the Haitian Economy: The Nineteenth Century Legacy', in Connolly, Michael B. and McDermott, John (eds), *The Economics of the Caribbean Basin.* Praeger, New York. Reprinted in Lundahl, Mats (1992), *Politics or Markets. Essays on Haitian Underdevelopment.* Routledge, London and New York.

The section on the predation techniques is based mainly on:
Lundahl, Mats (1997), 'Inside the Predatory State: The Rationale, Methods and Economic Consequences of Kleptocratic Regimes', *Nordic Journal of Political Economy*, Vol. 24.
Lundahl, Mats (1997), 'The Economics of Kleptocracy. Some Reflections on Underdevelopment and the Predatory State', in Roy, Kartik C., Blomqvist, Hans C. and Hossain, Iftekhar (eds), *Development That Lasts.* New Age International Publishers, New Delhi.

The example showing that it is easier to redistribute than to create new income is based on:
Olson, Mancur (1982), *The Rise and Decline of Nations. Economic Growth, Stagflation and Social Rigidities.* Yale University Press, New Haven, CT, and London.

Findlay's and Wilson's original model is published in:
Findlay, Ronald and Wilson, John D. (1987), 'The Political Economy of the Leviathan', in Razin, Assaf and Sadka, Efraim (eds), *Economic Policy in Theory and Practice.* Macmillan, London.

The significance of an external threat for economic development is discussed in:
Gunnarsson, Christer and Lundahl, Mats (1996), 'The Good, the Bad and the Wobbly: State Forms and Third World Economic Performance', in Lundahl, Mats and Ndulu, Benno J. (eds), *New Directions in Development Economics.* Routledge, London and New York.

13
The Predatory State: Haiti and the Dominican Republic

The traditional argument for government intervention in the development process rests on three foundations. The first one maintains that the market mechanism fails to allocate resources efficiently at a given point in time due to the fact that the goods and factor markets are imperfect. Furthermore, not even perfect markets are able to guarantee rapid growth of the economy. Finally, even if the price mechanism for some reason did manage to solve both the static and the dynamic allocation problem this cannot lead to an 'ideal' distribution of income, except by pure coincidence.

Most governments of developing countries have chosen not to rely exclusively on market forces. In earlier chapters we have seen a number of examples of this. Interventions, regulations and plans have played a great role in the development effort. In the 1950s this was self-evident. 'It is assumed by all that it is the state that must be responsible both for initiating the overall plan and seeing that it is carried out', wrote Gunnar Myrdal in an influential work of the time. This notion was applied in practice. The state made plans at regular intervals about what should be achieved in the near future. These plans often contained a relatively detailed description of the means to be used. A number of tasks that in developed countries are usually left to the private sector to handle were taken over by the state. Public goods and physical infrastructure were self-evident public activities. Business, domestic as well as foreign, was regulated. Individuals and firms were taxed in order to make room for public consumption, public investment and transfers in order to change the distribution of income. Assets such as land were redistributed.

The image of the state was positive, with or without support from the economic doctrine. The fact that interventions are not cost-free was disregarded or, at any rate, it was assumed that the costs involved were insignificant as compared to the beneficial effects of the interventions. It is, of course, not true that interventions are cost-free. In the preceding chapters we have seen many examples to the contrary. The fact that perfect markets do not exist does not mean that government intervention would solve all problems, however. Costs and benefits have to be calculated for the market alternative as well as for the interventions that may seem to be desirable at first glance. Only then will it be possible to make rational choices between systems that are imperfect in different ways.

In this context the assumptions to be made about the state are absolutely crucial. From the preceding chapters it should be perfectly clear that the state may not be as altruistic, impartial, well informed and omnipotent as the proponents of planning assumed in the 1950s. On the contrary, when studying the state and its economic role there is reason to scrutinize critically what its intentions and abilities are. In Chapter 12 we discussed the state as an interest group among many others, usually the most powerful one, and analysed how the state, in the extreme case, deteriorates and becomes a pure predatory state whose only interest is to redistribute income and assets from the people at large to the group of individuals that wield the political power. We also gave a number of examples of such kleptocracies, or predatory regimes.

In the present chapter we will continue our analysis of the predatory state. Our purpose is to give two very concrete examples of how political predators behave and what the consequences may be for the economy at large. The study objects are two neighbouring countries, Haiti and the Dominican Republic; these are countries that, at least until recently, have been characterized by a political culture where political power has been regarded as a 'right' to squeeze as much as possible out of political office for private purposes. The 'winners' have taken as much as they possibly could, and the citizens have been forced to foot the bill.

The emergence of a predatory state

In Haiti as well as the Dominican Republic the state has, as a rule, been primarily a source of wealth for the rulers and their friends. It is not possible to understand the turn taken by politics in these countries without keeping this fact in mind. Stable political institutions had few chances to develop. Politics lacked autonomy. All possible groups tended to get involved in the process. Haiti and the Dominican Republic turned into praetorian societies (i.e., societies where all conceivable groups are politicized: the Church, the universities, the bureaucracy, the trade unions and the firms). The lack of stable institutions led to direct – often violent – clashes between the contenders for power. Mechanisms for alleviating or avoiding confrontations did not exist. There have been no common views on how conflicts could best be solved. As a consequence, the political process in both countries degenerated during the nineteenth century, to the extent that both Haiti and the Dominican Republic still suffer from the consequences. Kleptocrats ruled both nations over extended periods of time.

During the nineteenth century, politics in Haiti and the Dominican Republic was characterized by sudden and violent changes. Revolutions, uprisings, plots and coups were the order of the day. The ruling groups were not strong enough to stay in power for longer periods of time. Their political legitimacy appeared low and was based only on their ability to exercise violence better than other, competing, groups. Their plundering of the population was based on that ability as well.

Haiti in the nineteenth century

The Haitian state displayed strong predatory features from the very beginning. These had their roots in the colonial era. When Haiti became independent in 1804, after thirteen years of liberation wars, the values of the new national elite were heavily influenced by colonial society. Saint-Domingue used to be France's richest colony, and its prosperity had rested on the labour of 450,000 slaves. The idea that the colonialists could do manual work was unthinkable. This attitude was inherited by the new rulers.

The first rulers had a difficult problem, however. The population had diminished by 140,000–150,000 people from 1791, when the uprising against the French began, until 1805. This implied that there was more land than anybody could use. At the same time, slavery had been abolished. The Haitians were free. Free peasants and free land are not, however, compatible with a non-working ruling class. It was impossible for the elite to exploit the peasants without tying them to the land. Collecting rent in a situation where the peasants could easily move and take up a new plot of land without being bothered with such burdens was, of course, impossible. The first rulers therefore returned to a plantation system based on forced labour. The former slaves were tied to the plantations and had to work under military supervision.

Beginning in 1809 the plantation system, however, broke down for good. The international market for Haitian sugar had shrunk as a consequence of the conflict with France and the unrest that resulted from the Napoleonic wars. At the same time, large parts of the capital stock had been destroyed during the liberation wars, and, as we already have seen, the labour force had diminished. Plantation-based agriculture needs markets as well as capital and labour. In 1809 Alexandre Pétion, president of the southern part of the then divided country, decided to start distributing the land to his officers and soldiers. Ten years later Henry Christophe, king in the northern part, followed his example. During the following decades plantation agriculture eventually disappeared and the peasant agriculture that still characterizes Haiti developed.

The land reform had paradoxical economic consequences. The elite were now deprived of labour-free income, since it was impossible to exploit free peasants who had ample access to land. Therefore the elite and groups competing with the elite (mainly the black army officers) focused on political power, because this power entailed the right to tax. The political game degenerated into a private struggle over the income produced by the state apparatus, and this apparatus was turned into an income-generating machine. Throughout the nineteenth century, until the American occupation in 1915, politics remained the affair of a few small cliques, all sharing the same goal: the highest possible private income.

Eventually a repetitive pattern emerged. Those who wanted to capture the political power and the state revenues recruited armies consisting of peasant mercenaries (so-called *cacos*) and marched towards the capital, Port-au-Prince, to topple the incumbent president and government. Between 1843 and 1915 more than one hundred revolutions and coups took place. During this time Haiti had 22 different presidents. Only one managed to stay in office for a full term. Four died, from more or less natural causes during their terms. The remaining seventeen were toppled, with or without violence. How can this pattern be explained?

The key to an understanding of the political history of Haiti in the nineteenth century is the fact that the competing groups, fighting for power, were relatively small. They did not represent any broad groups of the population but tried to gain economic advantages at the expense of others. We may then apply Mancur Olson's reasoning about the logic of small interest groups, which we explained in Chapter 10. It was exactly this logic that was brought to bear in Haiti after 1843. From that year until the American occupation the reins of power were taken over by one clique after another. All of these cliques, which could easily constitute themselves as they were small, did their best to empty the treasury chest and, if it was empty already, they did not hesitate to take up loans, at home or abroad, on practically any terms.

The seemingly endless series of coups, uprisings and revolutions illustrates Gordon Tullock's thesis that coups and revolutions virtually never stem from a wish to improve the situation of the majority. Revolutions do not aim at collective gains but at private profits. For those who organize the uprisings those profits are usually considerable, provided that the revolt is successful. Common citizens, in turn, have very little to gain from sticking their necks out. With bad luck they may lose their lives. If this reasoning is combined with Olson's small group logic it is easy to see why no genuine popular revolutions took place, but politics remained a matter for a small minority. The difference between the gain from toppling the incumbent government for the individual and that for the group was far too large, and if we also consider the risks of losing life and health because of a revolution, the incentives for the citizens to do something were totally negligible. They preferred to minimize the contacts with the state in order to avoid, if possible, forced recruitment to the army and taxation. In fact, they participated almost only when they were paid to do so.

It was not surprising that the masses had difficulties mobilizing any enthusiasm. After 1809 they could easily satisfy their two most cherished wishes: freedom and land. These constituted their driving force during the liberation wars of 1791–1803. Except for that there was little to be had. For the individuals directly involved in the political game the situation was entirely different. If they managed to topple the incumbent government they could take over its privileged position. The gains available were limited only by the ability of the new administration to tax the citizens, legally or illegally.

The predatory state as a club

In Chapter 12 we discussed briefly how rulers of a predatory state are faced with the problem of optimizing the size of the clique allowed to share in the revenues generated by the wielding of power. Nineteenth-century Haiti is an excellent study object in this respect. We will therefore consider more explicitly the model we just touched on in Chapter 12. This model focuses on the ruler's choice between revenue and security.

Let us assume that the ruler has a utility function with two arguments, his private income and the probability of staying in power:

$$U = U(Y, P) \tag{13.1}$$

where

$$U_Y > 0, U_P > 0, U_{YY} < 0 \text{ and } U_{PP} < 0,$$

that is, where the marginal utility of both income and security (probability of staying in office) is positive but decreasing.

The ruler's problem is that he cannot rule alone but is dependent on support from others to be able to line his pockets and cling to power. He needs a clique which increases his strength, military and otherwise, but how large should this clique be? The ruler has a problem similar to the one of determining the optimal size of a private club. The size of the clique affects both variables in his utility function. His net income will be given by the difference between his gross revenues, R, and his costs, C:

$$Y = R - C \tag{13.2}$$

The gross revenues as well as the costs are, in turn, functions of the size of the clique, M:

$$R = R(M) \tag{13.3}$$

$$C = C(M) \tag{13.4}$$

It is reasonable to assume that when the size of the clique supporting the president increases, its ability to tax the citizens increases, too, albeit at a decreasing rate: that is, $R_M > 0$ and $R_{MM} < 0$. The marginal cost of increasing the clique size can be assumed to be rising, however. Recruiting new clique members tends to become more and more costly, so that $C_M > 0$ and $C_{MM} > 0$.

The probability of staying in power varies with the size of the clique as well:

$$P = P(M) \tag{13.5}$$

Analogously with the case of net revenue, the risk of losing power may be divided into two components. The first one is the probability of being toppled by a rebellion initiated by competing cliques from outside the establishment. This probability is likely to fall when the size of one's own clique increases, but at a decreasing rate. The other component consists of the probability of being removed from office through a *coup d'état* led by members of one's own clique. The risk for this type of conspiracy is likely to increase with the size of the clique, at an increasing rate. Factions are formed within the ruling clique and, the larger the clique is, the more difficult they are to control for the ruler.

The assumptions we made regarding revenue and security generate the inverted U-shaped curves that we depicted in Figure 12.1. It is easy to see why the curves take on such a shape. The net revenue is the difference between gross revenue and costs at each size of the clique. As shown in Figure 13.1, this difference increases continuously up to a certain size and then begins to decrease.

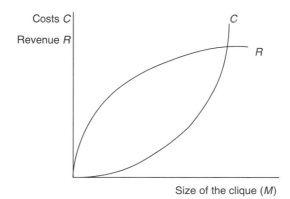

Figure 13.1 The ruler's costs and revenues as functions of the clique size

In a similar way the net probability for the ruler to stay in power is obtained. From the curve showing the probability that he will be able to thwart external rebellions we must deduct a curve showing the probability that he will be toppled in a *coup d'état*. (These two curves are analogous to the revenue and cost curve, respectively.)

In Chapter 12 we noted that the two inverted U-curves, for revenues and security, reach their maximum at the same size of the clique only by pure accident. In the general case the clique size that is optimal from a revenue point of view differs from the size which is optimal from a security point of view. Which one of the curves reaches its maximum first is a purely empirical question. In the case of Haiti, the curves seem to have had the positions indicated by Figure 13.2, where maximum revenue was reached before maximum security. We will return to the reasons for this shortly, but before we do we will take a look at the clique size interval between the values given by the two maximum points.

In this interval the ruler is forced to choose whether he prefers, at the margin, more security (larger clique) or more revenue (smaller clique). Formally we can find his optimal clique size by differentiating his utility function with respect to the clique size, M, while using (13.2)–(13.5): that is, we maximize

$$U[R(M) - C(M), P(M)]$$

We then obtain

$$\frac{dU}{dM} = U_Y(R_M - C_M) + U_P P_M = 0 \tag{13.6}$$

or

$$U_P P_M = -U_Y Y_M \tag{13.7}$$

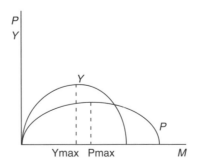

Figure 13.2   The Haitian rulers' choice between income and security

The utility gain made by the ruler because the probability that he remains in power increases with an increasing clique size must be exactly balanced by the utility loss he makes due to decreasing revenue.

The probability that the ruler will stay in office may be changed for reasons other than a changing size of the ruling clique. He may, for example, have stepped 'out of bounds' so grossly that a conspiracy has been formed against him. This results in a downward shift of the P curve, as indicated in Figure 13.3.

At each clique size, awareness of an ongoing conspiracy leads to an increase in the probability that a newly recruited person will turn out to be unreliable (and thus prefers to betray the ruler and join the conspirators). The P curve reaches its maximum at a smaller size of the clique. At the same time the ruler's ability to collect taxes will diminish. The R curve in Figure 13.1 rotates downwards as the conspirators, if they belong to the political establishment, increasingly prefer to pocket the tax revenues themselves, or, if they are outsiders, show the tax payers that there is an alternative to the incumbent government and thus undermine the tax morale. The slope of the curve will decrease at each size of the clique. At the same time, the C curve will rotate upwards since the conspirators, wherever they are, compete with the government for support, which in turn will increase the marginal cost of recruiting new members of the clique. The slope of the curve will thus increase. The Y curve shifts downwards, in the same way as the P curve, and will reach its maximum at a smaller clique size than before. (The area between the R and C curves is 'squeezed' and the maximum distance between the two curves occurs at a lower clique size than before.)

If large, the shifts in the P and Y curves may lead to a smaller optimal size of the ruler's 'club'. The marginal utility of recruiting new members decreases in terms of both security and revenue, while the marginal cost of recruiting increases. The ruler faces a situation where both his security and his disposable income are lower than before. This explains why a ruler tends to resort to weeding out potential adversaries when there are rumours of an imminent coup. It also points to the importance of creating mechanisms that minimize the risks of conspiracies which worsen the position of the ruler.

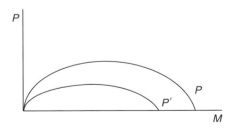

Figure 13.3 The effects of a conspiracy

These mechanisms must be capable of monitoring the ruler's environment to be able to stop potential rebels at an early stage, before they grow too strong. Secret police, paramilitary forces, intelligence organizations and other repressive bodies, whose strength should preferably be independent of the size of the ruling clique, are part of the picture. They are not free, but it is often much cheaper for the ruler to institutionalize repression than to increase the size of the clique in order to achieve a certain level of security. At the same time they may contribute towards increasing the tax revenues of the ruler, using mostly 'unorthodox' methods lacking a legal base.

The pattern of Haiti

Let us now see how our 'club model' may be used to explain the pattern that emerged in Haiti during the nineteenth century. After 1843, when President Jean-Pierre Boyer was removed from office, the political process degenerated. Power became a device for generating private income, and power thus easily justified the costs entailed by staging a rebellion or a *coup d'état* to topple the incumbent president. With time, these attacks tended to assume the character of one-shot raids for the treasury, which quickly tended to be depleted, which in turn led to a rapid deterioration of the loyalty of the president's followers.

Haiti during the nineteenth century was what could be called a security-inefficient state. The net revenue curve of the rulers reached its maximum at a smaller size of the clique than the curve indicating his probability of staying in office. Most of the presidents between 1843 and 1915 concentrated on the revenue aspect but were too weak politically to be able to stay in office for more than short periods. After 1883 *caco* armies more or less regularly marched towards Port-au-Prince, and the presidents were unable to put up much resistance. Then the treasury was plundered and the mercenaries were paid and returned home.

Haiti was a poor country, however, and it was not unusual that the treasury chest was nearly empty even before the rebels reached the capital. In that case the new rulers were forced to take up new loans from abroad or from within Haiti. Foreign loans were solicited, at exorbitant terms, in 1874, 1875, 1896 and 1910, and six domestic loans were issued between 1912 and 1914 (in the latter year, no fewer than four of them). The resources could not be stretched indefinitely, however. The Haitian presidents faced a permanent choice between security and revenues. If they limited the number of people who could share in the spoils they were easily thrown out of office. A contributing reason for this was that the *cacos* regarded revolutions as business, not as political activity. They sold their services to the highest bidders, who almost always were those not yet in power. The costs of staying in office thus tended to be high. Squeezing tax revenue from the population was not too easy either. Since the overwhelming majority of the presidents held power for just a short period they never bothered to create an efficient government apparatus and tax administration. The simplest possible methods were used, particularly export and import duties that were easy to collect. In the early 1880s no less than 98 per cent of the state revenue emanated from these two sources. The enforcement costs for widening the tax base to other sources than trade would have been prohibitive. Increasing the number of 'club members' would not have been of much help.

Hence most presidents were quickly removed from office. The consequences of this were seldom serious. Those who managed to stay in office for longer periods made an effort to invest in security systems: Faustin Soulouque (1847–59), Fabre Geffrard (1859–67), Lysius Salomon (1879–88), Florvil Hyppolite (1889–96), Tirésius Simon Sam (1896–1902) and Pierre Nord Alexis (1902–8). Soulouque had his *zinglins*, a paramilitary terror organization, Geffrard spent large sums of money on a network of spies and also had a secret police force, Salomon used similar methods, Hyppolite ruled through a system of warlords (*députés militaires*) at the province level and Nord had a *Police Centenaire*. At least five of the 'long-lived' presidents thus made special efforts to survive in office. At the same time they were kleptocrats and considered the state revenues their own. They differed from their more 'short-lived' colleagues in that they emphasized the security aspects more, but only marginally.

The Dominican Republic in the nineteenth century

In Haiti's neighbouring country, the Dominican Republic, a pattern very similar to that of Haiti developed. The country became independent in 1844, having been occupied by Haiti since 1822. A fight for power began immediately. The presidency saw a change of incumbent 50 times between 1844 and 1930 and innumerable civil wars and revolutions took place during this period. According to the Dominican historian, Frank Moya Pons, politics was the only 'industry' in the country apart from sugar and tobacco. The highest office of the country was usually held by some regional *caudillo* who relied on an army mainly consisting of mercenaries.

One of the *caudillos* who fought for power in the mid- nineteenth century was Buenaventura Báez. Báez was forced into exile at several occasions and then always took the treasury chest with him. After a while he used to return and eventually make his way back to the presidency, which he held no less than five times. His fund-raising methods included foreign loans at horrendous terms and printing money. Báez's main opponent between 1844 and 1866 was Pedro Santana. During this period Santana was president three times and Báez twice. Together they kept the country in a state of nearly permanent chaos.

The *caudillos* who fought for power during the nineteenth century usually sought financial and military support overseas. Pedro Santana asked Spain to re-annex its former colony and in 1861 Spanish rule was re-established. Three months later a rebellion broke out, however, resulting in a guerilla war against the Spanish. This war continued until 1865 when the Spanish troops left the country after severe losses. Thereafter the Dominican politics were fragmented, exactly as in Haiti. Earlier, only a few *caudillos* had competed for power. Due to the guerilla war dozens of military leaders entered the picture. They began their struggle over the presidency as soon as the Spanish had left. Between 1865 and 1879 the Dominican Republic saw 50 rebellions and 21 governments.

A certain political stability was introduced by Ulises Heureaux (1882–99). He was more concerned about security than the other Dominican presidents of the nineteenth century. Heureaux forced many of his adversaries into exile. Others were imprisoned or killed. He used large numbers of spies and spent huge sums on security. Heureaux led an extravagant life and in order to finance that, like Báez before him, he tried to lease Dominican territory to the United States. He also took foreign loans so large that he knew that he would never be able to pay them back. Finally, he printed bank notes on a large scale. Heureaux survived many murder attempts before he was finally killed in 1899. When he died the Dominican Republic was ruined and the enormous foreign debt he had accumulated finally resulted in the US taking over the Dominican customs, in 1905. Very little of the loans taken by Heureaux had been used for productive purposes.

After the death of Heureaux the fight between various military leaders continued. During 1903 and 1904 the share of military expenses in the government budget exceeded 70 per cent. The *caudillo* type of regime was to continue its domination of the Dominican politics until the American occupation of the country in 1916. At the onset of the occupation the Dominican army was so badly trained that it was virtually unable to suppress an uprising. The army was rather an instrument in the service of corruption and rebellion.

Trujillo and Duvalier

The United States occupied Haiti between 1915 and 1934 and the Dominican Republic between 1916 and 1924. The most important consequence of these two occupations was without doubt the reorganization of the military apparatus which took place in both countries. The regionally based private armies were disarmed and disbanded and in their place national guards were established, with a role between that of a regular army and a police force. These organizations soon came to play a decisive role for the political development both in the Dominican Republic and Haiti. On the surface political life calmed down, but the new armed forces prepared the way for a new type of predatory state.

In the Dominican Republic, Rafael Trujillo's way to power went through the ranks of the *Guardia Nacional*, and when he became president he used the Guard to crush his political opposition. In the neighbouring country, the *Garde d'Haïti* gradually became the paramount political agent, until the fateful year, 1957, when François Duvalier (Papa Doc) was elected president with its assistance.

In 1930 Rafael Trujillo became president of the Dominican Republic. He had been the commander of the National Guard and during his campaign he had used it as a terror instrument to force his political opponents to withdraw. When he became president he concentrated all power into his own hands and the regional *caudillos* who were opposed to his government were quickly eliminated by the *Guardia Nacional*. Trujillo managed to stay in office for over 30 years, until he was murdered in 1961.

The army was the backbone in the state apparatus created by Trujillo. Its numbers grew constantly. In 1931, 11.5 per cent of government expenditure was absorbed by it and by the end of the 1950s the figure had increased to 50 per cent. The military salaries were good and the army enjoyed special privileges. Apart from the army Trujillo had a national police force, created by himself, which could be used for suppressing revolts, a secret service, and a number of other intelligence organizations within and outside the country.

In order to protect himself against *coups d'état* and internal conspiracies Trujillo kept on reorganizing the military, the secret service and the bureaucracy. Nobody else was allowed to build up an independent power position. In all branches of government there were spies who reported to the dictator. To control the population at large Trujillo also used a state ideology. The educational system, the research establishment, the press, as well as literature and music were all involved in the service of the 'Benefactor'. They became pure instruments of indoctrination. Controlling the masses in this way was much cheaper than letting loose the repression apparatus. The latter could be reserved for special occasions. There is no doubt that the method was successful. The picture of Trujillo as a fatherly national figure for the country (and not a ruthless dictator) did not disappear with his death, but for many Dominicans it only faded away after many years.

Trujillo was an extraordinarily successful predator. He had no scruples whatsoever as to what the state machinery could be used for. This, combined with his inventiveness regarding plundering methods, soon created enormous wealth for Trujillo and his family. Thus it became impossible to get a government job without belonging to, and paying 10 per cent of one's income to, Trujillo's party (the only one allowed), and private firms had to pay the president if they wanted to stay in business. Trujillo also used taxation, of course, particularly taxes on foreign trade (coffee and cocoa). These taxes had to be paid in advance. Many producers therefore ran into difficulties and were forced to sell their land to Trujillo.

Moreover, the landowners were forced to sell to Trujillo at artificially low prices, unless he took over their land with more direct methods. The president thus came to control 60 to 80 per cent of the land and, additionally, 80 per cent of all businesses in the capital, Santo Domingo. Apart from this, a number of monopolies were controlled by Trujillo. The resources of the state were used directly for his private purposes. The reserves of the central bank and the rest of the assets of the banking system were used for building sugar processing plants, infrastructure that predominantly served his own properties, and so on.

Trujillo was particularly interested in the sugar industry, where he had a dominant influence, and he did not hesitate to use government money to develop his own business interests. Fields were cleared and sugar processing plants and roads were built. Finance was organized through special government funds. Soldiers and prisoners worked on the plantations. The big plant in Río Haina was built by forced labour under the auspices of the army and the government had to provide the money for an advanced water pipe to another sugar processing plant.

Using the government apparatus for his own benefit Trujillo ended up controlling between 65 and 85 per cent of the Dominican economy. He had accumulated a fortune, largely invested in foreign banks, of about $800 million when he died in 1961, which may be compared with the GDP of the Dominican Republic for the same year: 634 million dollars.

In Haiti the American Marine Corps suppressed the old *caco* armies and created a national guard like the one in the Dominican Republic: the *Garde d'Haïti*. The Guard had a commander, Démosthènes Calixte who for a while saw to it that the military stayed out of politics. Calixte was forced to resign in 1938, however, and after that the Guard became a political instrument. In the mid-1940s there was no longer any doubt about the army being the ultimate decision-maker regarding the time period a president could stay in office and enjoy its privileges. Dumarsais Estimé, who was elected President in 1946, had the army (which had forced his predecessor, Élie Lescot, to resign) behind him, and when Estimé had to leave office Colonel Paul Magloire became his successor. Haiti had turned into a praetorian state where the military was in charge.

The increasing importance of the military did not imply, however, that the predatory tradition had been lost. On the contrary: it had merged with the praetorian state. The American occupation power had made an attempt to clean up the Haitian administration, but when the American troops had been withdrawn it was obvious that the attempt had failed. When Sténio Vincent (1930–41) had been elected president, the predatory tradition of the nineteenth century was fully revived. Vincent, Lescot (1941–6), Estimé (1946–50) and Magloire (1950–6) all held similar opinions about what the presidential powers could be used for. All of them tried (some successfully) to stay on in office longer than the constitution allowed. Ultimately, the army decided the limit, however.

When François Duvalier (Papa Doc) was elected president, with the support of the army, in 1957, he was fully aware of this. He dismantled the existing power structure and built a new one with himself at the centre of the web. He was to dominate politics completely, like Trujillo, and even to the extent that it was possible for him to let his own son, Jean-Claude (Baby Doc) succeed him in office (1971–86).

The changes introduced in Haitian politics by Papa Doc had nothing to do with the revolutionary promises he gave during his election campaign. The predatory state did not disappear, but only the foundation it was based on. Exactly like Trujillo, Duvalier weeded out individuals in all groups and institutions that could possibly have offered some resistance to his regime: the army, the political opposition, the church, the mass media, the education system, the administration, and so on.

Particularly interesting is Duvalier's pacification of the army. As with Estimé and Magloire, he had assumed power with its approval. Since he understood that the army could remove him just as easily, Duvalier did not hesitate to introduce a policy that systematically transferred and retired senior officers, according to the same system as the one Trujillo had used. More than 200 officers were removed during Papa Doc's first eleven years as president. When he formally took over the position of supreme commander in 1964, all senior officers owed their promotion to him.

Instead of the army, which was stripped of its traditional role, Duvalier created a paramilitary force, the so-called *tonton macoutes*, who were used to terrorize real or imaginary enemies. Together with the regular army and the police force the *tonton macoutes* consumed between 25 and 30 per cent of total state expenditure. Apart from this terror organization, Papa Doc used the voodoo clergy and the local paramilitary sheriffs, the *chefs de section*. Both these groups had to plead allegiance to the president personally and towards the voodoo priests Papa Doc assumed the role of Baron Samedi, the *loa* (spirit) that guards the cemeteries. Finally he created a murky, 'revolutionary' ideology: Duvalierism.

When he had established himself securely at the state helm, Duvalier began to privatize government money for his own purposes. A number of methods were employed for squeezing out money that could be channelled into the pockets of the head of state. Tax proceeds were embezzled, deductions were made from the salaries of the civil servants and businessmen were forced to give 'voluntary' contributions to charitable government projects. To this can be added 'normal' extortion, theft and confiscation of property belonging to people with alleged sympathies for the opposition.

The result was overwhelmingly successful. While Magloire is believed to have stashed away between $12 and 28 million, Duvalier allegedly collected between $7 and 10 million *per year* (between $100 and $150 million all in all). The plundering continued successfully under his son. When Baby Doc was toppled in 1986, his wealth was estimated at about $450 million and that of his mother at no less than $1,150 million, to be compared with a GDP of $2,150 million in 1986.

Concealing the truth

We have in the preceding discussion implicitly assumed that a kleptocracy acts relatively 'openly': that is, that it does not really try to hide what it is up to. This is, of course, not the case in practice. One way of increasing both revenues and security at a certain size of the clique is to make the citizens believe that the ruling clique actually tries to promote the welfare of the population majority, or at least does not steal from the citizens.

Policies generally differ with respect to their transparency. It is clear what some measures aim at, while other interventions may be interpreted in different ways. An excellent example of this is the Swedish agricultural policy, which we discussed in Chapter 5. There we concentrated on the 'contingency' goal. The paramount goal during the postwar period has been another one, though: to guarantee the farmers an income comparable to that of other similar or corresponding (never fully specified) groups.

This target may be reached in different ways. The simplest, least distorting and clearest, for the citizens, is giving the farmers a direct income supplement without demanding anything in return. Then both production and consumption take place at world market prices, and the taxpayers realize at once that this is a transfer to the farmers that they have to pay. The second-best policy is a subsidy of the production (the low price policy) since this policy causes losses only on the production side, not on the consumption side. Its implications are less clear to the taxpayers, however, since it can be defended with the production goal: the alleged need to keep production at a certain level. Finally, there is the high price policy – the tariff policy – which distorts both consumption and production, but has the clear advantage that most citizens would not directly relate it to an income transfer from the tax payers to the farmers.

A similar type of reasoning can be applied to predatory governments to an even greater extent. The methods they use to enrich themselves are far from always the cheapest ones for the society. As we have seen already, predators are motivated by completely different reasons. Both their probability of staying in office and their revenue can be increased by using methods that effectively conceal what their real goals are, even if these methods are particularly expensive for society.

This reasoning can easily be included in our earlier model. Let us assume that the alternatives available for increasing revenues and/or security can be ranked according to how difficult it is for the citizens to see their true intentions (i.e., according to their degree of obfuscation). The latter, in turn, should affect both revenue and costs as well as the probability of the ruler staying in office, which means that instead of our earlier (13.3), (13.4) and (13.5) we have three new functions. On the revenue side we have:

$$R = R(M, O) \tag{13.8}$$

where a higher O represents a less transparent policy, and where $R_O > 0$ and $R_{OO} < 0$ (i.e., obfuscation displays decreasing returns) and

$$C = C(M, O) \tag{13.9}$$

with $C_O > 0$ and $C_{OO} > 0$ (i.e., the marginal cost of obfuscation is rising). These assumptions generate an inverted U-curve for the ruler's income (Y) as a function of the degree of obfuscation, analogous with our earlier case.

As to the probability for the ruler to stay in office we have:

$$P = P(M, O) \tag{13.10}$$

Whether the analogy with the size of the clique is valid here is more questionable. On the one hand, it is possible to argue that $P_O > 0$ and $P_{OO} < 0$: that is, that the probability of staying in office increases with the degree of obfuscation but at a decreasing rate. This is the simplest way. It is perhaps more realistic, however, to assume that an increasing degree of obfuscation is a signal for those working close to the ruler that he is increasing his revenues and that they would therefore regard it as more profitable to topple him. In that case the analogy with the clique size holds and we have P as a function of O, which also looks like an inverted U. The ruler can then cheat the citizens but not his own associates. In the optimum we then obtain:

$$U_P P_O = -U_Y Y_O \tag{13.11}$$

The increase (decrease) of security the ruler can get by increasing the degree of obfuscation is balanced by the decrease (increase) of revenue that this leads to. (If security were to increase monotonically with the degree of obfuscation it would always result in an optimum where more security can be obtained at the cost of less revenue.)

Some Haitian tricks

Finally, we will give some examples of obfuscation in practice, using Haiti as an source. The majority of Haiti's presidents have tried to conceal their real goals with varying success. Geffrard spent $20,000 per year on 'encouraging the arts and sciences'. His meat bill was footed by his life guard and his champagne bill was paid by the government hospital. The return from two government estates ended up in his own pockets. Salomon 'recycled' debt instruments issued by the *Banque Nationale*, which was forced to cash them twice, and when the matter was revealed it was hushed up as a 'non-deliberate mistake'. Simon Sam embezzled public funds when he 'consolidated' the state debt. Between 1908 and 1915 the tariff revenues of Haiti were regularly pawned to political leaders and, when the American occupation authorities started scrutinizing the government payrolls, they had to purge a number of employees who were 'dead, not working or gravely incompetent'.

Obfuscation and swindle continued after the occupation. When Sténio Vincent obtained a large loan in 1938 from the American Export-Import Bank for investments in infrastructure, the Haitian government tried to take direct control of the disbursements and force the American firm which had been contracted for the job to employ more people with good contacts in government circles. Lescot introduced mandatory deductions from wages and salaries for 'social security', but the deductions all ended up in his pockets. Estimé used the exhibition organized in 1949 to commemorate the bicentennial of the foundation of Port-au-Prince, at a cost three times as high as calculated, to line his own pockets. Under Magloire a big dam project was started in the Artibonite valley, where twice as much money as planned disappeared into corrupt pockets even before the first phase of the project was finished. Extensive roadwork and catastrophe aid to hurricane victims created more options for embezzling public funds.

Papa Doc introduced some new tricks into the repertoire. The most important one was the used of unbudgeted funds. The government tobacco monopoly, *Régie du Tabac et des Allumettes*, collected taxes on a number of goods: tobacco, matches, sugar, cement, flour, drinks, dairy products, chocolate and sweets. Despite repeated demands from the International Monetary Fund, the accounts of the monopoly were never audited. The money went to the *tonton macoutes* and to the Duvalier family. Moreover, funds that were included in the government budget were often used for purposes entirely different from what they were earmarked for.

Another trick was letting foreign interests participate in 'projects' which were funded either by taxes or government bonds. These funds were simply shared between the government and the foreign firms. When the projects were actually carried out they were often funded several times, such as the new airport, for example. Another lucrative project was organizing the annual migration of Haitian sugar cane cutters to the Dominican Republic. As a result of these arrangements, half of the total wage sum, $6–8 million per year, was sent back to Duvalier and his clique.

Duvalier's plundering was eventually organized in *Mouvement de Rénovation Nationale*, whose official purpose was to turn the little village of Cabaret into a model city. The financing included a fund for enhancing literacy, a compulsory state lottery whose winners remained unknown, 'liberation bonds' to finance the new airport and an unbudgeted pension system *à la* Lescot.

After the death of Papa Doc the Haitian predatory state went into a phase of 'fine tuning'. Some of the old tricks continued to be used. The unbudgeted accounts remained unaudited and the migration of sugar cane cutters to the Dominican Republic was still lucrative. Aid funds were embezzled, as in Papa Doc's time. This eventually became risky, however, as international opinion against Haiti hardened. The Duvalier clique therefore resorted to three new methods. The first one consisted of private business activities by the presidential family and its close friends, sometimes through fronts, in other cases more openly. The president's father-in-law, Ernest Bennett, in 1975 went into the export market for coffee with a market share of 1.1 per cent. After seven years he was the leading exporter and in 1986 he had 40 per cent of all export licences. Bennett was also involved in smuggling of, among other things, sugar, rice flour and cotton textiles, with the tacit agreement of his son-in-law.

More important, however, was that the Duvalier family controlled government enterprises. This opened the door for a number of manipulations, all of which were intended to create monopolies on the domestic market. For traditional public services – electricity, telecommunications and air transport – the customers were charged as much as the traffic could bear. Beginning in 1979, the state bought or established five large enterprises: soybean oil, wheat flour, sugar (two firms) and cement. None of these ever became profitable from an business or national point of view, but they all yielded big profits for those in power.

The Duvalier family had practically unlimited access to government funds. Blank cheques were issued on an account number in the administration, often without a receiver or simply to the holder. All ministries and government enterprises were affected, including the finance ministry, the tobacco monopoly, the state lottery, the government gambling commission, the wheat flour company, the telephone company, the electricity company, the cement plant, the government credit bank and the tax administration. Cheques of up to $6.8 million were issued. Plundering had become totally uninhibited.

Conclusions

Real states often differ considerably from the 'states' that appear in economics textbooks. This is most emphatically the case in developing countries. We discussed in Chapter 12 how the state, instead of reflecting the preferences of the population, may become an independent political agent, and how this, in the worst case, may lead to the emergence of a pure predatory state, where the overwhelming interest of the rulers is maximizing their own private income. In this chapter we have given two concrete examples of such states: Haiti and the Dominican Republic.

Haiti became a predatory state because the rulers were unable to squeeze out a surplus from the peasants without resorting to taxation. Control of the state was what guaranteed a work-free income for the presidents and their closest associates. The same pattern developed in the Dominican Republic. In both cases the state became a 'club' whose size determined the likelihood of the presidents staying in office and the size of the revenues they were able to secure for themselves. In both countries this pattern developed during the nineteenth century, but survived long into the twentieth century. Most of the presidents were soon removed because they tended to concentrate on the revenue aspect, and those who managed to stay on for longer periods were those who developed special methods for increasing security, ranging from terror organizations to ideologies. Their ability to conceal their real intentions was certainly significant.

Literature

The quotation from Myrdal is from:

Myrdal, Gunnar (1957), *Economic Theory and Under-Developed Regions*. Gerald Duckworth, London.

The empirical material on Haiti and the Dominican Republic is found in:

Lundahl, Mats (1979), *Peasants and Poverty: A Study of Haiti*. Croom Helm, London, ch. 6–8.

Lundahl, Mats (1983), *The Haitian Economy: Man, Land and Markets*. Croom Helm, London and Canberra, ch. 14.

Lundahl, Mats (1992), *Politics or Markets? Essays on Haitian Underdevelopment*. Routledge, London and New York.

Lundahl, Mats (1997), 'The Haitian Dilemma Reexamined: Lessons of the Past in the Light of Some New Economic Theory', in Rotberg, Robert I. (ed.), *Haiti Renewed: Political and Economic Progress*. Brookings Institution Press, Washington, DC.

Lundahl, Mats (1997), *Towards the Abyss? The Political Economy of Emergency in Haiti*. WIDER, Helsinki.

The club model emanates from:

Lundahl, Mats (1985), 'Government and Inefficiency in the Haitian Economy: The Nineteenth Century Legacy', in Connolly, Michael B. and McDermott, John (eds.), *The Economics of the Caribbean Basin*. Praeger, New York, reprinted in Lundahl, 'The Haitian Dilemma Reexamined'.

The extension that adds obfuscation is from:

Danielson, Anders and Lundahl, Mats (1994), 'Endogenous Policy Formation and the principle of Optimal Obfuscation: Theory and Some Evidence from Haiti and Jamaica', *Comparative Economic Studies*, Vol. 36.

14

From the Perfect Economy to the Predatory State: The Internal Logic of Distortions

A central thesis in modern economics is that the market system automatically produces the optimal allocation of resources provided that there is perfect competition in all markets. This was also the starting point of the present book. The purpose of the book was to show how it then comes that the theoretical ideal usually in reality is replaced by a system full of distortions – often initiated by economic policy – and which welfare effects this leads to. The theoretical instrument consistently employed in the book is a simple neoclassical model of the general equilibrium type.

Interventions in the resource allocation on the part of the state are justified if the above-mentioned conditions are not fulfilled. Otherwise interventions are distorting and should, in principle, be avoided. The fact is, however, that the state intervenes in the resource allocation in all modern economies, even for reasons not directly related to deviations from the ideal type of market economy. The usual reason for this is that the income distribution generated by the market is not accepted. A Pareto optimal allocation can, in principle, exist for any distribution of income. Which distribution is the 'correct' one is far from unambiguous, however, and various social groups try to change the conditions under which the economy works to their own advantage, with more or less success.

Redistribution of income is hard to realize, however, without also causing allocative effects. (Only lump-sum transfers have this characteristic.) Therefore redistributive policies usually introduce distortions of the economy as a side effect, not on purpose. It is also possible, however, to identify cases where the whole idea behind the intervention is to create distortions in order to favour a certain group in society at the expense of the population as a whole.

We started with a survey of our tools in Chapter 2: linearly homogeneous production functions, production isoquants and factor prices, relating factor and goods markets within a general equilibrium approach in the box diagram, the production possibility curve and its deduction from the contract curve, social indifference curves and the unambiguous relation between relative product prices, relative factor prices and factor intensities.

In Chapter 3 the marginal conditions of optimal resource allocation were deduced, and we showed that these conditions are fulfilled, under perfect competition in all markets, when the economy is characterized by free trade and *laissez-faire*. From a welfare point of view, free trade is superior to both pure autarky and trade limited by tariffs, provided that the losers are compensated by the winners. Some objections to free trade were also dealt with: lack of flexibility and rigid factor prices. The model in Chapter 3 is used as the ideal type and measuring standard for analyses and comparisons of different types of distortions.

In Chapter 4 various kinds of distortion were introduced. We distinguished between endogenous distortions, which are caused by market imperfections combined with *laissez-faire*, autonomous distortions which are unintended side effects of economic policy, and instrumental distortions which are brought about deliberately by economic policy.

Chapter 4 concentrated on a survey of the effects of endogenous distortions and how they may be eliminated. We found that the optimal technique is always to attack the cause of distortion directly. In the following chapters distortions introduced by economic policy, deliberately or not, were discussed.

Chapter 5 scrutinized one of the most obvious sources of distortions in the Swedish economy, agricultural policy. This is an example of instrumental distortions (i.e., it has been introduced on purpose). Agricultural policy was analysed here from a contingency point of view: that is, how the availability of foodstuffs can be secured if the country is cut off from international trade. Since the goal has been vaguely formulated in official statements, the implications of various definitions of it were analysed. It turned out that the high-price policy, followed in Sweden, is the optimal policy only in the exceptional case where the contingency goal was formulated as a direct import restriction. Otherwise, the best policy from the efficiency point of view is a combination of taxes and subsidies, not protectionism.

Instrumental distortions have also been used as part of a development and industrialization strategy in developing countries. Chapter 6 dealt with this issue. Also in this case the aim was to increase domestic production at the expense of imports. The idea was that new industries in developing countries need protection in order to survive and grow competitive. Thereafter, the protectionist measures can be dismantled, according to this argument. In reality, this strategy almost never worked as planned, however. A network of regulations was eventually built up with very large efficiency losses as a consequence. Industries with comparative disadvantages instead of advantages emerged, while the industries that could have been competitive in the export markets were often suppressed. The industrial structure that remains after the implementation of import-substitution policy has been difficult to change, however, not least because the industry sector is often represented by strong special interests.

One type of distortion that often overlaps those related to import substitution is the so-called urban bias. This issue was analysed in Chapter 7. The term, which alludes to systematic favouring of the urban sector at the expense of the countryside, emanates from Michael Lipton's works from the 1960s and 1970s and the discussion has, to a considerable extent, called into question whether such a bias exists at all. According to Lipton, urban bias is evident in many different ways: through public investments, through taxation and through the manipulation of relative prices, to the disadvantage of the countryside. The result is distorted commodity and factor prices with welfare losses as a consequence. Using our model, we showed that the effects are similar to those of import substitution.

Lipton's theses have been regarded as controversial, however. His fundamental terms are often unprecise and his handling of empirical data has been criticized for manipulating the facts to suit his theses. Nevertheless, many development economists feel that there is much to be commended in what Lipton says but that his ideas need to be elaborated and given a more exact form.

Chapter 8 concluded the discussion on the effects of distortions on a market economy. The chapter dealt with a distortion that emanates from the factor market but ultimately is based on an idea of racial inequality (i.e., racial discrimination). The South African apartheid system and its predecessors were used as examples.

The development in South Africa can be divided into three stages. In the first one the black population was deprived of its land because the immigrant Europeans needed it for their agriculture. In the second stage a mining and industry sector emerged which could use cheap labour. The availability of labour could be secured through continued crowding-out of Africans from the agricultural sector. At the same time some industrial jobs were reserved – at higher wages than in agriculture – for 'poor whites' who had also been crowded out of the agricultural sector. In the third stage the Africans had been concentrated in certain areas, which they could leave only with special permission. The labour force could be divided into an unskilled and a skilled group, but the jobs requiring skills were reserved for the whites. In certain cases discrimination was not directly distorting and sometimes it may not even have been economically advantageous for the whites. In order to explain the interventions we then have to resort to non-economic arguments, such as the 'security' of the white group.

Chapter 9 dealt with an extreme case, a situation where the price mechanism is practically eliminated: the planned socialist economies of the Soviet type. Although an efficient resource allocation, in principle, is possible in a planned economy, we showed here that the decision problems are so complicated that there is hardly any chance of success in reality. The structure is characterized by distortions at almost every level. Moreover, the planned economy tends to create other problems, mostly related to the incentive structure, which all speak against the possibility that a planned economy would be as efficient as a market economy. Some of the problems of the planned economy were related primarily to its ideological foundation, Marxism. The overemphasis on the production of goods at the expense of services was one of them. An application of our model shows that the end result, as far as the resource allocation is concerned, can be expected to be affected by virtually all the types of distortion that have been discussed earlier.

Chapters 4–9 analysed the welfare effects of distorting interventions in the resource allocation and compared these interventions with the 'perfect' economy of Chapter 3. The question is, then, why distorting interventions are undertaken in practice even when they are not optimal from an economic point of view. The explanation can be found in the fact that governments seldom or never let their activities be guided by the kind of social welfare functions that traditional textbooks start with. Instead, one way or another, they are representatives of groups and special interests or have to balance such interests against each other. The logic they are guided by emanates more from the behavioural assumptions of public choice theory than from the assumptions that welfare theory is built on.

In Chapter 10, with the starting point in Mancur Olson's work on the rationality of small groups, we studied the conditions that must be fulfilled for successful pressure groups to be formed. The principles regulating the behaviour of these groups were analysed, and we showed that it is usually easier for small groups to protect their interests than for large ones, that they tend to work for redistribution of a given pie rather than for efficiency and growth, and that their activities tend to damage the economy.

In Chapter 11 we looked into the effects of lobbying, starting from the assumption that these activities not only distort the resource allocation but also consume real resources. Several types of such directly unproductive profit-seeking activities, such as revenue, premium and tariff seeking, were discussed. It turned out – somewhat unexpectedly – that the effects of the activities are unambiguously negative only when the original state of the economy is free from distortions. In other cases, by improving the resource allocation, pressure by lobbies may contribute to the attainment of a second-best situation closer to the welfare optimum than the (distorted) original state. The net result may, however, just as well be a deterioration, either because the allocation gain is offset by the loss of resources that lobbying imposes on society, or because the resource allocation worsens as well.

Chapters 10 and 11 assumed that coalitions of citizens try to persuade the state to intervene in their favour. Chapter 12 discussed the possibility that the state itself functions as a special interest group. The starting point was then that that politicians and civil servants to some extent attempt to further their own interests before those of society. The conclusion of the analysis was that the behaviour of the state depends on the incentive structure of the power-wielding elite. If it can profit from promoting growth and development it will be developmental; otherwise not. The state may plunder the population and, at the same time, carry out measures that increase the efficiency of the economy. The incentives, in turn, depend on how the institutions of the economy are organized, and this is usually the result of a long evolution. There does not appear to be any self-evident relation between the propensity of intervention of the government or its 'benevolence' and economic development.

Chapter 13, finally, illustrated the general discussion of Chapter 12 with the aid of two examples of notorious predatory states, Haiti and the Dominican Republic. The kleptocracy form of government developed in both countries as early as in the nineteenth century, and this unfortunate heritage also dominated the activities of the state during large parts of the twentieth century. Politics has been a way of creating private income for the rulers, not a means for increasing the standard of living and welfare of the population. Small cliques have ruled the two countries and have done their best to conceal the fact that they have plundered the majority of the population.

For the functioning of the economy the activities of the state are of central significance. All states intervene in the economy but they do so in widely different ways. The traditional welfare theory that is the foundation of most of the chapters in this book assumes that the state sees to what is best for the citizens, that it therefore can and will correct market imperfections and that distortions, when introduced by the state itself, are aimed at promoting some goal that would further the interest of the citizens. This view is often naive, however, and needs to be corrected. States that are forced to balance group interests or which have completely different goals, such as amassing personal wealth, are not likely to act in the way that the traditional textbooks assume. There is a risk instead that their activities create more distortions than they do away with or correct for. This, in turn, makes the task of the economist difficult. Instead of postulating a certain behaviour we have to lay down empirically how governments act, analyse their motives and draw conclusions as to how their behaviour affects the economy and the welfare of the people that live and work in it.

Index

adverse selection   8
Africa   126, 209, 220
agricultural policy   *see* Swedish
   agricultural policy
Ahluwalia, Montek   127
apartheid system   9,131 ff, 245;
   abolishment   144–5
autonomous distortions   54, 244
autonomous state   204, 206,
   207

Baby Doc   *see* Duvalier, J.C.
Báez, Buenaventura   233
balanced growth   93
bantustans   *see* homelands
Bardhan, Pranab   205
Barone, Enrico   149
Bastable's test   94
Bates, Robert   127
Bennett, Ernest   241
black market   117–18
Bokassa, Jean-Bedel   207
box diagram   13, 19–20
Boyer, Jean-Pierre   232
Britain   175
Brunei   207
budget line   17, 31–3
budget restriction, soft   153
Burma   220
business cycles, political   203
Byres, Terry   127

Calixte, Démosthènes   236
caudillos   235
Central African Republic   207
centrally planned economies, reforms of
   the price system   150–1
central planning, routine   151–2
Chiang Kai-shek   221
China   127, 181
Christophe, Henry   226

civilized labour market policy   132,
   135 ff
collective action, application of
   theory   174 ff
commodity prices   31; relative   13, 244;
   relation between factor prices and
   commodity prices   34 f
conspirators   231–2
consumption loss, from free trade   62
contract-based view of the state   205
contract curve   19
Costa Rica   181
coup d'état   209–10
crowding out, in the labour
   market   138 ff
Cuba   147
Currie, Lauchlin   125
cybernetics   150
Czechoslovakia   151, 202

democratic state   206
demonstration effects   47
developmental state   220–1
directly unproductive profit-seeking
   (DUP) activities   10, 184 ff, 2203,
   213; classification of   187; revenue-
   seeking   188, 246; lobbying   187;
   premium-seeking   187, 246;
   smuggling   187; theft   184–6;
   tariff-seeking   187, 195, 246;
   evasion of tariffs   187
distortions   1, 3, 53 ff; autonomous   54,
   244; endogenous   54, 244;
   instrumental   54, 74 ff, 244; in
   planned economies   159–61;
   classification of   54; in the labour
   market   135 ff; reasons for   210–11
Domestic Rate of Substitution
   (DRS)   40 ff
Domestic Rate of Transformation
   (DRT)   40 ff

Dominican Republic 11, 224 ff., 247
Duvalier, François 207, 237, 240
Duvalier, Jean-Claude 237

East Asia 175
Eastern Europe 201
economic efficiency 2, 177
effective tariff protection 101
efficiency goal, in Swedish agricultural
    policy 76
Ellis, Frank 117
emergency policy in Swedish agricultural
    policy 76 ff
endogenous distortions 54, 244
endogenous tariffs 168 f
equity 1, 2; horizontal 2; vertical 2
Estimé, Dumarsais 236
Euler's theorem 34
exchange value 148
exploitation-based view of the state
    205
export-based development model
    103–5
export of 'wrong' goods 61
export pessimism 93
export promotion 103–5
external effects 66; factor-
    generated 68 f; in
    production 58 ff; negative 6;
    positive 6

factor diagram 13, 16 f
factor-generated externalities 68 ff
factor intensity 244
factor prices 243; inflexibility 49;
    relative 13, 244, 311; relation to
    goods prices 34 ff; divergences
    of 63 f
Findlay, Ronald 216
Foreign Rate of Transformation
    (FRT) 40 ff
foreign trade, the fundamental theorem
    of 41 ff; in planned economies
    157 f; gains from 39 ff
France 176, 226
free-rider problem 171
free trade, dynamic effects 46 f;
    consumption loss 62; and factor

mobility 48–9; and inflexibility of
    factor prices 49 f; specialization
    gain 62
functional planning 151
futures markets 7

Geffrard, Fabre 233, 239
Germany 176
Ghana 221
goods production in planned economies,
    overemphasizing of 156–7
government failure 202
government relations 99

Haiti 11, 207, 224 ff, 247
Harris–Todaro model 121
Hayek, Friedrich von 149
Heureaux, Ulises 234
high-price policy, in Swedish
    agriculture 75
homelands 132
Hume, David 200
Hungary 151, 202
Hussein, Saddam 209
Hyppolite, Florvil 233

imperfect competition 5
import substitution policy in developing
    countries 91 ff; intermediate
    production 101; investment
    goods 101; consumption goods
    industry 101; and exports 103;
    and agriculture 103; and capacity
    utilization 102; and capital
    formation 102; and luxury goods
    industries 102; and
    employment 103; and
    growth 101; and foreign
    dependence 102; results of
    95 ff
incentive problem in planned
    economies 152–4
income goal, in Swedish agriculture 76
India 108, 126 f, 205
indifference curve; social 13
Indonesia 207
infant industries 93 ff
infant industry argument 95

inflexibilities, in resource allocation
    48–9
influx control   138
inputs, in planned economies
    154–5
institutional economics   165
instrumental distortions   54
interest groups   164 ff
intermediaries, mark-up   63
intransitivity   28
investment goods   47
invisible hand   3
Iraq   209
isocost line   17

Japan   175, 176
job reservation   132

Kantorovich, Leonid   150
kleptocracy   200, 238, 247
Korea   207

labour cost approach   148
labour market policy, civilized   132,
    135 ff
labour market, crowding out
    138 ff
labour theory of value   148
Lal, Deepak   204
land market, segregation   132 ff
Lange, Oskar   149
Latin America   126, 210
learning-by doing effects   94
Lescot, Élie   236, 240
Lewis, Arthur   92
linearly homogeneous production
    function   13 ff, 243
linkage effects   92; backward   92;
    fiscal   92; forward   92; via
    consumption   92
Lipton, Michael   108 ff, 180, 245
lobbying   10, 165 ff, 187, 246; for
    abolishing of tariff   194; and
    economic efficiency   177;
    preconditions for   170 ff
low-price policy in Swedish
    agriculture   75
lump-sum tax   4

Magloire, Paul   236
Marcos, Ferdinand   207, 210, 212
market failure   5 f, 202
market socialism   149
market, missing   7; insurance   8;
    black   117–18; futures   7
mark-up (by intermediaries)   63
mark-up school   148
Marx, Karl   147, 149, 156
middle-price policy   76
Mill, John Stuart   200
Mill's test   94
Mises, Ludvig von   149
Mobutu Sese Seko   207
monopoly, natural   5
moral hazard   8
Moya Pons, Frank   233
Myint, Hla   204
Myrdal, Gunnar   126, 224

negative externalities   6–7
newly industrialized economies
    (NIEs)   220
Nkrumah, Kwame   221
nomenklatura   218
Nord Alexis, Pierre   233
North Korea   147
North, Douglass C.   203, 205

offer curve   55; derivation of   55–6
Olson, Mancur   165, 174 ff, 184, 202,
    227, 246
operative plan   152
optimal tariff   56 ff
optimal taxation   114–15

Papa Doc   *see* Duvalier, F.
Pareto optimality   2, 3, 149, 243
perfect competition   3
perspective plan   152
Pétion, Alexandre   226
Philippines   207, 210, 212, 220
planned economy   10, 190 ff; principles
    of functioning   147 ff; inputs
    154–5; distortions   159–60; foreign
    trade   157 f; scarcity of goods
    155–6; overemphasis on goods
    production   156–7

planning, functional 151; sectoral 151; territorial 151
planometric optimization approach 148
political business cycles 203
political economy 1
Port-au-Prince 227, 240
positive externalities 6
praetorian state 236
predation, techniques 211 ff
predatory state 11, 200, 206 ff, 243, 247; limitations 214–15; bureaucratic 218–19; methods 211 ff; obfuscation 238–9; optimal size of 228 f; productive 215 ff; as a club 228 ff; emergence of 225 ff
premium-seeking 187, 192 ff, 246
price regulations, of agricultural goods in developing countries 116
price system reforms in planned economies 150–1
principal–agent problem 209
production function 13; linearly homogeneous 13 ff
production isoquant 16 f, 243
production possibility curve 13, 20 ff; shape of 24 ff; derivation from the box diagram 20 ff; convexity 24 ff
production target in Swedish agriculture 76
public choice school 165, 201, 203, 246
public goods, and group size 172 ff; optimal level 173–4; sub-optimization of 177

racial discrimination *see* apartheid system
reforms of the price system, in centrally planned economies 150–1
regimes, totalitarian 207
regional (territorial) principle 151, 152
rent-seeking, *see* directly unproductive profit-seeking (DUP) activities
resource allocation, inflexibilities in 48–9

returns to scale 14
revenue-seeking 187, 188 f
Rybczynski theorem 139, 143, 161, 190

Saint-Domingue 226
Salomon, Lysius 233, 240
Sam, Tirésius Simon 233, 240
Santana, Pedro 233
savings 46
scale economies 14
scarcity of goods, in planned economies 155–6
second-best 3–5, 8, 246
sectoral planning 151
Seers, Dudley 125
segregation, of the land market 132 ff
Smith, Adam 3
smuggling 187
social indifference curves, derivation of 27 f
soft budget constraint 153
soft state 205
Soulouque, Faustin 233
South Africa 9, 131 ff, 245
South Korea 215
South Vietnam 220
Soviet Union 147 ff, 151, 153, 155
Spain 233
specialization gain, from trade 62
staples 91–2
state, as an interest group 199 ff, 247; autonomous 204, 206, 207; democratic 206; economists' view of 20 ff, 224–25; exploitation-based view of 205; contract-based view of 205; soft 206; different types 204; factional 204; as an interest group 199 ff, 247; as predator 11,204, 206 ff, 211 ff, 214, 215 ff, 225 ff, 228 ff, 247; totalitarian 207; developmental 220
Suharto 207
Swedish agricultural policy 9, 74 ff, 244; high-price policy 75, 82; middle-price policy 76; low-price policy 75

Taiwan   207, 215, 221
tariff-seeking   168 f, 187, 195–6, 246
tariffs   45; effective   101 f; demand
    for   166; endogenous   168 ff;
    Swedish agriculture   75; evasion
    of   187; supply of   167–8
taxation, and equality   115–16;
    optimal   114–15
territorial planning   151, 152
Thailand   210
theft   184 f, 187
tonton macoutes   237, 240
totalitarian regimes   207
transaction costs   215
Tullock, Gordon   184, 227

union activity   9
urban bias   9, 108 ff, 180–1, 245;
    definition of   109–10; in
    India   126; in China   127;
    components of   111; critique
    of   123 ff; and taxation   112 ff;

and efficiency   110; and agricultural
income   120; and equity   115; and
credit   118–19; and marketing
services   118; and migration   121 f;
and public investment   111–12; and
price policy   115 ff; and exchange
rates   118

vicious circles   201
Vincent, Sténio   236, 240

West Germany   175
Wilson, John   216
World War, Second   92

X-inefficiency   213

Yugoslavia   151

Zaire   207
Zimbabwe   207